ASIAN DAWN

Recovery, Reform and Investing in the New Asia

ASIAN DAWN

Recovery, Reform and Investing in the New Asia

Callum Henderson

McGRAW-HILL BOOK CO

Singapore Malaysia Thailand Korea
Taiwan Hong Kong Philippines Indonesia
New York Auckland Bogotá Caracas Lisbon London
Madrid Mexico Milan Montreal New Delhi Paris
San Juan San Francisco St. Louis Sydney Toronto

McGraw-Hill

A Division of The ***McGraw-Hill*** *Companies*

ASIAN DAWN

Recovery, Reform and Investing in the New Asia

10 9 8 7 6 5 4 3 2 1
20 9 8 7 6 5 4 3 2 1 0
FLF TOP

When ordering this title, use ISBN 0-07-116479-0

Printed in Malaysia

ACKNOWLEDGEMENTS

This book marks the third in a trilogy on Asia that began with **Asia Falling**, written at the height of the Asian crisis. Since then, Asia has come a long way. Interest rates have fallen sharply, fiscal policy has been expanded and Asian currencies have recovered some ground - not least the *yen*. At the microeconomic level, companies and banks have been restructured, though not sufficiently, as some would argue. Whatever the case, the Asian recovery has occurred far more quickly, has been far more dramatic than most anticipated, including myself. The aim of this book is to provide a critical analysis of the recovery, how it happened, its relevance in a global context and where Asia goes from here. In this endeavour, I am profoundly grateful for the advice and encouragement I have had from my colleagues and counterparts within the financial industry, and to those individuals within the financial authorities who were gracious enough to give of their time. Necessity dictates that most of these remain anonymous.

To Jon Eley, Peter Farley,
Steve Boyajian and Sanjay Arora

INTRODUCTION

At the best of times, IMF annual meetings are hardly occasions of unbridled levity or celebration. They are usually more sombre, more serious affairs where the self important discuss important matters. For a journalist, they represent an orgy of interview opportunities, where correspondents from around the world do battle to gleam one word of wisdom from a passing delegate. For an economist or analyst, they are a chance to shine, to be seen, or alternatively to ponder on the subtleties of new velocity of money theories and other such weighty topics. They are glorious spectacles - full of drama, and passion and power playing.

Serious affairs to be sure, they are also occasions of self indulgence and targeted flattery. No expense is spared (courtesy of the tax payers of the developed world). It was this aspect of levity which was particularly lacking at the IMF's annual meeting in October 1998. By IMF standards, it was positively austere. Indeed, the whole meeting was overshadowed by a pall of gloom and despondency. Nobody felt like partying, not even the journalists (and that is saying a lot). It is no exaggeration to say that the organisers and most of the delegates were despondent. Russia had just devalued and defaulted in August of that year, the "Asian economic miracle" lay in ruins and in Latin America the first signs of trouble were emerging. There was a real sense of nervousness, almost fear in the air. People talked openly about a global financial crisis. The idea of globalisation, so recently seen as a major benefit in opening up trade and capital markets for the world economy, was put in the dock for lengthy and vigorous cross examination. Easy answers were sought and found, and those who did so for their own ends blamed globalisation (i.e., foreigners).

Emergency action by the Federal Reserve that Autumn, cutting U.S. interest rates three times in less than two months, had saved the day in averting a total meltdown in global financial markets but for how long? In the "real economy", amongst ordinary people not focusing on economics or markets and simply going about their daily business, such tensions were clearly undesired, but a nuisance rather than anything more serious. At the time, those in the financial markets were frightened of what tomorrow might bring. It was that serious. We were that close to a global financial meltdown.

Consequently, the despondency which filled the corridors of the IMF's annual meeting in October 1998 was perfectly understandable. How different the atmosphere the following year, however, at the 1999 meeting, how stark the contrast. Having devalued in January 1999, Brazil had bounced back much quicker than expected, Asian economies were booming, Japan was starting to recover and there were even hopes for Russia. Granted, even the most optimistic official or delegate would admit that problems remained. Ecuador had delayed payment on its "Brady" bonds, becoming the first country ever to default on "Brady" debt[1]. Argentina remained a concern, with the economy sliding into a deep recession, the fiscal situation worsening and the question ever present as to whether the authorities would consequently have the will to hold its currency pegged to the dollar. Still, there was much to be hopeful for, much reason to slap each other on the back and drink yet another glass of champagne.

The crisis, or to use a medical analogy the virus that had emerged in Asia, which had proved so contagious spreading through Central and Eastern Europe, into Latin America and briefly in the U.S. and Europe themselves, had been contained, isolated and dealt with. There were still pockets where it was virulent, but one by one they also would be dealt with. The nightmare of "Contagion" appeared to be over and better times seemed ahead. In October of 1999, global economic prospects appeared to be steadily improving, as economies outside the U.S. picked up. From a modest of level 1.8% in 1998, global growth at that time was forecast at 2.5% for 1999 followed by 3.1% for 2000. More specifically, in Asia, economic forecasts continued to be upgraded. Thailand, where the virus was first sited, was expected to grow by 4% in 1999, the first growth for three years after it had seen its economy contract by 1.3% in 1997 and 9.4% in 1998. Korea was expected to grow 10%, a stunning turnaround from the near 6% contraction it experienced in 1998. To return to the medical analogy, the patient seemed to be showing signs of recovery, had been moved out of the ER and was recuperating in an open ward (or private ward depending on the country concerned).

When I wrote **Asia Falling: Making Sense of the Asian Currency Crisis and its Aftermath** (McGraw-Hill, 1998), it is no exaggeration to say that the Asian region was falling down around my ears. There was complete panic. Financial markets were in uproar. Businesses collapsed overnight, tycoons were made penniless, people committed suicide. The real wealth destruction at the individual level was phenomenal. Given the apparent recovery we have before us, it is hard to remember those desperate times, but remembered they should be, not least because of the stark contrast which the current recovery represents. In addition, however, they should be remembered also for what went wrong, for the reasons of the Asian crisis. While I am reasonably optimistic on Asia's prospects, some of those reasons, and the lesson therein, have yet to be learned. It is by no means assured that we will not see the re-emergence at some stage of the virus. The patience's health has been stabilised but remains fragile and there is usually an unhealthy tendency for its relations and friends to be more optimistic than realistic as to its prospects.

Asia Falling was meant partly as a descriptive piece of those torrid, exciting, exhausting days, partly as an explanation of what went wrong, why the subsequent events were so violent and why the virus spread so rapidly from one host to another. Finally, it was intended as a prescription for what *should be* done. What it *was not* was a predictor of what would happen. In truth, it held few predictions, nor was it intended to do so. Frankly, if anyone in those times had suggested with any degree of certainty the fate that would befall the region, he/she would have been rightly called delusional - this is not to say that many did not attempt that feat. However, one of the few predictions I did make in the book was to suggest that the most bearish of forecasts seemed overdone. It was extremely fashionable in those days to suggest - with scant evidence to back the suggestion, but why spoil a good story with the truth?! - that the Asian crisis was similar in every way to the Latin American debt crisis of the 1980s. Somewhat tentatively, I suggested that on the contrary, Asia had a number of fundamental strengths which could well cause it to recover and more speedily than many anticipated. At the time, this was quite a risky suggestion to make - and indeed from at least one publication it received considerable scorn. Nonetheless, I repeat here, and with no little relief that it proved reasonably accurate!

"So is Asia falling? Or is this just a temporary stumble in its long-term rise? Some analysts would suggest that Asia faces the prospects of a 'lost decade.' This is the fate that befell Mexico and subsequently much of Latin America after the debt crisis of 1982. The sheer immensity of the debt problems in much of Asia could well lead one to such a tempting conclusion.... The Asian go-go years of growth are no more, but they do not have to be replaced by a 'lost decade' if - and only if - the problems are dealt with now. Hard decisions, involving the liquidation of companies and resultant expansion of unemployment and other nefarious side effects, have to be taken now, or the risk is that when they are eventually taken, the 'illness' will have become considerably more serious."[2]

The purpose here is by no means to go in for self congratulation. To attempt to do so is unfailingly self defeating and in any case the day economists start to believe unflinchingly in their own forecasts is the day their track record will respond most eagerly to gravitational forces. Rather, it is to focus on the issues which were and remain key to the future of Asia and indeed the global economy. The Asian patient, somewhat unwillingly at times but nevertheless acquiescent, has taken the IMF's medicine and now appears to be on the mend. Trade and current account deficits have become healthy - and in the case of Korea, massive - surpluses, inflationary pressures have abated, asset market valuations have become more appropriate and the Asian consumer is now tentatively making his or her way back into the shops. Some hard decisions have indeed been taken, yet the events which we saw last year in Korea with the Daewoo Group, in Indonesia with Bank Bali and in Thailand with the Krung Thai might suggest to the sceptical - and being a dour Scot, I am most assuredly in that camp - that at the very least there remains much to be done.

This is not to doubt the achievements that have been made in the last three years. During 1997-1998, Asia suffered its worst regional recession since World War II. Only two years after such a cataclysmic collapse, the region appears to have secured full economic recovery. Yet, there lies the possibility that not all hard decisions have been taken. Towards the end of 1999, despite some vigorous efforts by the Thai authorities to deal with their many and varied financial problems, non-performing loans in the Thai banking system still amounted to just under 50% of the total. In Indonesia, whose banking system is still in the ER - to continue the analogy - despite the best efforts of IBRA, the Indonesian Bank Restructuring Agency, the figure was around 70%. Asia, as a region, has a number of fundamental strengths - as well as weaknesses which have helped it to recover, not least its entrepreneurial culture, social cohesion, high savings' ratios and hard work ethic. Demographics also played a part in the Asian "miracle" and will continue to do so going forward, albeit to varying degrees. It is without doubt that many other regions would still be in a state of economic shock, while Asia is in contrast attempting to sort itself out, attempting a full recovery from its debilitating collapse. Yet, while the term "recovery" seems satisfactorily appropriate, the word "full" seems at the least questionable. It depends what you mean by full recovery. If you mean a return to the economic growth rates prior to the crisis, it is not inconceivable that that could be achieved, indeed the last time Korea's economy posted such a strong economic performance as it did in 1999 was in 1995, when it grew 8.9%. Taiwan should match its 1996 growth of 5.7% while Singapore should expand a healthy 6%. For the year 2000, much will depend on year-on-year basing effects, that said with domestic demand following in the wake of a strong rebound in exports and corporate inventory re-stocking, the platform for continued growth in the near term seems reasonably assured.

However, something has been lost, not least the previous appearance of invulnerability and superiority of the Asian economies and the Asian model. A lot of unmitigated rubbish was written about "Asian values". The Asian economic "miracle" - so described by the World Bank in a 1993 report "The East Asian Miracle - Economic Growth and Public Policy" - which involved regional economic boom for at least two decades had solid economic underlying reasons - as did the subsequent crash. The Asian model was different in some respects but not *that* different, some central tenets of economics still held true, not least the laws of gravity from which economists have frequently borrowed. The economics' world should be indebted to the

MIT Professor Paul Krugman for so cogently and eruditely targeting the "myth" of the Asian miracle in 1994 and subsequently in 1999, by questioning the sustainability of the Asian recovery.

Most of the other Asia watchers are now considerably more cautious than they used to be - or at least, they should be, though one fears for the worst in some cases - and Asian politicians and financial officials do not have the same ability to manipulate market forecasts as they once did. Some may rail against the nefarious activities of foreign investors, yet those same investors - having been badly burned in 1997 - have also learned a lesson. No-one *has to be* in Asia. Even China is not immune from this realisation. The continuing decline in foreign direct investment commitments into China is an eloquent testimony of this. In 1996 and 1997, Hong Kong felt like a new Klondike, an Asian gold rush where money could be made easily. In retrospect, when sectors of the economy which have had no previous knowledge of or interest in financial markets start speculating, attracted by the promise of unfettered riches, you should start to worry. Hindsight is of course 20/20, but an investor who had packed, on their hasty trip to Asia to plunder local asset markets, the likes of Charles Kindleberger's seminal work "Manias, Panics and Crashes" would have been amply rewarded or rather suitably protected. It is never *that* different.

In contrast to **Asia Falling**, the purpose of this work**, Asian Dawn: Reform, Restructuring and Investment in the New Asia**, is to enter that dangerous world of prediction. It is said that prediction is always a dangerous pursuit, particularly of the future. This work, then enters dangerous territory indeed, yet for that it is territory which all market watchers enter every day of the week. Whole rain forests are felled every week in the pursuit of providing a plethora of economic and financial predictions. This is good news and bad news. Bad news for carbon monoxide emissions, good news for economists whose forecasts are frequently lost in the crowd (and many times deservedly so). Where are those individuals who predicted 20,000 for the Hang Seng by the end of 1997 I ask myself?! Were they punished for such irrational exuberance? Certainly not. In any case, predicting or forecasting is by no means an exact science or indeed any type of science. Economic analysis is at its most useful in providing a platform, a framework for investment prediction. Those who expect more from it could be lucky - or not as the case may be. The purpose of this book is thus to provide a framework for examining where Asia goes from here, Asia's future importance in the world as a whole, what the world can learn from the Asian virus - and whether that virus has as yet been eradicated - and finally what investment opportunities might be present as a result of all this. Like **Asia Falling**, this book is aimed at the general public who have an interest in international affairs, rather than specifically at economic specialists. What happened in Asia and where Asia goes from here has profound relevance to all of us.

Because lessons cannot be learned without an analysis of mistakes, Chapter 1 is a deliberate reminder of the key dynamics of the Asian crisis, a reminder of the smell of fear and panic, of companies going bankrupt by the hundred, of millions made unemployed and poor, of paper fortunes rendered worthless, of speculators and maverick political leaders, of rioters in the streets, of houses burning, and of a region which prided itself on irresistible economic growth and social stability brought to its knees. It is a reminder of how the Asian virus subsequently spread to other emerging markets, to the likes of Russia and Latin America. While there were specific differences in some cases, all the currency collapses and debt crises which subsequently occurred had key similarities. The sense of impending doom and gloom which prevailed during the height of the crisis has faded, but that is not necessarily a good thing. For one thing, as the patient feels better, he/she sees less reason for more medicine. Fiscal tightening is now seen as inappropriate, while corporate restructuring might no longer be necessary, and fiscal loosening has surely run its course. Understandable arguments but flawed. Many of the key vulnerabilities present in Asia before the crisis of 1997-98 remain in place. Without continued medicine, they could spread virulently once more, doing further damage to the "body". Such vulnerabilities also remain elsewhere in the emerging markets - and one could argue also in some of the emerged markets.

It should not be surprising that financial market turbulence between rather than solely within markets is inter-linked since that was one of the very purposes of globalisation, namely that financial and economic transmission would become more efficient. Well, it is - of the bad as well as the good. What emerged in Asia, spread, in various forms to the likes of Russia, the Czech Republic, Brazil, Argentina, Colombia, Ecuador, South Africa and Turkey. After Russia devalued and defaulted in August 1998, the first signs of credit crunch conditions appeared in Europe and in the U.S.. Such conditions did not occur because of high interest rates which dissuaded borrowing, but instead because of panic and hysteria in the market which caused credit lines between financial institutions to be reduced or cut altogether. In turn, lines to hedge funds and low-rated corporates were reduced as credit departments became increasingly risk averse. Yet such actions, while prudent on an individual bank basis, together added to the drying up of global liquidity. Without exaggeration, the actions of the Federal Reserve Chairman Alan Greenspan and his colleagues on the FOMC in September and October 1998 saved the world from global financial meltdown. In the aftermath, markets responded tentatively at first and then more vigorously as it quickly became apparent that the disturbance to real economies had been but slight. The individual countries themselves responded in varying ways.

In Asia, where the virus had been most virulent - as opposed to in Russia where one could argue it was self induced - the IMF led the external side of the restructuring effort, followed by the U.S. Treasury and Federal Reserve in the specific case of Korea and finally, bringing up the rear, investors seeking to pick through the debris for nuggets of gold. The very idea of receiving help from the IMF was not initially welcomed by the likes of Thailand and Korea, yet such was the damage done that in the end they had little choice. Considerable structural damage occurred in these two countries, along with a complete meltdown in Indonesia, the emergency imposition of capital controls in Malaysia and the need for stock market intervention in Hong Kong. Asian governments sought a variety of means of coping with the crisis at hand. Chapter 2 examines this process and looks at the relationship between the IMF and the respective Asian governments and whether or not the IMF's policies helped or hindered the region. At the time, several leading commentators, notably Harvard's Jeffrey Sachs, were quick to criticise IMF policy remedies as being overly harsh. Certainly, in my own view the initial implementation of Indonesia's programme was a dismal failure, causing panic and the complete meltdown of what remained of that country's shattered banking system. Yet it is questionable as to whether any policy, whether focusing on fiscal consolidation, raising interest rates or whatever could have coped with or helped alleviate satisfactorily the situation which prevailed at the end of 1997 and the initial months of 1998. Put simply, what money could flee did flee. Asian countries simply did not have enough reserves to stem the tide. Ironically, Malaysia's imposition of capital controls and Hong Kong's intervention in the stock market - both actions which were widely lambasted at the time - were the only actions which were specifically targeted at stopping or limiting the effects of investor flight. Meanwhile, coincidentally or not, not a single country which had gone under the IMF programme escaped seeing their currency devalue. The strategies which these Asian countries attempted in order to cope with the crisis are useful to analyse not only for their individual merits or faults, but also in the context of what are surely global economic seismic shifts which remain ongoing.

In 1999, after two years of desperate recession across the Asian region, the first signs of economic stabilisation and actual recovery in some specific cases were sighted. Chapter 3 seeks to examine just how sustainable are these economic recoveries and to what extent they are being flattered by temporary factors such as inventory re-stocking and year-on-year basing effects; that is to say, companies re-stocking their shelves *in the hope* that consumers will start buying again, rather than actual signs of increased consumption, and secondly the natural ability of a country's economic performance to look rather good in the year after it has contracted by 8% or so. The IMF packages have poured billions of dollars into national coffers, social programmes have been enacted to help the poor, trade and current accounts have turned around, to the benefit of national balance of payments and foreign exchange reserves. Yet, are the solutions which the Asian governments and the IMF have sought that different from the initial causes of Asian economic expansion, thus forming at least one of the major causes of the crisis itself? Those who argue that there was in fact no Asian "miracle", but rather that Asian economic expansion was simply a case of excess inputs relative to savings - that is, higher government and private investment relative to the national savings - now suggest that the recovery we are now seeing is simply a resumption of investment, in this case investment initially from the IMF and then from foreign investors anew. What it does not reflect is an increase in productivity, which the proponents of this argument suggest is the key to long-term sustainable growth. How accurate or not is this argument? We will look at this question which is crucial to the sustainability of Asian regional economic recovery in this chapter.

As fragile as that regional recovery remains, there are some positive cases which shine out from the pack, which lead the way. Chapter 4 examines the specific case of Korea, which we noted earlier grew 10% in 1999 after contracting to almost 6% in 1998, an economic rebounding of almost 16% points, a stunning achievement by any standards. Why is Korea doing so well? The answer is relatively easy. Because Korea has done what many others have not yet done, or at least not to the same extent - cut debt. More specifically, Korean banks have been forced to reduce domestic non-performing loans and repay external debt, and Korean corporates, the *chaebol* have been obliged by government mandate to reduce significantly their debt/equity ratios. In short, Korea has achieved a re-liquification of its financial system, allowing the resumption of credit growth - its money supply figures are ample testimony to this - which is after all the oxygen of any economic recovery. The likes of Thailand and Indonesia are still faltering in this regard. Korea is a clear example of taking hard decisions, an example not only to the rest of Asia but more specifically to Japan which continues to struggle, a decade after its own financial bubble burst. Indeed, contrary to initial expectations, Asia has not waited for Japan to lead it out of recovery. In the case of Korea, it has given to rather than taken from a lesson from Japan.

Chapter 5 seeks to examine Japan's changing role in the Asian region. At one time, it was seen as the lead for the "flying geese" theory whereby Japan was the lead "goose" and the Asian economies flew in formation behind it. In the wake of the Asian economic and financial crisis, Asian governments have sought to re-examine the relationship between Japanese manufacturers and Asian markets. If Japan was the lead "goose", it was so because it crowded out domestic manufacturing, whether deliberately or not in its effort to use Asia as an export platform to the U.S. and Europe. Somewhat belatedly, Japanese companies and banks saw Asia as a domestic consumer opportunity and greatly increased their exposure to the region, only for that region to collapse. It seems that both sides are re-examining their roles. However, while it remains reluctant to take a political leadership role in Asia for historical reasons, Japan has little choice but to at the very least maintain its financial role in the region, particularly as the influential shadow of China looms ever larger.

As we start the year 2000, the Japanese economy appears in somewhat better health, though serious problems remain, not in the least the persistently high level of non-performing loans and bad debts in the financial system. What lessons, if any, can Japan learn from Asia? One obvious example is the need to reduce debt levels rapidly once the economy has been initially stabilised. Japan should have done this from 1992, yet to be charitable it hesitated. It is only quite recently that the various agencies looking at the NPL question have been given any real teeth and yet they are still unable to force banks to write off their NPL exposure (granted, in the case of some, it is too large to be done at one shot) or to close it. The Japanese crisis of 1990-1 has recently been compared with its later counterpart in Asia in 1997-98 and indeed there are some similarities. Put simply, both were bubbles fuelled initially by excessive investment which led to speculative activity, inflated asset prices and eventually financial catastrophe. To return to the medical analogy, Asia contracted in 1997 a highly infectious and potentially lethal virus which has only recently subsided. A similar event occurred in Japan in 1991 as the Nikkei 225 crashed from just under 39,000 to its eventual low of around 12,000 in 1998. A combination of fiscal and monetary medicine, along with meddling by the Ministry of Finance to ensure that as little real deregulation and reform occur as possible which might reduce their influence, has stabilised that virus. Yet, the existence and growth of massive non-performing loans and bad debts within the Japanese financial system has resulted in what some have termed 'a wasting disease', where the body dies slowly, almost irrespective of what cures are attempted. And Japan has attempted many cures (short of the ones which would do the job, but which in the short term would put people out of a job by reducing capacity). The Bank of Japan has cut interest rates almost to zero and the government has attempted fiscal package after fiscal package. Most of these packages have been ineffectual and inappropriately targeted but which have resulted in a budget deficit of some 7% to the GDP, a level which if it was in an emerging market country, would usually result in stern words about the need for fiscal prudence from the IMF. Whether or not Japan's problems are the same as those of the Asian region, it is clear that its government and financial authorities have yet to find the solution to overcome them, though there are signs of hope to be sure. The pulse of domestic demand has shown flickering signs of recovery, though to what degree this is due to; public or private investment remains uncertain. Recent construction data at the least puts into question the idea of self-sustaining economic recovery which the much-maligned Bank of Japan has for long been trying to achieve.

Japan is stuck in a classic liquidity trap, where debt and capacity overhang frustrate the usual policy responses of monetary and fiscal expansion., indeed whereby monetary transmission becomes blocked. As a result, interest rates have been cut to near zero and Japan's fiscal deficit has ballooned without any major corresponding response from the Japanese consumer. Indeed, economic data show that retail prices are still falling. Faced with rising job insecurity, an economy which continues to under-perform the expectations of what most Japanese have been brought up to expect of their country and finally a political system which is at the very least from inspirational (i.e. cankerous), the Japanese population is - quite understandably - bunkering down, saving for a rainy day on the assumption that there will be a downpour for some time to come. Yes, Japanese are saving even more - this despite the fact that the savings' rate remains at around 30% relative to a negative savings' rate in the U.S. - this is a time when Japan is already running a current account surplus of 2.8% of GDP. Meanwhile, from an external perspective, Japanese investors, continuing Japan's role as the world's biggest net creditor, are exporting trillions of *yen* of capital, the other side of a current account surplus being of course a capital account deficit. Adding to this scenario of high savings, paltry consumption and the exporting of much needed capital, the fact that credit growth remains muted at best as banks are still faced with the crushing burden of existing non-performing loans, and we can quickly see why cash is both "king" and scarce! What to do about this? Current policy responses have at best had mixed results. Frankly, unless the recovery maintains its momentum in 2000, one can safely say that they have failed.

We are then presented with a dangerous situation. Monetary policy is as expansive as it can be in terms of absolute interest rate levels and on the fiscal side there appears to be little room for further major expansion with the budget deficit already so high. Then, Japan is truly faced with a crisis. This is not necessarily a bad thing. If Japan is to get itself out of its present mess, it needs a crisis for emergency action to be taken, for new and radical answers to be sought and found. The times I have been to Tokyo in the mid and late 1990s, I have not once felt that Japan faced economic, financial or political crisis. This is not because of any oriental inscrutability but because the average person on the street and the average bureaucrat or corporate executive truly did not feel that there was any crisis, as the economy continued to stumble and falter like a drunk almost a decade after the bubble burst. While I certainly do not intend to present what I would do to solve Japan's problems here in the introduction, following are a teaser of those ideas:

1. Japanese consumers are saving rather than consuming so cut consumption taxes and hike savings' taxes.
2. Japan needs corporate transparency and minority shareholder rights in order to break up and reform corporate Japan. In short, Japan needs the Mike Milkens of this world!
3. Japan needs inflation. The expectation that prices will stop falling would be a further catalyst for consumption.
4. And finally Japan's debt restructuring agencies such as the DIC (Deposit Insurance Corporation) need real teeth in order to *force* banks and other types of financial institutions to cut their debts.

Chapter 6 carries on from where my second book, **China on the Brink: The Myths and Realities of the World's Largest Market** left off. While there are signs that Chinese exporters have faced the worst and are coming back, thanks in large part to the Asian regional recovery, the domestic economic picture remains mixed at best. China continues to suffer from deflation, a similar situation to that of Japan and due to the same problems - significant overhang, whether of the manufactured or the debt kind. In the past, China could export its excesses but 1998 and the first half of 1999 were tough times for Chinese exporters with the result that massive inventory overhangs built up. The situations in China and Japan are indeed remarkably similar, both with the problems and the solutions which both countries have sought to resolve. Indeed, it is probably fair to say that the central banks of the two countries are both deeply scarred institutions, scarred by the previous experience of allowing asset bubbles and retail price inflation to build up to the extent that the central banker's goal of long-term sustainable growth was clearly threatened. In Japan, the BoJ continues to refuse, somewhat stubbornly, to opt for quantitative monetary easing because this could be inflationary - despite the fact that Japan continues to suffer from deflation - while in China, the People's Bank of China (PBOC) does not have the option of quantitative easing, in part because of the relative lack of sophistication of the Chinese money markets to date, but also because this would inevitably put intolerable pressure on the Chinese *yuan* at a time when the Chinese authorities continue to insist that the stability of the *yuan* will be maintained at all cost. China still has some room to cut nominal interest rate levels, but it will inevitably be faced with the dilemma of the need to boost domestic demand superseding the political or financial imperative of maintaining a managed exchange rate. Indeed, China's entry to the WTO will eventually necessitate that the *yuan* be allowed to float. It is a question of when, rather than if. Given that China continues to enjoy significant trade and current account surpluses, one could well argue that the *yuan* should be *re-valued* rather than devalued, but this is clearly not an appropriate or desirable option. As a result, China's leaders could decide some time in 2000 or 2001 that it is expedient to create a trading bound for the *yuan* as a further step in the deregulation of the Chinese foreign exchange market towards the full convertibility of the currency, both on the capital and current accounts. Unofficially, the Chinese authorities have pledged to make its currency fully convertible by 2004 and this would be a further important step towards that goal. The PBOC would thus have the policy flexibility to counter any appreciation pressure in the *yuan* by either cutting interest rates or through quantitative monetary easing.

Taking a step back for a second from individual country analysis, Chapter 7 seeks to examine the regional fundamental strengths of Asia which allowed it first to boom for two or more decades and then to recover so speedily from what was a catastrophic collapse. In addition, it also seeks to respond to the criticisms of the Asian model, both to agree with some specific points and to disagree. Asia's fundamental strengths have been long debated. Indeed, at one time - hard to believe now - it was widely thought in the West that Asian growth was an inalienable right and feature of the region and that the mantle of regional economic leadership was indeed passing from West to East. Utter nonsense of course, but such was the time. Near term, no country will even come close to the United States in terms of global economic leadership, though as a region this is clearly the aim of the euro-zone. Asia still has major long-term fundamental strengths such as social cohesion, a hard work ethic, low labour costs, and a focus on high standards of education, yet it also has serious flaws. At a regional level, its capital markets remain woefully inadequate.

Readers of **Asia Falling** will be familiar with the subject of the need to create "institutional infrastructure", but I shall return to it for the purpose of including recent developments in the likes of Hong Kong and Singapore to develop and expand their capital markets and also to examine the fundamental role which capital markets and more specifically debt raising through the capital markets playing in the transmission mechanism of an efficient economy. At the corporate level, transparency and bankruptcy laws remain inadequate. Some progress has been made, and this book shall endeavour to look at the specific efforts with regard to Thailand - and the work that still has to be done there and elsewhere - yet on a fundamental basis the corporate system in Asia has to change. This can only be done by giving minority shareholders the rights which are enjoyed elsewhere in the world. Corporate performance should be the *only* barometer of financial reward at the highest levels in Asian companies and they should be forced to open their books fully and to account for their operations according to international (i.e. western) standards or to face appropriate sanctions. Why? Because the alternative is to allow shareholders (whether western or oriental) and ultimately domestic populations to continue to be exploited. Most importantly, it is in the interest of Asians that Corporate Governance and banking regulation be tightened significantly. It is no coincidence that the two places where these are most rigorously enforced experienced the least structural damage from the Asian crisis. Any response to the effect that matters of western-style corporate governance are in conflict with Asian values should be seen for what it is - entirely self serving. In any case, as we shall see, there are ways of combining Asian values with Western corporate governance standards to create a harmonious fusion.

Chapter 8 delves into that dangerous territory we talked about earlier, namely that of prediction, or more precisely where the Asian regional economy goes from here. What we have seen in 1999, and particularly in the second half of that year is an impressive turnaround in the real economies of Asian countries, most notably in Korea but also in the likes of Thailand, Malaysia, Singapore and even Hong Kong, burdened as it remains by the straightjacket of a currency board system which does not allow the currency depreciation by which others have ultimately benefited. Yet, how sustainable are these recoveries? Much depends not only on developments within Asia, but also on the global economy as a whole and more specifically on the economy of the U.S.. The bottom line scenario for the U.S. economy is that of a soft landing, both for the country's equity market and for the economy. Growth should slow modestly in 2000 in the U.S. to around 3.6% from 4.2% in 1999, a level the Federal Reserve Board should be well pleased with as long as it is still accompanied by moderate price pressure in the system. This has important implications for the Asian region. Equally, Japan is expected to grow some 2.0% in 2000 after around 1.3% growth in 1999. Asian exporters, in relative terms, will thus concentrate more effort and focus on Japanese demand relative to that of the U.S.. Equally, Japanese capital, one of the very building blocks of the Asian "miracle" in the first place is likely to come flooding back to the region, albeit to a lesser extent than in those heady days of the late 1980s and early '90s. The scenario for 2000 and 2001 will not be completely rosy however. Significant fiscal and monetary expansion were the chief causes of the Asian recovery in 1999, along with the massive bailout packages from the IMF. The availability of these three sources of liquidity is likely to be significantly less in 2000 and certainly in 2001 than they were in 1998-99. Indeed, at the heart of my prediction for the region is that without major micro-economic reforms the Asian recovery could stumble and falter once more.

At an individual level, there will be some good opportunities for investment, and this is the issue with which Chapter 9 is concerned, not so much in terms of individual companies - I am well content to leave that difficult task to the job of the equity analysts - but more with regard to asset classes and types of industrial sectors. In addition, I will look at the individual Asian currencies which I think will outperform throughout 2000 and those which are likely to suffer, and the reasons for both. In **Asia Falling**, I put my cards on the table and said my favourite country in the region is not China but India, a statement which clearly looked foolhardy in the wake of India's regrettable decision to test its first nuclear device. We shall re-examine the idea of India as an investment, of the pros and cons of the country's economic fundamentals, and its prospects. To complete this chapter, I shall give brief summaries of each major Asian country, where I see them going and what will be the specific opportunities and pitfalls. A dominant theme of this chapter is the idea that the governing elite in many of these countries will try to resist fundamental change, but that the move towards such change will eventually prove irresistible. Power, in this modern world of the "information economy" comes not from the barrel of the gun but from satellite television and the internet (and let us hope it stays that way). Those who resist are merely fighting a delaying action, and they know it.

Finally, in Chapter 10, we look at the implications of the Asian experience for global emerging markets around the world and for the global economy as a whole; what Asian recovery means for the world, and what faltering within that recovery scenario might equally mean. The argument that "globalisation" is to blame for Asia's woes is clearly flawed; rampant corruption at the local level and inefficient economic systems have as much to do with the subsequent collapse of the Asian "miracle" as global forces. Indeed, is it any coincidence that the likes of Mexico, Thailand, Brazil and Russia all had significant black market economies and they all saw financial and economic crisis?! No, it is no coincidence at all. The very existence of a large and flourishing black market economy is testimony to the fact that the real economy is not working efficiently and fairly. Emphasis on the rule of law is a clear lesson which emerges from the Asian crisis, at both the corporate and individual levels. A further lesson is that productivity does matter! The sustainability of Asia will be put into question without the reforms we talked about earlier. In some cases, efforts are being made in this regard. In others, they have barely begun or are actually being fiercely resisted. The reduction of liquidity provided by the IMF and the World Bank and the need to limit fiscal expansion will put Asian countries - and their leaders - to the test in 2000 and 2001. Without reform, the law of diminishing returns could ultimately mean that international investors once more shun the region. For some, this could mean the "Japan-isation" of their economies whereby they fall into Japan-type liquidity traps, unable to sustain domestic demand and unwilling to make the reforms and changes necessary in order to re-liquify their financial and economic systems. This year and the next will be the turning point for the Asian region. Given that Asia represents over half the world's population, it could well be a turning point for the world as a whole. Back in 1996, when the Mexican economy started to recover, international investors acted as if this were a one-off event, localised only to that country. Barely a year later, the Asian crisis was triggered. Presently, there would appear to be the re-emergence of that type of dangerous complacency - the Asian crisis is over, move on. At the IMF 1997 meeting in Hong Kong which I attended, a

Mexican Finance Ministry official said - without the slightest trace of irony - that the Asian crisis was purely an Asian phenomenon and Latin America in general and Mexico in particular did not suffer from such fundamental problems! Such is the duration of memory in financial markets! I said at the time (in **Asia Falling**) that if one was to hear an Asian official saying the same kind of thing about the next Latin American crisis this was surely as good a sell signal (on Asia) as any investor was ever likely to receive. Thankfully, Asian officials have - to date - been admirably reticent in this regard, though they still have time. Watch this space in 2000.

The Asian crisis of 1997-98 must not only be seen for what it was, the bursting of a financial bubble which showed up the economic flaws of the Asian "Miracle". It must also be put in context - in the context of other market crises, whether of the "emerging" or the "emerged" variety, down the ages. The crisis in Asia had of course particularly Asian characteristics but it was also part of a wider process of financial and economic deregulation without the necessary infrastructure to cope with the deregulation. Such inadequacy of infrastructure (institutional and "real") was also seen in the Mexican crisis of 1994/95, in the Czech crisis of 1996, in Russia and finally in much of Latin America in both the 80s and the 90s. Indeed, the bursting of the Japanese bubble in 1990 also has similarities with the Asian crisis. Where Asia differs however with the rest is how it has coped. Latin America "lost a decade" in the 80s following the 1982 crisis. The Czech Republic is still in recession. Russia is also still suffering from its crisis.

The Asian recovery remains extremely fragile but only Asia has recovered to any extent with such speed. To some criticism, **Asia Falling** predicted this. Victory has not yet occurred in the fight against recession, in the pursuit of recovery, but it is in sight. There are lessons in this for the rest of the world, most of all for Japan. While Asia still has a considerable way to go in terms of reform and indeed in recovering from the full effects of the crisis, it is coping significantly better than Japan has done for much of the last decade. Why is this? One could argue that emerging markets should of necessity be considerably more flexible than their emerged cousins, in the same way that a small company should usually be more flexible than a large one, but this is surely not the complete answer. Japan's population has for long been governed by those who saw themselves as unaccountable, whether by politicians or bureaucrats. Lip service was paid to the popular vote but the actions of the polity and certainly of the bureaucracy were symptomatic of times past rather than that at the end of the 20th Century, of paternalistic warlords jockeying for power and influence, albeit be-suited rather than in armour. The Japanese people have paid a heavy price for the arrogance and the self interest of these groups. It is not an accident that the Japanese economy failed so miserably in the 1990s relative to those elsewhere and certainly relative to its performance in the previous two decades. It was not so much rank incompetence as cankerous self interest. In a very Soviet communist way, those who saw themselves as elevated to the level of being responsible for the interests of the people, in many cases used the opportunity, deliberately or not, to merely serve their own. This is a lesson for Asia, just as much as the Asian recovery and the speed of the Asian regional response to the crisis is a lesson for Japan. While Asia has indeed outperformed, recovering much faster than was the case of Japan in the early 1990s, those who resist reform within Asia should at least examine the subsequent decline in the land of the Rising Sun. That decline could have been prevented, but was not. It is my sincere belief that in Japan there will come a day of reckoning, a day which would be of enormous benefit to Asia, for learning from the mistakes of others is by far the best route to success.

Callum Henderson,
London, April 2000

Table of Contents

CHAPTER 1

THE CRISIS - DAYS OF FEAR AND LOATHING ON EMERGING MARKETS

Cast your mind back to the autumn of 1998, not that long ago, and one word dominated the financial headlines - "Contagion". Granted, some may not want to conduct this exercise, painful as that time was for many, yet in a period of relative euphoria where such considerations are all but forgotten it is well worth a reminder of how truly awful the year 1998 was for global emerging markets.

While U.S. retail investors watched the valuations of their U.S.-invested mutual funds climb ever skyward, investors elsewhere were left to sweep over the ashes of what was left of the Asian asset markets, burning and smouldering as they were in the first half of 1998 in the wake of the regional economic collapse. Like a brush fire which suddenly catches once more, devastating all in its wake, or a virus which re-emerges to disable the host, the woes of Asia spread to other markets, most notably to Russia. For much of the year, the Russian financial system had seemed on the brink of collapse in any case, but two factors held back many from predicting one - Russia, either in its modern or Soviet form had never defaulted on its debt and the IMF in July 1998 provided it with a USD4.8 billion loan tranche which was aimed at shoring up the financial market and economic confidence. Hindsight is of course 20/20, but both these factors represented the hopes of those who expected Russia to seek to pursue logical economic and financial policies (whatever the policies of the past), hopes that were to be proved bitterly disappointed by the subsequent - and seemingly suicidal move - by the Russian authorities, both to devalue their currency and default on their debts. By then, however, Russian local dynamics were not the only or even the prevailing force driving events which had taken on a much more global nature, overwhelming all before them.

Much as had been the case with the Thai *baht* on July 2, 1997, the devaluation of the Russian *rouble* on August 17, 1998 stunned global financial markets; not so much a butterfly flapping its wings, as a bear brought low with an earth-shaking thud. Ironically, yet with little apparent sense of irony - or memory - the IMF quickly moved to welcome the devaluation of the *rouble*, just as it had done initially with that of the Thai *baht*. The subsequent default by Russia on its domestic debt market was greeted however by a deafening silence. The reverberations of those events in Russia were felt instantly all around the world, and not just in the emerging markets but also in those of the emerged or developed world which had up until then seen this process as merely the latest developmental stage in such markets. In the financial markets, pressures quickly moved to Latin America, more specifically to Argentina and Brazil. Increasingly risk averse, investors began to hedge or reduce their emerging market investments and many banks began to take a more conservative view about lending exposure. Across Wall Street, credit line exposure to emerging markets or those to leverage were severely reduced, thus to a certain extent fuelling both the subsequent decline in assets as liquidity dried up and the ensuing credit crunch conditions. However, some brave souls took a completely contrarian view, seeing in the Russian devaluation a golden opportunity to buy into the plunge on the view that the *rouble's* un-competitiveness would be eliminated and interest rates would come down, thus causing a significant recovery in Russian asset markets. In those chaotic August days, buying into such a market was like trying to catch a falling machete. They were cut to pieces.

In London, New York, Singapore and Tokyo, trading rooms were in uproar as markets convulsed in the wake of the Russian turmoil. While the initial reaction to the Thai devaluation had run the gamut from disbelief to relief, elation and despair, that to the Russian devaluation and default was unanimous: unequivocal horror. Investors felt utterly betrayed and just as importantly the credibility of the IMF was seriously damaged. The Central Bank of Russia had tripled interest rates and spent billions of dollars in defence of the *rouble* and once again it had all been for nothing; bitter memories of the Thai *baht* devaluation. This time investors and corporates would not be caught out again. The selling pressure spread instantly, reaching epidemic levels, hammering with hurricane-like force the ramparts of such far away shores of Argentina and Hong Kong. In the latter, the HKMA was forced for a variety of reasons to intervene in the stock market, spending over HKD100 billion to burn speculators and discourage market manipulation. Hong Kong's Financial Secretary Donald Tsang, in a speech in London in the wake of these events, vigorously defended these actions, adding pointedly with regard to the interconnectedness of global financial markets that Brazil was the "line in the sand", that multilateral organisations and the major economies of the world could not allow Brazil to fail as Russia had failed - or face the consequences. For such an eloquent speaker, it was a surprisingly blunt message, but such were the times. International authorities responded with more vigorous leadership. The Federal Reserve Board cut interest rates three times - on September 29, October 15 and November 17 - and the IMF expressed support for Brazil's economic policies, putting forward a financial support programme of some USD41.5 billion for the country towards the end of that year. As with the Russian *rouble* however, it was all for nothing. Late on Wednesday, January 13, 1999, Brazil widened the trading band of its currency, the *real*. On Friday, January, 15, it gave up and scrapped the band altogether. In a single day, the *real* plummeted by some 12%, reminiscent indeed of the 15% swan dive by the Thai *baht* a year and a half earlier.

What had started out as an Asian crisis, an "Asian flu", had become a truly global phenomenon, indeed a global financial crisis. The fear of contagion, of contracting the emerging market virus was both cause and effect. It took the emergency actions of the Federal Reserve late in 1998 to calm the situation somewhat and the resolute defence of the Argentinean and Hong Kong dollar pegs to stop the virus from spreading still further. In order to gain a full understanding of the Asian recovery which is currently alleged, we have to first understand the full extent of the damage caused by the initial crisis, how that crisis spread to other regions and what fundamental forces stopped the Asian currencies and asset markets from falling. Just as with the initial Asian crisis itself, the transition period has seen a number of major stages, the first being of course the initial fallout. Indeed, at the macroeconomic level, the Asian crisis became a model, what I have termed the **"Classic Emerging Market Currency Crisis" model** for the asset class as a whole, one possessing four key phases. Throughout it, I refer liberally to the example of Thailand since it is widely seen as the catalyst for the Asian regional crisis, yet readers should note that this model applies to global emerging markets as a whole - it works well with regards to the Brazilian and Russian crisis, and indeed fits neatly with the ERM and sterling rises in the more emerged markets:

PHASE I: THE DEVALUATION OF THE LOCAL CURRENCY

Initially put in place to create policy and economic stability, the Asian currency pegs did their job too well. They caused such stability, such lack of volatility that investors and corporates alike were lulled into a false sense of security - though that false sense of security in some cases lasted for a decade or more. The result, along with the macroeconomic policy mix which Asian governments adopted in the late 1980s and 1990s (fiscal rationalisation, strategic industrial intervention, encouraging high savings' rates), was massive capital inflows, both of the portfolio and of the foreign direct investment kind. Yet, investors are a fickle lot. While they were generally keen to take advantage of the apparently high returns available in the Asian emerging asset markets, the lack of a track record on defeating inflation in many of these countries relative to emerged market levels necessitated high risk premiums in local bonds and money markets. Despite the fact that the region was running significant fiscal surpluses throughout the 1990s, interest rates remained substantially higher in most Asian countries than they did in the anchor country of those currency pegs, the U.S.. This was not a problem at the public or governmental level since most Asian governments did not seek to expand domestic borrowing. It was a problem however for the domestic private sector. Those same currency pegs which allowed for economic and policy stability and consistency allowed local private sector corporates and financial institutions to borrow offshore, usually in the dollar bond or loan markets and then swap back to the local currency.

In a time of currency stability, this seemed not only prudent but profitable and for many it certainly was. Significant external debt burdens were thus built up, but unlike the case of Latin America in the 1980s, this was in the private not public sector and thus went largely unnoticed in the public accounts. Such was the degree of capital inflow that it was far too much for the fragile institutional structures of these markets to absorb efficiently. As emphasised in **Asia Falling**, the lack of deep and liquid bond markets in Asia caused a heavy price to be paid subsequently for the resulting inefficient allocation of these capital inflows. The money went into the local stock and property markets, into get-rich-quick schemes of all sorts, shapes and sizes and was ultimately recycled into the external debt markets, adding further to these countries' private sector external debt burden. Yet as beneficial as capital inflows are - and as characteristic of an emerging economy as they also are - one of the few economic laws in reality necessitates that significant capital account surpluses lead to significant current account deficits. Most things in economics are opinion or interpretation, but this is a pretty sound law which holds true. The larger the inflows, usually the larger the current account deficit. By 1996, Thailand was running a current account deficit of some 8% of the GDP.

How does this happen? Clearly, significant capital account inflows are a major fundamental positive for a currency. The very nature of emerging markets is such that they are perceived to be growing at a faster rate than the emerged markets and thus absorb greater amounts of capital relative to their ability to absorb it. Faster growth rates also suck in imports, as do the infrastructure and building projects which were financed by those capital inflows. This creates the beginnings of a trade deficit.

On the currency side, the central bank usually attempts to sterilise such flows given the dampening effect they have on interest rates and the potential inflationary effect they have on domestic prices (too much money chasing too few goods), but eventually such is the scale of those capital inflows that the Central bank has at some point to stand aside, no longer draining that liquidity out of the money market through daily operations. In terms of the currency, this is a turning point. Rising demand and reduced supply is an irresistible combination and the result is inevitable - a strengthening local currency. This would not be a problem on its own except that the currency usually strengthens to such an extent that it becomes significantly un-competitive on a Trade-Weighted and REER (Real Effective Exchange Rate) basis. In turn, this exacerbates the degree of economic external imbalance, that is to say the trade deficit widens at an accelerating rate as exports become increasingly un-competitive due to the strength of the currency.

This is precisely what happened in the case of Thailand. Indeed, it is a central part of the model which we are looking at. The way to avoid this is to loosen capital controls gradually relative to the construction of institutional infrastructure, that is the ability to absorb capital inflows. Deep and liquid capital markets have to be created first and the appropriate regulatory bodies to oversee both the capital market and the domestic banking industry. It is no coincidence whatsoever that the least degree of economic structural damage as a result of the Asian crisis occurred in Singapore and Hong Kong where the degree of institutional infrastructure development was the greatest and the extent of regulatory supervision the most vigilant. The subsequent collapses in Thailand, Indonesia and Korea say a considerable amount about the efficacy of institutional infrastructure development in those countries.

Now, just because a country has a large trade deficit does not necessarily mean that its currency will inevitably collapse. The U.S. is a fine example of this, possessing a significant trade and current account deficit in the years of 1995-1998 and yet seeing its currency appreciate against the Japanese *yen* from around 80 to a high of 147. Capital flows in this modern world of ours significantly exceed trade flows which means a country can run a trade and current account deficit for quite some time - decades perhaps - without experiencing significant disruption to its asset markets and eventually its currency. There needs to be a catalyst, a trigger which changes investor perceptions and thus reduces and eventually reverses those capital inflows. What the history of currency market crises teaches us is that the trigger can vary enormously. In Thailand, there were two key triggers. Firstly, in the fourth quarter of 1996, Thailand recorded a budget deficit, the first for a decade. Memories in the financial markets are notoriously short, but in the aftermath of the Mexican crisis in 1994/1995, investors were still keenly aware of the potential pitfalls and dangers of twin fiscal and current account deficits. The second trigger was political; Thailand threw out one notoriously corrupt regime only to get one which did not seem to be any better. The system itself appeared flawed, at least that was the perception to many. Investors became increasingly wary of putting new cash into the Thai asset markets. Because Thailand had by then a current account deficit of some 8% of the GDP, it needed increasingly large sums of capital inflow in order to offset that current account deficit. It didn't get them. Instead, by the first quarter of 1997, capital was starting to head out the door.

The result was that Thai interest rates started to edge upward and the Thai *baht* started to weaken. Note that this was *not* due at that stage to speculative activity but instead to so-called "real money" investors taking an increasingly defensive turn towards Thai investment. Up until then, local Thai companies and banks had taken a relatively relaxed view towards the concept of currency hedging. Indeed, the perception was that there was little need to hedge as there was little prospect of currency risk given that the Thai *baht* was pegged to the dollar. Not content with such inaction, some took it a step further and effectively speculated on currency and interest rate risk by borrowing offshore in dollars, swapping back to *baht* and then lending that *baht* out, making a very healthy profit on the interest rate differential. Increasing risk aversion on the part of international investors towards Thailand however started to cause a re-think on the part of the Thai corporate base (though for many, that re-think was much too late). Perhaps there was a currency risk after all. By then, such was the size of external debt built up in the private sector, largely through the Bangkok International Banking Facility (BIBF) that hedging of that currency risk started to involve some serious dollar buying going through the foreign exchange market. Meanwhile, one or two speculators - somewhat belatedly - arrived on the scene. Indeed, objectively, if they can be accused of anything, it is of tardiness. The signs of fundamental imbalance in the likes of Thailand and Indonesia were there long before the first hedge fund showed its face and started to sell the *baht* or the *rupiah*.

By this time, the capital account had turned negative on a net basis, meaning that more capital was flowing out of the country than into it. This coupled with a current account deficit and a fiscal deficit increased the pressure on both the *baht* and the Thai interest rates. The Bank of Thailand responded by intervening in the currency market and hiking official rates. Still the selling pressure increased, if anything it accelerated. In May 1997, the BoT tried to ambush the market, stopping Thai banks from lending the *baht* to the offshore market, hiking interest rates dramatically and intervening very aggressively. The dollar collapsed against the Thai *baht* and the Thai overnight borrowing rate skyrocketed to 3000% before "settling" at around 1500%. There was no question that many speculators were severely burned by that move, but more importantly it was extremely painful for Thai companies and banks. To focus on the speculators was - and is - to miss the point. The *baht* had been coming under pressure due to what we call "fundamental" rather than "speculative" flows, that is to say Thai manufacturing companies and banks were by far the main sellers, followed by foreign mutual funds. Hedge funds did not cause the Asian crisis. They showed up somewhat late and made some belated, opportunistic money - though some were burned in both Thailand and Indonesia - it is utter nonsense to lay the blame for the subsequent devaluations at their doorstep - though at the time it made perfect political sense to do so. If you face domestic instability, seek an external diversion. Hardly a new strategy as it has been around since the times of von Clausewitz and long before, Sun Tzu ("The Art of War").

Eventually, the selling pressure simply became too much. Leading Thai financial officials met and said candidly that their reserves were simply running out, that they would soon run out of ammunition with which to fend off a Thai *baht* devaluation. In addition, punitive interest rates in order to defend the currency were killing the economy. The peg had to be scrapped and the *baht* had to be floated, and on July 2, 1997 that is what happened. So much for the first phase!

PHASE II: THE TRADE ACCOUNT IMPROVES

Needless to say, Phase I is the most spectacular, full of fire and brimstone, the stuff of high drama. Phase II, the smell of cordite still wafting over a battlefield strewn with the vanquished is by contrast an anti-climax for most, the source of utter despair for those who had been involved in trying to defend the currency in the first place. The devalued currency overshoots, and usually dramatically so - in the case of Thailand, the *baht* went from 25 *baht* to the dollar to 56, while in Indonesia the *rupiah*'s fall was even more spectacular, collapsing from 2,300 to 17,000! The threat of imported inflation which such a collapse - in the case of Indonesia, a complete meltdown - that usually entails, requires a combination of tight monetary and fiscal policy, both to dampen that price pressure and also to stabilise the currency. With the country's monetary credibility having been cut to pieces in the wake of the devaluation, emergency measures are needed in order to stem the tide and stop complete panic. Such measures usually cripple the economy, and in the cases of Thailand and Indonesia that is indeed what happened. In 1998, the Thai economy contracted by some 9.4%, while that of Indonesia contracted by a stunning 13.2%. At street level, such a degree of macroeconomic contraction means bankruptcy, tragedy and despair. In the Asian crisis, millions lost their jobs or were made homeless. Companies went bust by the thousand. The extent of the calamity had to be seen to be believed. Thailand and Indonesia were by no means exceptions, though they were extraordinary to the extent of the collapse. Similar phenomena have been seen elsewhere around the global emerging markets of the world, for a start in the rest of Asia, but also in the likes of the Czech Republic, Mexico, Brazil, Colombia, Ecuador, Russia, Romania, Bulgaria and the Ukraine.

This brings us to an interesting paradox, which we shall deal briefly with here, but return to later on in the book: the possibility that there is a fundamental difference between emerged market crises and their emerging market counterparts. After all, in the cases of the UK in 1992 and the ERM in 1992 and 1993 (one could even count the dramatic fall in the dollar from 1993-1995 as a mini crisis), currency devaluations did not result in an economic catastrophe in the same way that this occurred in Asia, or the rest of the emerging markets for that matter. Indeed, as far as the UK is concerned, the ejection of the sterling from the ERM was the best thing that ever happened to the UK economy (a repeat of the UK's ejection from the Gold Standard and with similarly beneficial results). Equally, the widening of the ERM bands in mid-1993 was positive rather than negative for the EU economies, allowing them greater policy as well as exchange rate flexibility to cope with the economic dislocation. In the emerging markets, by contrast, currency devaluations were seismic events with similarly catastrophic consequences to those of an earthquake. Why the difference? It is a gross oversimplification to say, but that notwithstanding, that the emerging market crises were the result of excess capital inflows relative to the ability to absorb them, of financial bubbles which were spectacularly burst. In this regard, the Asian crisis bares a strong resemblance to that of Japan in 1990-1991, at least in terms of what happened to the local asset markets and subsequently to the economy. The *yen* did not come under pressure in the same way as the Thai *baht*, for instance, because of the relative immense size of Japanese trade flows to capital flows. In the UK and the EU, by contrast, the devaluations were not so much the result of financial bubbles (though those played a part, to be sure) as lack of policy credibility. The UK, at the time, was mired in a vicious recession with a clearly overvalued currency and a widening current account deficit. For the UK to defend its currency with higher interest rates and intervention was simply not credible. In September of 1992, when the Bank of England raised UK interest rates to 12% and then to 15%, the market barely reacted. Such a move, when the dole queues were getting ever longer and the housing market was in tatters as to the high mortgage costs resulting from those interest rates, was simply not credible. The market did not believe that the UK was prepared to take the pain in order to defend the sterling, and (thankfully) it was proved right. Equally, ERM-member countries were pursuing questionable economic policies were put to the test, and found wanting.

The economic fallout from the emerging market currency crises was thus partly the result of their stage of development and partly because they occurred at or close to the height of the economic cycle. Concerning the latter, the dollar remains vulnerable to this type of currency crisis, and even if this happens the policy response from the U.S. authorities is likely to be substantially different to those pursued by the likes of Thailand and others. Having finally achieved a considerable degree of inflation-fighting credibility, the U.S. authorities would only protest dollar weakness if its decline threatened imported inflation or if the degree of the move resulted in a lack of two-way risk in the market. Thailand, Indonesia and others did not respond in this fashion, partly because they were told how to respond by the IMF - the fact that they had to ask for IMF loan programmes being the result of having sought to defend their currencies through massive intervention and thus having thrown away most of their foreign exchange reserves - and partly because they did not have such policy credibility. The damage was already done and to a large degree it is questionable whether any policy framework would have stopped the slide. Several leading commentators have been critical of the IMF policy response to the Asian crisis, saying that the combination of extremely tight fiscal and monetary policy represented a worse cure than the disease itself. While I have some sympathy with this view, particularly given that the public policy adjustment is not necessarily the appropriate policy response to private sector imbalance (too many Asian companies borrowing too much in dollars and speculated too much in their own stock markets), this still does not answer the question as to what one does to stop the local currency from falling, an important consideration bearing in mind that the collapse of the *rupiah* resulted in the bankruptcy of almost every company in Indonesia. Whether you favour the argument of the IMF's Herbert Neiss or Harvard's Jeffrey Sachs, it is pretty irrelevant. By then, the damage was already done, the battle had already been lost. By then, it was a question only of damage limitation.

The example of the Brazilian crisis, however, suggests that some refinements to the standard IMF policy response have been considered - not least at the IMF - in the wake of the Asian crisis. When the Brazilian *real* devalued in January 1999 and subsequently fell to a low of 2.2200 to the dollar from a band level of around 1.20, many forecast 2.50 or even 3.00. Yet, the *real* managed to regain substantial ground, rebounding to just above 1.60. Why? Clearly, the appointment of Arminio Fraga as the new head of the Brazilian central bank was an important step. Fraga had considerable experience of the financial markets. Indeed, he left Soros Fund Management in order to take up that post at the central bank. Once there, he and the Brazilian Finance Ministry conducted a superb PR campaign to assure the markets that the appropriate policy responses would indeed be conducted, that fiscal rationalisation would take place - here the government succeeded in passing a number of important bills through the parliament despite substantial opposition - and that the focus was on internal price stability through appropriate monetary policy settings. The currency would eventually find its natural level and it was up to the markets themselves to set that level.

While this effort has so far been relatively successful, needless to say governments cannot rely on PR exercises alone, certainly not if their fundamental economic policies remain mis-aligned. That said, there is a case to be made that emerging market authorities should focus on internal price stability, even at the expense of devaluation of their currency. In those days of crisis, however, it was already much too late for such considerations.

Why did the Asian crisis cause economic catastrophe for two years, while Brazil took only a couple of quarters to recover (a fragile recovery to be sure)? For one thing, Brazil's problems are far from over. More importantly, however, by the time the Brazilian *real* was devalued, the degree of market inter-connectedness had been greatly reduced as investors became increasingly risk averse and went home to their own regions. Meanwhile, the ability of speculative, leveraged accounts to take on huge positions had also been greatly reduced as banks became more cautious in lending to this sector after the debacle over Long-Term Capital Management (LTCM). As a result of these two developments, the potential for transmission of "contagion" was short-circuited. Markets were volatile in the wake of the Brazilian devaluation, but such volatility paled in comparison to the typhoon which had devastated Asian markets in the second half of 1997 and their economies the following year.

Those developments, beginning at the end of the first quarter of 1998, were the first signs that the huge external imbalances which the Asian economies had developed were being corrected, albeit at the expense of the domestic economies of those countries. Few in Asia would have found comfort in that at the time and understandably so, yet to return to the medical analogy this was surely the first blip on the patient's heart monitor after a period - brief in historical terms but no doubt endless to the patient - of flat-lining. The key element of Phase II is that the collapse of the domestic economy causes a collapse in imports. This in turn forces the trade deficit first to decline and then to become a surplus. This is a fundamentally positive development, however severe the pain incurred in achieving it, yet during the initial part of this second phase, threats to the economy remain substantial. In the cases of Thailand and Philippines, the devaluation of their currencies caused an initial spike in domestic price pressures both because of imported inflation and shortages. The presence of inflation and more importantly of rising inflationary expectations was a clear threat with the potential to fuel a renewed devaluation of local currencies, in turn forcing a further wave region-wide of currency and asset market depreciation and competitive devaluation in sympathy. The fiscal and monetary screws had to be tightened even further, despite the near-term, added cost to an economy already wracked by severe dislocation.

In Indonesia, the *rupiah* lost an unbelievable 85% of its value against the dollar, causing justifiable fears of hyper-inflation. As a result, interest rates were raised to over 80% compared to a "paltry" 24% in Thailand after the *baht* was devalued. By the third quarter of 1998, the trade account of most Asian countries involved in the crisis and who had seen their currencies devalue was starting to see significant improvement. The exception to this obviously concerns "Greater China" and more specifically Hong Kong and China whose currencies remained pegged, in one form or another, thus distorting the timing and extent of the phases of the emerging market currency crisis model which we are looking at here. Even in the case of Taiwan, the model's natural progression was distorted by the fact that the Central Bank of China managed (and still manages) the exchange rate in such a strict and un-free manner, not allowing it to fall or rise sharply and punishing those banks found to be aiding perceived speculative forces in the market.

Yet, for the most part, Asian trade and current account balances were improving significantly. Simultaneously, the domestic price pressure abated or at least stabilised. In turn, Asian currency markets had begun to stabilise. Once again, the price movements which theoretically should have occurred as part of Phase II of the model were briefly distorted in the wake of the May 1998 riots in Jakarta. However, from July onwards that year, the process worked remarkably well. Phase II of the model is where the local currencies appreciate, not because of any real or perceived fundamental improvement in the domestic economy, but because the defeat of inflation and the significant and positive shift in the trade and current account balances has allowed interest rates to stabilise and then to fall. In other words, market tensions which are stretched to a breaking point in Phase I finally relax and liquidity returns to the system. Phase II is where local currencies experience liquidity-based rallies - and this is precisely what happened in the cases of Asia

(1998), Brazil (1999), Mexico (1995), the Czech Republic (1998) and others. The patient has not yet sat up and walked around the ward, but at least the pulse is stronger!

PHASE III: THE ECONOMY HITS BOTTOM

While Phase II remains ongoing, the economic patient is still showing no major sign of recovery. Phase III, by contrast, deals with the first inclination of improvement in the vital signs. Put bluntly, the economy hits bottom and a period of stabilisation ensues. Readers should note that the economic stabilisation does not mean the same as recovery, in the same way that the hitting the ground after a fall from some height does not entail recovery (indeed, if the height is sufficient there is unlikely to be any recovery!). Both processes usually entail a prolongation of pain, but at least the pain is not getting worse. Thankfully, economies are not as frail as the human body. They can indeed fall from great heights, smack down hard on the concrete with a sickening thud and yet still recover; the timing of that recovery depending crucially on the extent of the fall.

At the micro-economic level, companies are still continuing the process of rapid de-stocking of their inventories. Individual consumers remain extremely cautious and in the shops and department stores, the rental agencies and the real estate agents, prices are still falling. Yet, by this time, the liquidity-based rally in local currencies which we looked at in Phase II and most importantly the fall in interest rates which that entails provides crucial support for cash-strapped local companies and banks. Sensing this, at the local level companies seek to plan for better times to come by hastily completing their inventory de-stocking process, switching most of that supply to export markets unaffected by the crisis where possible (in Asia, many Asian companies were quick to switch exports destined for fellow Asian countries to the U.S. where domestic demand remained very strong) and starting the process of re-stocking. At the international level, both in terms of offshore and onshore investors, the reality of the economy hitting bottom, as evidenced by declining contractions economic indicators, leads to the expectation of Phase IV, economic recovery.

Phase III is not plain-sailing for local currencies however. As domestic economies stabilise, so do imports. Indeed, year-on-year basing effects accelerate that process. Thus, what we usually see in Phase III is the trade and current account surpluses peaking on a monthly basis. During Phase II and the initial part of Phase III, trade flows are actually more important than capital flows - as most offshore investors have already left by then, taking their capital with them. Reduced trade surpluses thus have a greater effect on market movements than would otherwise be the case, serving to weaken the local currencies - and again, that is exactly what we saw in the first quarter of 1999 in Asia. More specifically, the Thai *baht* rose to a high of 35.65 against the dollar from its record low of 56.30, only to fall back to around 38. The same thing happened to the Indonesian *rupiah*, the Philippine peso and the Singapore dollar (note that the Malaysian *ringgit* was pegged to the dollar on September 1, 1998 at 3.80, hence it did not experience this renewed setback, nor for that matter did it experience the fundamental recovery which most Asian currencies enjoyed in the second quarter and part of the third quarter of 1999.

In the case of Brazil, Phase II and Phase III occurred much more quickly, partly because Brazil, unlike in Asia, was alone in its devaluation and was not affected by region-wide devaluation. In addition, it continued to benefit from strong demand for its exports, both from the rest of Latin America and perhaps even more importantly from the U.S.. Finally, at the corporate level, there was not nearly the same degree of structural dislocation as Brazilian corporates were by then well aware of what had happened to their Thai and Indonesian counterparts and had already begun to hedge external liabilities long before the *real's* final devaluation in January 1999.

The case of Russia is special for many reasons, not least because several key elements of the Russian government were not informed of the decision to devalue the *rouble* and default on the domestic debt market until the actual announcement was made. In addition, the size of the black market economy relative to the real economy and the seemingly persistent state of chaos in the Russian government has somewhat distorted price and economic development as anticipated by the model. Nonetheless, the key aspects of the model - the turnaround in the trade account, the defeat of inflation, the liquidity-based rally (we have not got to Phase IV yet in Russia or anything like it!) - still hold true.

So Phase III sees a decidedly more bumpy ride for emerging market currencies than Phase II, indeed for many this means a reversal of some of the gains made in Phase II. Yet, economic stabilisation, all else being equal, gradually becomes economic recovery - the person eventually picks him/her self off the floor after lying there in pain after the fall.

PHASE IV: ECONOMIC RECOVERY – THE LOCAL CURRENCY RALLIES

What does economic recovery mean and how is it different from mere "stabilisation?" It is the equivalent of the patient on the one hand getting back his/her vital signs but still remaining essentially horizontal, and on the other wandering around the ward. There is a clear difference! In economic terms, recovery means that real economic indicators such as retail sales, industrial output, imports and so forth are no longer contracting, but actually rising, first year-on-year (due to basing effects compared with the previous, depressed year) and then month-on-month. Indeed, the first sign of economic stabilisation in Asia was that the pace of contraction in imports began to slow. Equally, the first sign of recovery at the theoretical level was that imports actually began to rise. More practically, at street level, recovery was - and is - evidenced by more people out on the streets, shopping and driving around - the streets of Seoul seemed deserted of cars for many months in 1998, while individuals sold their personal gold in the national effort to raise money for the country. In comparison, the return of the Korean shopper and motorist was one of the first practical signs of economic recovery. On a trip to Seoul I made in October 1999, the shops were jammed full, while at key times so were the main highways - lamentably so for anyone trying to get somewhere at the time! Clearly, one should not exaggerate this analogy. Traffic jams do not of necessity mean economic recovery. Indeed, they can suggest decidedly negative aspects of the economy, not least lack of adequate infrastructure. That said, the combination of increased retail demand for goods, whether of clothes or cars, is a clear, cyclical sign that things are on the mend. You do not go out and buy a car or luxury goods if you are afraid you might lose your job tomorrow. The elimination of corporate de-stocking which had hitherto been a drag on growth, coupled with lower interest rates and looser fiscal policy which provide support for weak domestic demand, help boost economic growth. Corporate *re*-stocking of inventories gives a further lift to the growth take off.

In terms of trade balance, inventory re-stocking accelerates the recovery in imports, in turn accelerating the pullback in monthly recorded trade surpluses. However, by this time, capital flows have begun to offset and then to exceed trade flows once more as investment returns to the region. This was the key driving force for the Asian currency strength in the second quarter of 1999. Indeed, it is my contention that but for the specific concerns over Y2K which emerged in the third quarter of that year, Asian currencies would at the least have remained stable in the third quarter and more likely have continued their strengthening process. Two further factors conspired to hurt them in that period. Firstly, there were in truth specific fundamental concerns at the microeconomic level. In Korea, the necessary restructuring of Daewoo caused significant volatility in Korean asset markets, encouraging an accelerated sell-off in local stocks and bonds and not only of Daewoo paper. In Thailand, the health of the domestic financial system was put in question as banking sector non-performing loans remained at a high 47% of the total despite increasing signs of economic recovery. More specifically, the health - or rather the ill-health - of state-owned Krung Thai Bank was put under the spotlight, for many an appropriate reflection of the inadequacy of the Thai financial sector reform up until that point. Meanwhile, in Indonesia, the scandal of Bank Bali first soured local market sentiment - and then offshore market sentiment as the Indonesian government refused to allow the publication of the full report from auditors PWC - only for the East Timor issue to take centre stage, the Indonesian armed forces' inability or unwillingness to deal with the massacring of East Timorese by pro-Jakarta militias obliging the multilateral organisations such as the IMF and World Bank to cease further disbursement of loans from their respective aid programmes.

In addition to these specific concerns, at the global level the U.S. Federal Reserve changed the rules of the game. At its June 30 meeting of the Federal Open Market Committee, the U.S. central bank raised interest rates for the first time since its March 25, 1997 meeting. The

Fed hiked the Fed funds' target rate by 25 basis points to 5.00% from 4.75%, however it was not so much the degree of the move as what that move itself signified - the end of monetary easing. To recap, the Fed had cut interest rates three times from September-November 1998, and by 25 basis points each time in order to provide emergency liquidity to a market that was verging on a global meltdown. The message at the June 30, 1999 FOMC meeting was that the market conditions no longer warranted such extraordinary, emergency monetary easing and that those rate cuts would gradually be unwound. Whether or not one likes it, the Federal Reserve remains the de facto Central bank of the world, the provider of global liquidity. Fed tightening of necessity means less favourable conditions for *global* markets, both of the emerging and the emerged variety. Indeed, this was the start of a major reversal in Asian currencies and asset markets, in line with a generally more defensive line in global emerging markets across the board. Gradually, through a number of Fed official comments and through testimony by Fed Chairman Alan Greenspan, it became clear that the Fed was seeking an orderly and gradual reversal of those three fate cuts. At its August 24 FOMC, the Fed again hiked its Fed funds' target rate by 25 bps, bringing its benchmark interest rate to within 25 bps of the 5.50% level from which the monetary easing had begun.

Candidly, the problem with any economic model is that it does not, and cannot take account of what we call "event risk". That is to say, it cannot by definition allow for events which occur unexpectedly and which can potentially - and often do - cause temporary or even extended reversals in market sentiment. The classic emerging market currency crisis model is no different in this. Its aim is to provide a framework for tracking various emerging market economies according to the specific phase in which they find themselves and thus anticipating how their respective currencies might perform, *all other factors being equal*, based on the developments of that phase. Of course, in reality, in many instances, all factors are most certainly not equal and event risk plays a major part in distorting price action. In the specific case above however, a model which is aimed at targeting the various phases of emerging market currency crisis cannot include such external factors such as Fed policy since the latter does not of necessity track events in the emerging markets, indeed the rate cuts of last year were a very rare exception to the rule. As we said at the start of this examination, the model provides a useful framework for market and economic analysis, albeit with caveats., the best one can hope for with any model. Despite those caveats, it provides an accurate reflection of what happened during the various stages of most of the emerging market currency crises in the 1990s.

PUTTING THE ASIAN CRISIS IN CONTEXT

For many in Asia, those turbulent, violent times of 1997-1998 remain too painful for recollection or analysis. A region which once prided itself on seemingly endless economic growth and political stability, a virtuous combination to be sure, was brought to its knees, leading many to question the very existence of the Asian "miracle". Yet, while there is clearly an argument to be made that the "miracle" was flawed, such flaws eventually being brought to light and the result being the ensuing crash, or indeed that higher inputs (i.e. investment) will inevitably lead to higher output (growth). Equally inevitably, it will lead to increasingly diminishing returns and a crash if not accompanied by higher productivity. Yet, despite the merits of this argument, it does not of itself explain why Asia massively outperformed the African and Latin American regions during the 1980s and the half of the 1990s. Asian countries such as Indonesia did not suddenly become corrupt in 1997. They were so long before, yet unlike in the case of Africa, in some countries in Latin America or Russia corruption did not act as a hindrance on growth for quite some time - and by that I mean over a decade. Why the difference? Some of the same domestic factors which eventually brought down the region were behind its growth phase, namely the inter-connectedness of local companies, banks and politicians, emphasis on networking rather than on individual aspirations and a focus on top line development (sales, in other words) and market share. Yes, growth was boosted substantially by investment without producing sufficient productivity gains to offset either real or financial asset inflation (thus leading to a decline in real returns), but that growth did not happen everywhere. It did happen in Asia and at least partly because of some of Asia's long-term fundamental strengths, as well as it weaknesses. In that sense, there *was* an Asian "miracle", but that "miracle" was not indefinite, its time would come to an end, albeit spectacularly so, as indeed many boom periods do. Indeed, for every boom, there is usually a bust. Looked at in a long-term historical context, the Asian crash of 1997-1998 could be seen as merely an evolutionary step in the region's economic development, a step which Asia's more "emerged" counterparts have periodically seen on a number of occasions.

Though many have sought to compare the Asian crisis to past crises in the emerged world, notably the Latin American debt crisis of the 1980s, I would suggest that this is a useless exercise. Whatever the appropriate comparison - if indeed there is an appropriate comparison which can be made - going forward what matters is not the past but the specific responses at this time of the Asian countries to their financial and economic situations. At least initially, there was a wide variety of responses to the crisis, varying from acceptance to recrimination at cries of revenge at the verbal level. Enemies were sought and easily found, but whatever the truth or not of the charges levelled against the speculators - and it is the contention of this book that the vast majority of these charges were ill-informed, nonsense at the very least and cynical political expediency at a more realistic level - the damage continued to be done to the Asian financial markets and economies alike in the second half of 1997 and the first half of 1998.

With several countries running out of reserves with which to defend their currencies or to provide adequate funding for their combined fiscal and current account gaps, they turned one by one, albeit grudgingly to the IMF for economic aid. Such aid did not come without strings attached. Fiscal and monetary policies were to be tightened significantly in order to stabilise the domestic currency and reduce the external imbalance and the concept of market intervention was discouraged in favour of seeking appropriate medium-term policy settings. In 1998, the IMF did somewhat of an about-face and allowed those countries which had aid programmes - Thailand, Korea, Indonesia and the Philippines - to loosen policy settings in order to alleviate somewhat the effects of previously tight policies on the domestic economy. Going forward, while the likes of Thailand is now emerging from the IMF programme, no longer needing to fund itself through external, multilateral sources, the influence of both the IMF and the World Bank remain extremely profound on region-wide policy. Indeed, any examination of how Asian countries sought to cope with the initial stages of the crisis and how they are presently striving to secure economic recovery would prove fruitless without an analysis of the role of these organisations, most notably that of the IMF.

To put it mildly, the past three years have been trying times for "the Fund" as it is widely known. In not a single instance where the Fund went in to provide financial aid for an Asian economy did the local currency not devalue afterward - and usually in a spectacular fashion. The IMF's emphasis on tight fiscal and monetary policies was roundly condemned, notably by Harvard's Jeffrey Sachs - an unloved figure within the corridors of the Fund - but also by such luminaries as World Bank chief economist Joseph Stiglitz, resulting in an ongoing spat between the two organisations. High drama indeed, though this un-edifying spectacle of the world's two leading multilateral organisations feuding over how to deal with the Asian crisis did not play well with those most immediately involved with the worst effects of the crisis in Asia itself. Either with or without the efforts or such organisations, Asian countries went about their way, trying initially to limit the damage and then to provide some support for stabilisation and then recovery. What ensued is a remarkable story, of some that followed the IMF medicine to the letter and now appear to be emerging from the other side, albeit in frail shape, of others that refused the medicine and took the "nuclear" option of adopting capital and exchange controls, of still others where truly brilliant economic leadership super-ceded any need to seek external help. How Asia coped and is coping is the focus of the next chapter.

CHAPTER 2

THE FIGHT-BACK - ASIAN STRATEGIES FOR COPING

Asian countries initially sought to deal with attacks against their currencies through the usual means, namely by hiking interest rates and by vigorous intervention in the foreign exchange market. In addition, several authorities including those of Thailand, Indonesia and the Philippines imposed limits on currency swap trading. The Bank of Thailand was the first Asian central bank to see its efforts go for nought, to be soundly - and no doubt bitterly - defeated by the markets, but it was by no means the last. Those of the Philippines, Indonesia, Malaysia, Korea and Taiwan subsequently gave way to the massive waves of currency selling pressure which devastated Asian markets in the second half of 1997. Even the much respected (and feared) Monetary Authority of Singapore allowed the Singapore dollar to trade with substantially more flexibility than its trade-weighted value - which the MAS tracks - might otherwise have allowed for.

The initial reaction from many Asian authorities to the beating their currencies and asset markets took was entirely predictable, encapsulated most memorably by Dr. Mahathir Mohamed on September 20, 1997 at the IMF conference in Hong Kong. Those newsworthy comments, lambasting the currency speculators of the developed world for deliberately impoverishing developing countries were extraordinary only for their vehemence and their candour. They know doubt expressed in public the sentiments which many Asian officials privately shared. External reasons and "forces" were sought and found to explain the tempest which had struck poor, innocent Asia, from western speculators, and financial neo-colonialists to the Jews. To a westerner not directly involved in or affected by the Asian crisis, such sentiments seemed irrelevant nonsense at best, and utterly disgraceful at worst. More to the point, whatever the merits or otherwise of the view that the causes of the Asian crisis were largely external, this did nothing to alleviate or stop the crisis itself.

THREE STAGES OF RESPONSE TO THE CRISIS

Subsequent to the initial devaluations of Asian currencies, the response from Asia in terms of deeds rather than mere words, and externally from multilateral agencies and western governments and institutions came in various stages. We shall look at these various stages in great detail, up until and including present day Asia and current strategies being adopted to try and secure economic recovery in Asia, but first it is important to list the individual stages themselves:

1. Undoubtedly, the first stage reflected no doubt galling capitulation, the humiliation of having to go cap in hand to the IMF and other multilateral financial organisations for financial and economic aid. First, Thailand, then Indonesia and finally Korea went down this route. Armed with its standard approaches to systemic crises, the IMF arranged massive bailout packages for these three countries concerned, but attached severe criteria and conditions, necessitating that a clear programme of macro- and microeconomic measures needed to be strictly followed for regular loan disbursement to ensue. To summarise, these criteria reflected an emphasis on tight fiscal and monetary discipline to reduce economic overheating, crush imported inflation, close external imbalances and last but not least to stabilise the currency which up until then had been in free-fall.

   Thailand accepted this bitter medicine with grim resignation. Indonesia initially agreed to it, then sought to restructure that agreement and finally accepted a more palatable accord, more for reasons of face than anything else since the core elements of the agreement remained. As for Korea, it needed extra help in the form of a debt restructuring agreement by the international banks in order to stop the slide.

2. Yet the initial IMF rescue plan was far from the parachute which it professed to be - the 'chute did open briefly but only for it to "Roman candle", the hapless victim left to plummet to earth with a sickening thud. In financial market terms, the announcement of the IMF bailout programmes did nothing to stop the slide in the Thai *baht*, the Indonesian *rupiah* or the Korean *won*. Indeed, that selling pressure intensified, climaxing in late December of 1997 and early January of 1998 only when most of the capital that could leave those currencies had finally managed to do so. This second wave of the Asian currency crisis despite international rescue efforts - or as some perceived, *because* of the nature of those efforts and the attached conditions - caused the IMF to come under significant criticism, not only from within Asia, but also from western private sector economists and finally from none other than the chief economist of the World Bank, Joseph Stiglitz, hence resulting in a rather embarrassing and damaging public feud between the two agencies while Asia "burned". Whatever the merits or criticism, to give the IMF credit, it changed tack in 1998, allowing its programme member countries substantially more fiscal and monetary policy leeway than had first been envisaged in order to try and boost growth. Together with the resulting policy loosening by Asian financial authorities, this marks the second stage of the response to the crisis.
3. The third stage concerned those countries which did not put themselves under the IMF loan programme, either because they did not need financial aid or because they refused to accept such indignity. The policy responses from these countries varied to some extent though they can largely be grouped into those which applied IMF-type policy responses despite not being under the IMF programme, those which sought more specific responses to their own economic needs, and finally the exception to the rule, Malaysia, which changed the rules, doing the unthinkable by imposing capital and exchange controls. Aside from the case of Malaysia, two further cases deserve special mention: Singapore and Hong Kong, the first for superb economic management at a time of extreme financial and economic strain, the second for defeating speculative forces where all others had failed and baring the pain.
4. The fourth stage examines the attempts by the various Asian countries to limit the damage at the micro-economic level and seek to deal with what microeconomic infrastructure there was left standing in the wake of the crisis. These attempts varied from the vigorous in the case of Korea to the resigned in the case of Indonesia. Not surprisingly, region-wide, these attempts have met with varying degrees of success. Such is

the scale of the damage that it will take years in some cases (notably Indonesia) for the extent of microeconomic recovery to be significant.

5. Finally, the fifth and last stage looks at the policies put in place by Asian authorities in 1999 in an attempt to initiate and then to secure economic recovery. Ahead of finalising or developing sufficient microeconomic reform, the emphasis has been on creating a sound macroeconomic platform for economic stabilisation and recovery. The good news, as we shall see in Chapter 3 is that this appears to have been largely successful. The bad news is that inadequate reform and restructuring at the microeconomic level could stall that recovery unless such reforms are accelerated and deepened.

THE IMF TO THE RESCUE

Returning to stage 1, we find ourselves at the scene of battle, the victors - of whatever nationality or origin - riding off into the sunset with their spoils, the vanquished left to survey a vista of devastation, of bitter defeat. After initially refusing to accept the prospect of having its nation rescued by external elements, the Thai government capitulated on August 20th 1997, financial support for Thailand in the form of a USD17.2 billion aid package that was approved by the IMF. Indonesia followed suit on November 20th and Korea on December 4th of that year. For Thailand, a nation which has never in its history been colonised, succumbing to the pressures of the global market and requiring a national bailout package must have equated to national surrender and subjugation. A package of some USD17.2 billion was put together by the IMF involving multilateral aid from itself, the World Bank and the ADB, plus bilateral aid from Japan, Australia and a number of Asian countries. The specific break up of this is as follows:

Thailand:

	commitments
Multilateral	USD6.6 billion
IMF	3.9
World Bank	1.5
ADB	1.2
Bilateral	USD10.5 billion
Japan	4.0
Australia	1
China	1
Hong Kong	1
Malaysia	1
Indonesia	0.5
Brunei	0.5
Korea	0.5
Total	USD17.2 billion

Source: Official Data

Yet, the IMF-arranged bailout package did not come with out strings attached, without a strict programme of terms and conditions which governments had to follow in order to receive further loan disbursements from the package. The IMF stepped into the crisis, armed with its standard programme of belt tightening and austerity measures to cure the ills of any emerging market crisis. In the specific case of Thailand, this is interesting because IMF officials had warned that country's government on several occasions that the size of their current account deficit was becoming unsustainably large and that it would eventually cause economic dislocation. One must presume that the economists concerned conducting this analysis, whether in Washington or Bangkok extended that analysis to the reasons behind such a significant expansion of the current account deficit and in addition that deficit's implications. If they had extended that analysis - and surely the presumption is not unreasonable - they would have discovered that the underlying "cause et effet" was over-investment in private sector projects relative to what was already stratospheric savings' rates by Western standards. Armed with this knowledge, they might subsequently have examined the public fiscal account for evidence of imbalance - and found little or none.

How to explain this? This surely did not fit the standard model?! Here, one has to say that such an extension of what is pretty basic economic analysis is itself relatively elementary and basic. No great leap of intellect or imagination is required, though admittedly data transparency was an important issue. It is mere logic to assume that someone seeing substantial imbalance and taking the trouble to note that would look for the causes of that imbalance and - bearing in mind the many lessons of the Mexican currency crisis of 1995 - would equally examine for imbalance elsewhere, notably in the fiscal account. Let us assume then that the IMF did exactly that. And as a result, they brought out a report warning the Thai government as to the danger of running such a large current account deficit. They might not have known the size or degree of the Thai corporate short-term foreign currency debt - indeed they probably had no idea of this given that the Thai government seemed similarly unaware - but they must have known that the current account deficit was produced by private rather than public over-investment - remember, that one way of expressing the current account balance is simply savings minus investment. The fact that the public accounts had been in surplus for a decade up until the fourth quarter of 1996 would have confirmed this.

They might, or might not have subsequently examined the available data on private debt, more specifically the data from the Bangkok International Banking Facility (BIBF). If they had done so, they would have tied the two ends together - excessive private investment being fuelled by private, short-term debt, most of it in foreign currency.

Of course, I admit fully that much of this is speculative. What is a fact however is that the IMF produced several reports warning Thailand as to the potential economic dangers of its unsustainably high current account deficit. A further fact is that Thailand did absolutely nothing about these reports so a considerable degree of blame for the ensuing crisis must be put firmly at the door of the Thai authorities themselves. This does not however detract from what is a reasonable assumption, that the IMF looked at the reasons behind that growing current account deficit. If one can accept that assumption, then one must come to what is an uncomfortable conclusion. After all, the IMF implemented its standard programme of conditions in Thailand, yet the assumption that the IMF examined specific reasons for Thailand's current account deficit requires an expectation that they found those reasons, and equally the realisation that these said reasons potentially required different policies and conditions for implementation within the overall bailout programme. Theoretically, the IMF officials responsible for Thailand might have suggested an entirely different and more specific set of policies, based on their greater knowledge of the situation on the ground and the IMF might have completely ignored this and applied their standard programme of remedies despite this being ill-suited to the crisis concerned. This is the uncomfortable conclusion that one might come to, armed only with the words and deeds of the official IMF statements. Speculative? Undoubtedly, but by no means a leap of faith. Either the IMF surveillance procedures in place before the Asian crisis did not work, and thus the IMF must itself accept part of the blame (though we know this was not the case given the IMF warning to Thailand), or they did work. But if they did work, why did the crisis happen in the first place? There are two possible reasons: one is that the IMF board ignored their reports, the other is that the countries concerned ignored the warnings. In all likelihood, both were the case.

This had profound implications not only for the initial onset of the crisis, but for its subsequent worsening and for the policies aimed at stopping its progress. Those policies, whatever the findings of IMF staffers or their surveillance procedures, were the same, standard IMF medicine, the same policy responses which the IMF would use in most if not all crises no matter what their characteristics, above all the same IMF mind-set:

- Tighten fiscal policy
- Tighten monetary policy
- Liberalise and deregulate capital markets
- Strengthen supervisory institutions

Most or all of these might seem eminently reasonable to readers, yet the combination of these was not necessarily appropriate in the case of the Asian crisis. For one thing, they were aimed at public spending profligacy, a characteristic of the typical Latin American debt and currency crisis. For another, by combining loan bailouts and tightening the fiscal and monetary policy with the additional requirement of market opening and tighter supervision, they potentially confused the essential aim of the bailout plan itself. Was it to stop the slide, or was it to manage the economy? Here, the criticisms of some Asian countries, namely that more should have been done at an earlier stage, that more money should have been lent and without conditions are potentially valid. If larger loan packages had been arranged at an earlier stage, without market opening conditions and private sector debtors and creditors had been encouraged to negotiate debt rollovers, far less financial and economic chaos might have ensued. If...only. But such criticism is largely self-serving in any case. For one thing, it is not for a beggar to decide the terms of aid. For another, like the CEO of a corporation, a national government is ultimately responsible for the successful running of its country's policies. Failure is and should be met by summary dismissal.

The blame for Asian currency and economic imbalance must rest in large part with those whose job it was to run their economies - inexperience and incompetence being treated with equal severity by the markets. Yet, there is a case to answer that the actual IMF policy prescriptions for Thailand and subsequently for Indonesia and Korea were not fully appropriate and equally that they were not sufficiently focused on financial stabilisation, that demands for simultaneous opening of markets unnecessarily confused matters. This was especially the case for Korea which could in truth have been handled better. No Korean candidate for the December 18, 1997 Presidential elections could be seen to be fully and unequivocally endorsing the IMF loan terms, with the result that the voiced objections to these terms by all candidates caused significant market concern and distress. This was entirely unnecessary and could have been avoided if the IMF loan package had been made without public conditions, those conditions to be made public only after the election.

The Question of Appropriate IMF Policy Response

The IMF itself responded to the criticisms it received for its programme focus in several reports, notably in "The IMF's Response to the Asian Crisis" (January 17, 1999) which gave a preliminary assessment of its programmes for Indonesia, Korea and Thailand, for the most part defending its actions although it admitted that lessons had been learned during the crisis. In the case of the Asian crisis, the IMF saw its role primarily remaining in the defence and safety of the global financial system, and secondly helping to restore confidence to the economies affected by the crisis. Its goal was thus to provide financial programmes which might provide the foundation for economic stabilisation - and this is indeed exactly what it did. The pillars of this platform were consequently:

1. Temporary monetary tightening to stop exchange rate depreciation
2. Concerted action to correct the weaknesses in the financial system, which contributed significantly to the crisis
3. Structural reforms to remove features of the economy that had become impediments to growth (such as monopolies, trade barriers, and non-transparent corporate practices) and to improve the efficiency of financial inter-mediation and the future soundness of financial systems
4. Efforts to assist in reopening or maintaining lines of external financing
5. The maintenance of a sound fiscal policy, including through providing for rising budgetary costs of financial sector restructuring, while protecting social spending. Once the severity of the economic downturn in the affected countries became clear, fiscal policy was oriented toward supporting economic activity and expanding the social sector safety net.[1]

It was consequently NOT the IMF's specific job to attempt or help with the stabilisation of the financial markets through the implementation of short-term measures, which could well prove contrary to the medium-term economic stabilisation requirements. That said, a key lesson of the crisis which the IMF did take on board was the need to co-ordinate with the private sector, particularly with regard to private debt rollovers and restructuring, providing key support in particular to the roll-over of Korean short-term debt, negotiations which took place between December 1997 - March 1998.

Many of these points are well made. It most certainly was not the job of the IMF to bail out the Thai, Korean and Indonesian corporate sectors after these had found themselves both over-leveraged and under-hedged. Equally, the IMF cannot be blamed for inadequate regulatory supervision in several Asian countries affected by the crisis, for those countries are lack of sufficient institutional infrastructure for the lack of corporate, market and data transparency. It also cannot be held accountable for the lack of checks and balances which existed in several Asian countries, resulting in significant levels of corruption and vested interests in the case of some.

Indeed, the IMF programmes sought to address many of these important issues. Throughout the Asian crisis, IMF policies and programmes attracted substantial criticism from a host of different quarters, some in the U.S. taking the view that it should not provide any bailouts, others in Asia saying that the bailouts were too little too late, yet others who said its key focus on fiscal austerity was misplaced since Asia's public finances were already in surplus, and finally those who argued that the IMF should have stopped the crisis from happening in the first place. Some of these criticisms were reasonable, some ridiculous, and some betraying the most profound ignorance of the situation. The point about fiscal austerity is notable, and a criticism with some validity given that Asian countries were by no means fiscally lax, that the deficits were at the corporate rather than the public level, yet this was a key aspect of the policy programme aimed at closing Asian external gaps (trade and current account deficits). Granted, this was a brutal way to do it given that it implied that the domestic economy had to pay the price, bad to take the adjustment required to achieve this. But then so be it. The IMF did not create the debts problems. The IMF did not create the current account deficits, indeed in the case of Thailand it issued several warnings on that score. Indeed, the IMF is not a global financial supervisor as some take it. In the event of a financial crisis, it arrives after the fact and whatever its power and influence it cannot order the implementation of its programmes if a programme member is not fearful of getting the loan disbursement ceased.

THAILAND

Returning to the example of Thailand, whatever the theory, the Thai government set about in a decidedly practical fashion to follow the IMF policy prescription to the letter. Taxes were raised and spending programmes were savaged. Shortly after the initial devaluation of the *baht*, the Thai government increased the ceiling for foreign ownership in Thai corporations from 25% to 100%. Along with the fiscal strait jacket which it applied, the Thai authorities, albeit with some reluctance, closed down 56 finance companies which had found themselves over-exposed to the domestic property sector in the wake of the asset market crash which took place before and after the devaluation of the *baht*. Subsequently, the authorities allowed foreigners to own a majority stake in the 56 finance companies - if anyone wanted to.

There can be no question that the Thai authorities applied the terms of their bailout package with the IMF most rigorously and fully. Indeed, such was the determination of Thailand to take the medicine given to it, however bitter, that it did not shirk the cost, and the cost was high. Indeed, in addition to the middle classes and Northern peasants demonstrating in the streets of Bangkok, in addition to what one commentator called the "decapitation" of the Thai middle classes, the bankruptcies, the hundreds of thousands who lost their jobs and were forced into poverty, it cost the very existence of the Thai government itself. New coalitions were formed and once the presence of the Chavalit government had been removed, Chuan Leepkai of the Democrats returned to power. This caused jubilation and hope among offshore markets, though some investors with long memories would recall that it was the same Chuan Leepkai who as part of his programme of financial liberalisation created the BIBF, the well-spring of so much of the short-term dollar debt and therefore of the resulting financial chaos in the first place.

Still, with Thai asset markets seemingly being priced at bargain-basement value, one or two foreign investors started to return, started to sift through the rubble of shattered balance sheets for occasional gems. Thailand saw a contraction in 1997 of -1.3%, only for this to increase dramatically to -9.4% in 1998 as the initial government programme of fiscal rationalisation and monetary tightening added to the collapse in domestic demand resulting from the currency devaluation. As a consequence, the external gap was more than closed, indeed Thailand produced substantial trade and current account surpluses for 1998. The cost of that was the domestic economy, but in large part that was precisely the aim of the IMF programme. The domestic economy had to bear the brunt of the adjustment in order for the current account deficit to be reduced and ultimately eliminated. At the macroeconomic level, that swing in the Thai current account balance to a surplus of 12.8% of GDP in 1998 from a deficit of -2.1% in 1997 and -7.9% in 1996 represented a healthy improvement in medium-term fundamentals, albeit at the expense, temporarily of the domestic consumer. Left at that, things would have been fine. The economy would have gradually recovered by itself.

Yet, the degree of current account surplus in 1998 and equally the degree of economic growth contraction betrayed deeper ills that might otherwise be solved by such general, sweeping macroeconomic measures. At the microeconomic level, the deterioration of the Thai *baht* and the consequent revaluation of dollar debts had eviscerated most Thai corporate and banking balance sheets, bringing low even renowned Thai conglomerates or at the very least burdening them with massive foreign exchange losses.

With the Thai banking system saddled with bad debts of 40% of total and rising, local banks were neither able nor willing to lend to the corporate base or to consumers. Instead, they sought first to seek to repair their own shattered balance sheets by buying up every long-dated government bond issue they could find at auction and in turn borrowing the funds for those purchases from the bank of Thailand through its repo window, thus making the spread between those two interest rates. The fiscal side was being tightened, interest rates were being kept high in order to support the weakened currency and in addition banks were showing no willingness to lend whatsoever.

From a financial crisis, Thailand had been thrown into a deep economic recession, verging on outright depression. Meanwhile, if it were possible, the situation in Indonesia was even worse.

INDONESIA

The second country to go to the IMF for financial aid, in November of 1997, Indonesia under the leadership of President Soeharto, prevaricated, stalled, delayed, changed and twisted like a chameleon, infuriating IMF officials and Western governments alike. At once accepting the strictures of the initial IMF programme approved by the IMF board on November 5, 1997, Soeharto seemingly reversed course without warning, announcing budgetary measures including the re-opening of banks which were shut down supposedly as part of that fiscal rationalisation and which were subsequently re-opened.

The same pattern occurred with the IMF demand for the closure of 16 out of the country's 260-odd banks. Several of these were to re-open, some simply by virtue of changing their name. This was a further issue which could have been better handled by the IMF given that it played an undoubted part in the complete meltdown of the

Indonesian banking system as panicked depositors, unsure of which banks were to be closed, withdrew their funds en masse. The issue is not whether the closure of the 16 banks concerned was correct, but rather that the demand for closure should have been pre-empted by a national guarantee by the Indonesian authorities, with multilateral assistance if necessary, of Indonesian banking deposits. The specific disaster which was visited upon the country's banking system as a result of this demand need not have happened and the IMF and the Indonesian authorities themselves must share the blame for this.

The IMF made further demands in the latter months of 1997 and early January 1998, more specifically concerning the complete dismantling of the state cartels on primary products, such as palm oil, wood and so forth, and the lifting of subsidies on oil, flour and other basic commodities. In the context of free trade theory, this made perfect sense. Yet applying this theory to the case of Indonesia at the end of 1997 and early 1998 was perhaps not best appropriate. In practice, the dismantling of price and trade controls on palm oil resulted in a massive spike in its price, leading to violent bursts of social unrest from a domestic peasantry, already bemused by mounting job losses. In reaction to this, Soeharto then ordered the banning of palm oil exports, in complete breach of the IMF trade requirements. Soeharto's dealings with the IMF can best be characterised by a combination of expediency and evasion. Oversight by a Western multilateral organisation such as the IMF was certainly not deemed desirable in the first place, but in the latter months of 1997, when the *rupiah* was in free-fall and Indonesia's economy was steadily being destroyed on a daily basis, such oversight - and more to the point, financial aid - was deemed necessary.

Evasion was also necessary, in part because many of the IMF programme demands clashed with the financial and economic interests of the Soeharto family, in part because Soeharto was after all the leader of a nation which had rid itself of colonial domination by the force of arms. It is in this context that the January 15, 1998 signing of the second IMF agreement by Soeharto, seemingly cowering before the erect figure of a grim-faced Michel Camdessus should be seen. To many in Indonesia, this was a humiliating replication of colonisation. For many in the West, this may seem an extreme analogy, but it was not the West which was suffering from its greatest economic catastrophe since the war. A leader of Indonesia who could be so humbled by the West, who could be seen as so powerless to defend his country's interests was potentially a leader who was dispensable and expendable. Soeharto came to power in 1966, after all, as a result of a military coup - historical purists will point out here that elements of the military deemed leftists staged a coup against the Sukarno regime, possibly aided by the PKI, the Indonesian Communist Party. There is little question however that the Soeharto faction in the military knew ahead of time of such plans, allowed them to be played out, only to use these as an excuse for a military take-over of the country and a bloody putsch of perceived opposition elements, or more specifically anyone who was thought to be a Communist.

Actions by Asian governments emerging from colonial domination and subsequent internal turmoil cannot be seen exclusive to that historical backdrop, particularly those undertaken by the Soeharto government. It is in this context that we find ourselves on January 20, 1998, with Soeharto stunning the world by announcing the appointment of BJ Habibie as Vice President. At the time, the parliamentary confirmation of this appointment through the MPR was merely a rubber stamp. International reaction was at first bemused and then highly critical. As a minister responsible for national industry and technology, Habibie had been responsible for the creation of a number of industrial projects, including a national aircraft manufacturer, using substantial public investment. He was also responsible for the wholesale acquisition of the (rusting) East German military fleet after the unification of Germany and finally for the economic thought process which many dubbed "Habibienomics", characterised most clearly by the idea of alternating interest rate loosening and tightening.

Rightly or wrongly, his appointment as Vice President was viewed in the West, in the governments of the U.S. and Europe, and in the IMF, as an unmitigated disaster. Soeharto was showing his hand, that he and he alone was the supreme ruler in Indonesia. Yet, the appointment of Habibie had wider implications. As well as being a champion of national industrial projects (however ill-advised given that most of them lost money), Habibie was also an active promoter of "pribumi" (indigenous Indonesians) and Islamic interests. He was after all head of an important Islamist group, the ICMI (Indonesian Association of Muslim Intellectuals). As such, he had reportedly on occasion openly promoted "pribumi" and Islamic interests over those of the Christian religions and Chinese ethnic minorities. His elevation was thus seen also as an elevation of Islam in the national political psyche, an important departure from the previous government's policies which had brutally if effectively dealt with any Islamist elements deemed fundamentalist or against the binding national ideology of "pancasila".

Subsequently, elements of the Indonesian society appeared to see this as a green light for the public promotion of "pribumi" interests with some calling for the expropriation or redistribution of ethnic Chinese wealth among the pribumis. What had started as an economic recession was rapidly developing nasty and serious socio-political and ethnic overtones. While sporadic rioting outside of Jakarta was gradually taking on an ethnic, anti-Chinese flavour, minorities were initially protected by the security forces in the capital itself. Coincidence? Surely not! It was most likely a graphic demonstration by Soeharto again of who was in charge and the chaos that might ensue if that iron grip on control was ever let slip.

Yet, Soeharto had other tricks up his sleeve, on the economic as well as the political side. In particular, he stumbled upon one trick, the idea of a currency board. It is unknown quite how Soeharto came upon this idea, though it seems doubtful that it originated from his own economic and financial technocracy, particularly since the very concept of a currency board necessitates the theoretical elimination of discretionary control by a country's central bank over its monetary policy, if not the complete elimination of the central bank itself. For a central bank or a finance ministry to suggest such an idea would be tantamount to suicide. Whatever the case, Soeharto's "discovery" of the idea of a currency board coincided with the public promotion of the same idea by a university professor at John Hopkins University in the U.S., one Stephen Hanke. The IMF programme conditions were not only against the financial interests of the Soeharto Family. The full implementation of liberalisation, the shutting down of debt-ridden corporations and banks and the elimination of price controls were tantamount to a demand for the regime itself to commit political suicide given the social and political backlash which would inevitably result from these policies. Yet, Soeharto undoubtedly needed the significant funds attached to that IMF programme. Hence, he needed to be seen to be willing to go along with the programme, thus attracting initial loan commitments, if not actual disbursements from the programme while at the same time playing for time in terms of applying the terms and conditions of the programme, to avoid the worst consequences of these conditions for the regime itself and at the same time to seek a classical, economic alternative to those conditions.

The currency board idea thus suited Soeharto's objectives perfectly. Hanke was soon invited to Soeharto's "court" - given that Soeharto seemed in every respect the modern incarnation of a traditional Javanese King, this analogy seems apposite - where one must presume he discussed the intracacies of the currency board concept with the great man and his hangers-on, and its application to the Indonesian situation.

It must also be presumed that the IMF, which seems to deem itself the economic arbiter of the last resort, is not used to or tolerant of economic alternative ideas, to its stated policy recommendations. Certainly, the IMF public reaction to the currency board idea was far from positive, not only because it was deemed unworkable, but because the very fact of an alternative idea was unwelcome. A currency board requires the subjugation of monetary control to a fixed peg or exchange rate, extreme fiscal discipline, the backing of the monetary base by foreign currency reserves and the national resolve to accept that the economy henceforth takes the pain of adjustment rather than the exchange rate resulting from financial over-valuation. On its own, Indonesia did not have the reserves to back its monetary base commitment to a currency board. In order to do so, it would need extra funds from the international community and the IMF was at that time ideologically opposed to the idea of a currency board in Indonesia since this ran in direct opposition to its existing policy prescription. Even if it had the necessary funds for this purpose, given the shattered state of its economy and more importantly of its banking sector, the market would most likely test Indonesia's commitment to a currency board, necessitating initially sharply higher interest rates to defend the currency board peg. Those who argue that Indonesia's banking system could not under any circumstances have withstood the requirements of a currency board system ignore the precedent of Argentina whose banking system was in similarly perilous state before the implementation of a currency board in 1991 and equally the fact that the discipline of the currency board saved both the economy and the financial system of that country.

So much for theory. There can be little doubt that Indonesia, unlike in the case of Argentina, did not have the resolve to follow through on the currency board idea. When Soeharto learned the requirements of a currency board, he most probably would have dismissed the idea out of hand, albeit privately given that the stratospheric interest rates needed to defend the currency board initially would have caused potentially explosive social unrest. The best that can be said of the currency board idea in Indonesia was that it could have worked theoretically if the government had had the unswerving resolve to implement it fully, but in the end Soeharto rejected the idea for very practical reasons. In the meantime, however, Soeharto pretended to continue to consider the idea. This served two useful purposes. On the one hand, it kept the IMF occupied, and away from demanding the implementation of their own programme conditions. On the other, it had the hitherto unexpected benefit of causing the Indonesian *rupiah* to stabilise and even strengthen. The *rupiah* had by that time hit a distant and record low of 17,000 to the dollar (as against around 2,400 before the devaluation), only to slowly crawl its way back from that abyss after the signing of the second IMF agreement. At a time when it was still trading around 12,000 to the dollar, official leaks suggested that a currency board might be implemented at between 5,000-8,000 to the dollar, immediately causing currency traders to cover short *rupiah*, long dollar positions, by buying back the *rupiah*, just in case such a seemingly far fetched idea was actually implemented. This provided at least some degree of platform for economic stabilisation while Soeharto tried to keep the IMF at bay.

While the Western media speculated that Soeharto might actually implement a currency board at an exchange rate of 5,000 to the dollar, as per official leaks, in order to bail out much of the Indonesian corporate base linked to the First Family - a policy which would have seemed eminently reasonable on the face of it to a Javanese King - it seems likely that Soeharto, at least in the latter stages after he had been made to understand its implications, had no intention whatsoever of actually implementing a currency board given the likely consequences to the banking system and the country as a result of yet higher interest rates. Soeharto was thus, yet again, the Javanese puppet master in an elaborate puppet game. Neither

Hanke nor Soeharto were to remain unscathed from this episode. In the case of the former, he was publicly castigated by many commentators, most famously by the MIT Professor Paul Krugman as the "*rupiah* Rasputin", a description seemingly aimed more at capturing the media's headlines rather than adding to the level of economic debate.

Meanwhile, Soeharto continued to court alternatives to the IMF. In March 1998, Habibie toured Japan, pleading for financial aid. The then Japanese Prime Minister Hashimoto followed this up with a visit to Jakarta in April, bringing commitments of financial and food aid, notably of basic commodities such as rice. Japan had a major vested interest in not allowing Indonesia to go under since its banks were thought to be exposed in Indonesia to the tune of USD24 billion. Japan's trading houses were thought to be even more exposed than their Japanese banking counterparts. Japan's commitment to helping Asia up until then had met with significant controversy. In mid-1997, it had proposed an idea subsequently to be dubbed an Asian Monetary Fund, reflecting a reserve facility upon which Asian authorities could draw in times of need. This idea had gone down like a lead balloon in Washington, publicly because there was no need to replace the existing facilities of the IMF, and privately because it represented a fundamental challenge to U.S. dominance of the global financial system. Japan's loans to Indonesia and Thailand and the subsequent Miyazawa Initiative, named after Finance Minister Kiichi Miyazawa and reflective of this initial idea of a Japanese-dominated and created loan fund for Asian countries in need, were controversial with Western governments because they too represented a key challenge to Western domination in Asia. Yet, they were surely reflective merely of what the West had long since demanded, namely a more assertive Japanese presence on the world's political and financial stage.

Japan's loans were the catalyst for donations from other Asian countries, but though they delayed the IMF's demands on Indonesia, they did not serve to deflect them. The IMF continued to demand its trademark brand of fiscal and monetary austerity coupled with market opening and supervisory regulations. Without these, IMF loan commitments would not become actual disbursements. Soeharto's delaying tactics had frustrated and fooled many, but they did nothing to solve the underlying problem. The Indonesian corporate base was to all intents and purposes completely bankrupt, its banking system in tatters. Unemployed urban workers were being herded into trucks by the military in order to avoid major public demonstrations or unrest. Soeharto faced two alternatives, both potentially unpalatable. One was to give in completely to the IMF demands and thus risk complete social and political disintegration and more importantly his own removal. The other was not to give in and to continue to delay, thus getting IMF and international loan commitments but few actual disbursements. The country would thus continue to stagnate, more companies would continue to go bankrupt. In the end, Soeharto seems to have chosen a combination of going down fighting, while protecting his own.

In this regard, Soeharto's last hurrah was his move on May 5, as he left for an emerging market summit in Cairo, to eliminate all price controls on basic commodities for a year which he had up until then been delaying on the view that such price control elimination would be socially disastrous. The result should have been predictable. Within a week, Jakarta's Chinatown district was in flames as the city's primarily Muslim disadvantaged used the perceived wealthier ethnic Chinese Indonesians as the scapegoats of their own misfortune. At the time, several newswires reported the suspicion that elements of Indonesia's special forces, then under the command of Soeharto's son-in-law Lieutenant General Prabowo, were responsible for fuelling and inciting the riots which wracked Jakarta in May of 1998, involving the killing and raping of ethnic Chinese. Subsequently, an Indonesian military court ruling confirmed this reported suspicion. In total, around 1,120 people died in the May riots, including several hundred looters who perished in a building which they were in the process of looting and which was mysteriously set on fire. Subsequently theories abounded that Prabowo had been attempting a coup while Soeharto was away. This view - denied by Prabowo - gained prominence because ABRI (Armed Forces of Indonesia) Commander General Wiranto was also away from Jakarta at the time. Whatever the case, Wiranto returned and restored order to the streets of Jakarta through a combination of stern orders that looters would be shot on sight, and attempts to negotiate with demonstrators and student groups. When Soeharto returned to Jakarta, his capital was effectively under martial law. Once more, he had demonstrated that he - and by implication the military from which he came - were "the only game in town". Yet again, he had "proved" himself indispensable to the West (i.e. the IMF) in keeping Indonesia in one piece. Yet, the underlying fundamental condition of Indonesia continued to worsen. Indeed, that degree of deterioration had just been multiplied several times over as a result of the May riots. The essential calamity which was destroying the very fabric of Indonesian society, let alone its economy, could not be outrun by Soeharto's delaying tactics.

On May 17, Soeharto had claimed emergency powers from the MPR, only for House Speaker Harmoko to call for Soeharto's resignation the following day. Daily student demonstrations climaxed in the storming of the parliament itself. ABRI Commander General Wiranto had plenty of opportunity to shed significant blood if he had wanted to, but instead he seemed reluctant to fight such public expression of discontent through force of arms on the streets of the capital.

The bottom line had been that Indonesia, its fiscal and current accounts badly holed below the water line was sinking fast and needed money immediately to plug the gaps. With Soeharto in power, Indonesia was unlikely to get it. This realisation now coincided with widespread public demands for Soeharto's resignation. On May 20, the unthinkable happened. Soeharto stood before the world's media and announced his resignation, handing over to his Vice President BJ Habibie. The Western media recounted the end of a 32-year reign, as if the old man, now stripped of formal office, was also stripped of all influence. This was very far from the truth and to many a case of wishful thinking. Habibie was after all like an adopted son to Soeharto, dating back to the time when Soeharto as a young army officer had stayed at the Habibie home in the outer islands. Despite having his own financial resources, Habibie owed his elevation in government circles almost entirely to his "father" figure. To then say that Habibie mounted a coup against Soeharto is thus nonsense. General Wiranto almost let slip the reality when he stated publicly that no member of the Soeharto Family nor their assets would be allowed to come to harm, this while the houses of rich ethnic Chinese who had done much to finance the regime were allowed to be ransacked and burned. It is in this context that the initial elevation of Habibie to Vice President should be seen. Yes, he was put in place as a transition President, but also one who would protect the interests of his "father" Soeharto, either deliberately or otherwise. In the Javanese puppet game, Habibie played his part, an important part to be sure, but the puppet-master had not changed. Soeharto still pulled the strings. To be sure, there had to be sacrifices, examples which could be held as proving the new administration's reforming spirit. Right after Habibie was handed the reigns of power (subsequently to be confirmed by a vote of parliament), he removed from ministerial office "Bob" Hasan, Soeharto's golfing partner, and "Tutut", his daughter, a very public gesture of reducing the influence of the First Family. While filling technocratic positions with his own supporters, Habibie did everything possible in the public arena to please the U.S. administration and the IMF, promising free and fair elections the following year. He made the Bank of Indonesia separate and independent from the government by an act of parliament. He supervised the setting up of the Indonesian Banking Restructuring Agency and the Indonesian Debt Restructuring Agency. Western officials must have been pleasantly surprised. Certainly, the markets were. In truth, however, little had changed. Soeharto still held considerable influence, if only by his sheer presence and force of personality. The interests of his family had not been realistically threatened let alone expropriated. Meanwhile, the economy continued to deteriorate, the debt burden to get ever larger.

The first effort in Tokyo in May 1998 to restructure and rollover foreign bank loans to the domestic banking system had seen its talks come to nothing. Subsequently, in June of that year in Frankfurt, an agreement was tentatively reached with Indonesia's leading creditors, allowing a 3-5 year grace period for the repayment of the principal. Indonesian Debt Restructuring Agency (INDRA) was set up to provide foreign currency, though in a crucial departure from the Mexico 1982 bailout INDRA did not guarantee to subsidise the translation exchange rate to be used for debt restructuring. There was thus little incentive for an Indonesian corporation or bank to use INDRA.

KOREA

Even more melodramatic and colourful events had been taking place some way North of Indonesia, in Seoul, Korea. At the end of November 1997, Korea, the 11th largest economy in the world and recently promoted to the OECD, had come within a whisker of defaulting, saved at the 11th and three quarterth hour by a combination of the U.S. administration and the IMF. The first days as U.S. Treasury Secretary in December 1994 and January 1995 of

Robert Rubin had been a baptism of fire in having to deal with the Mexican currency crisis and its international market ramifications. His already extensive market experience notwithstanding, this period an ideal training ground for the task of leading the decidedly more complex international effort to speed up the loan packages, particularly to Korea and to persuade commercial and investment banks to roll over debt obligations owed to them. On December 24, subsequent to the announcement by the Korean government of a package of reforms designed to restructure the financial system, accelerate and deepen capital account liberalisation, introduce market-based measures to stem the outflow of short-term capital and speed up measures to open the real economy to foreign trade and investment, Rubin made the following statement:

"We have supported a broad international effort to restore stability in Asia. This effort is critically important to U.S. economic and national security interests. We welcome the steps announced today to the Korean government to strengthen and accelerate its reform programme. These important steps demonstrate the commitment to sustained reform that is essential to a successful programme to restore confidence and return Korea to a path of growth and stability...The G7 and other nations have announced today their support of action to advance by early January existing commitments of official finance, in the context of a sustained commitment by the Korean authorities to implement an intensified programme and in the context of a significant voluntary extension of the maturities of the existing claims by international bank creditors on Korean financial institutions and adequate progress by Korea towards accessing new sources of private international finance. The United States is prepared to join with the G-7 and other countries in this effort"[2]

The efforts by the U.S. financial authorities, in the form of the Treasury and the Federal Reserve, along with other Western nations has been crucial in seeking to avoid mass Asian corporate and banking defaults - and, for that matter, a consequent spike in Western bank loan write-offs. Indeed, without these efforts, the IMF loan packages would not have been enough.

The model adopted by the IMF for the bailout package of Korea did not quite reflect the subsequent U-turn in its fundamental macroeconomic thinking which was to come, but it did represent an important change, perhaps, in that direction. For the international (i.e. Western) community, it also represented an important change. Up until then, the response from the U.S. and Europe had been sympathetic, but far from unequivocal in terms of concrete support. The U.S. sought to ensure strict terms and conditions for the IMF packages, as fundamental analysis might indeed justify however this was also in full knowledge that U.S. banks had only moderate loan exposure to Asian debtors - the lessons of Mexico 1982 and Mexico 1995 having been well, if painfully learned. The EU, meanwhile, had far greater loan exposure to Asia, European banks having greedily sought to fill the gap left by Japanese banks who quietly started to depart the scene or at least to reduce their exposure in 1996. The option of demanding tough terms was thereby not open to EU officials, not in any case given to demonstrations of resolve against any but the weakest of emerging market countries. On the contrary, they pleaded for softer terms than their U.S. counterparts, fearful that Asian debtors might default, while paying the greater share of IMF contributions, the purpose of which was of course to ensure that default did not occur.

Korea was different in many respects to Thailand and Indonesia, most notably because it had vital geopolitical and strategic interest to the U.S., in addition to its new-found economic status. Put simply, Korea was vital to U.S. national security interests - seen most visibly by the U.S. military presence on the DMZ - and Thailand and Indonesia were not, or not so much. Korea could not be allowed to fail. The bailout was arranged along two lines, the first concerning the IMF negotiations with the Korean government, the second regarding pressure from the Federal Reserve, Bank of England, Bundesbank and others to persuade the international banking community to roll over short-term foreign currency debts, allowing the Korean government the time theoretically to fill the gap through new debt issues.

For Korea, the avoidance of default in December 1997 had been a very close run thing indeed. The New York Fed has summoned senior officials of the 6 largest banks to its Liberty Street headquarters for a meeting on the Korean situation. Korea was experiencing net outflows of over USD1 billion a day and its usual foreign exchange reserves were not much more than USD5 billion. The banks were encouraged to maintain credit lines to Korea on the view that it was in their own interest given that a Korean default would pose systemic risk to the global financial system. The banks' agreement on this and subsequent agreement by UK and Europe provided Korea with the necessary, though brief breathing space in which to seek options for funding itself, stopping the outflows and boosting reserves.

The devaluation of the Korean *won* from around 800 to the dollar to a record low of 1985 had meant the amount of *won* needed to repay dollar debt had more than doubled and given that just under USD30 billion in short-term debt was due by the end of March 1998, this meant potential bankruptcy without outside aid. Korean corporate foreign currency debt from the top 30 *chaebol* and their numerous affiliates amounted to around USD60 billion. Following the foreign banks' agreement to maintain credit lines, the Korean parliament in the first week of January passed the government's proposal to extend some USD20 billion in government guarantees and to issue a total of USD10 billion in new debt. In late January it was announced that the Korean banks and a group of 13 leading international banks had agreed to extend the maturities of almost USD25 billion in short-term debts to the Korean banks, a further major step in the stabilisation of Korea.

On the Korean side, at one and the same time, the Koreans treated the crisis much like any other crisis of their history, as a national struggle for survival, and simultaneously as an opportunity for more hard-bargaining. On the edge of a financial precipice Korea might be, but its new government under President Kim Dae-jung was not without skill or guile in seeking to obtain more favourable terms. Kim was particularly well aware of the country's need for new international private finance. One of his first acts as President was to invite George Soros, founder and head of the Soros Fund management, for a private meeting. In a press briefing afterwards, Soros reportedly said that he was seeking to "increase significantly" the investment of his lead fund, the Quantum Fund, in Korean asset markets, though he first wanted to see significant corporate restructuring - which would inevitably result in painful but necessary heavy layoffs - greater corporate balance sheet transparency through the consolidation of accounts and labour market flexibility.[3] That statement worked wonders for improving Kim Dae-jung's reputation as a free-market reformer, and at the same time potentially attracting the interest of other Western institutional investors to the country. It was a masterstroke. Kim went further, reintroducing the concept of anonymous bank accounts which his predecessor had banned. The initial ban had caused discreet and black money to flee the country, putting pressure on the currency and interest rate markets. In opening up the economy to foreign ownership, while simultaneously promoting Korean national interests, Kim had to walk a tightrope. It was a high-wire act done with consummate skill, but not without compromise. A reformer he was - and is - but he was not about to tear down the structure, the very fabric of Korean corporate or political society. Kim's other major success was in getting the unions, militant and moderate alike to agree to mass layoffs in return for unemployment pay, a concept inconceivable under previous Korean administrations.

Yet, while he led the reform element in the hope of attracting the necessary foreign capital to keep the economy and the financial system afloat, not all elements within Korea supported his efforts. The ruling party prior to Kim, which now formed a majority in the national Assembly did not appreciate seeing its corporate allies of long year forcibly restructured or rendered bankrupt and sought to frustrate the restucturing process through stalling bills in the parliament. Equally, the *chaebol* themselves, having gorged for years on cheap credit were hardly keen to go on a forced diet which in many cases involved the forced sale or liquidation of many of their own affiliates and subsidiaries. Many did not fulfil their part of Kim's compact with the unions by paying unemployment pay, either because they wouldn't or because they couldn't meet such obligations. Meanwhile, the economic cost of the fiscal belt tightening which the IMF demanded continued to bite into the soft flesh of the economy, hurting healthy and insolvent companies alike.

The IMF's U-Turn

Somewhere along the way, the IMF had a change of heart. Though the ideological spat with the World Bank's Joseph Stiglitz is unlikely to have caused it directly, that did serve to cause the IMF to defend publicly their programme's principal condition of fiscal austerity. In addition, the near collapse of Korea, a country which had only recently been elevated to the OECD - and thus presumably getting as close to an emerged status as a country can be while remaining "emerging" - caused a realisation that the problems of first Thailand, then Indonesia and finally Korea were not isolated incidents, but part of a regional, if not a global crisis and that the private sector had to be more involved in the resolution of the debt crisis. In addition, there was the realisation, however belated, of the sheer catastrophic degree of damage done to the Asian economies as a result of the currency devaluations and consequent debt re-valuations, economic damage which had actually been exacerbated by the IMF's own demands for fiscal austerity. Certainly, there was the realisation within the IMF that more effective procedures had to be created to involve the private sector in emerging market currency and debt crises. In addition, there was the belated recognition of the specific nature of private rather than public debt crises. Two IMF internal reports appeared to call into question the randomness of bank closures and the appropriateness of fiscal austerity.

Once Asian external gaps had been closed by the end of the first quarter of 1998 and currencies had been stabilised, the IMF finally started to listen to Asian government requests for flexibility in terms of the fiscal account given the extent of the pain being felt by their economies and populations. Indeed, the IMF went so far as to allow Thailand, Indonesia and Korea to run significant budget deficits for both 1998 and 1999 in return for further moves to open up their markets, reduce and restructure corporate debt and strengthen institutional infrastructure. From a budget surplus of +2.2% of GDP in 1996, Thailand ran a budget deficit of -1.0% in 1997 (initially targeted at a surplus of +1.0% by the IMF) followed by -2.3% in 1998 and -6.0% estimated in 1999. Korea is also expected to have recorded a budget deficit of -6.0% in 1999, after -2.9% in 1998, such was the extent of the IMF U-turn on fiscal policy. Credit where credit is due: this reflected the realisation that financial conditions had been stabilised and the priority going forward was to stabilise the economic situation and alleviate the suffering of domestic populations. The fact that the programme countries were now running trade and current account surpluses (because their economies had collapsed and thus imports had collapsed) provided a much needed funding cushion and in addition acted as a stabilising factor for Asian currencies, allowing them greater flexibility in this regard.

In particular, the IMF allowed for programme-member Asian countries to expand social spending to mitigate against the worst demand factors resulting from the effects of the crisis and the initial fiscal and monetary austerity which had been necessary in order to close external gaps and to stabilise currencies. In the case of Indonesia, the overall budget cost of social safety net programmes was initially put at 8% of the GDP per annum, a financial hole which the IMF helped plug. Up until the first quarter of 1998, the programme member fiscal targets remained contractionary, but after that they became expansionary as the IMF allowed the three programme members to increase social spending, seeking to reduce the worst of the burden on the poor. There was a condition however and that was that deficit spending had to be financed through viable borrowing rather than monetary creation in order to avoid the potential threat of further inflationary impulses. In addition, there was the deliberate attempt to avoid increased fiscal deficits resulting in higher domestic interest rates. Through the joint efforts of the World Bank, deficit spending was aimed to help the poor, and to provide the necessary funding for the cash-strapped corporate sector. Monetary policy was similarly allowed to be expansionary, in line with easier fiscal policy after currencies were stabilised.

This belated flexibility on the part of the IMF was welcome. There were however Asian countries which suffered similarly or even equally amidst the hurricane of the Asian crisis which did not go the way of the IMF. These were divided into two types: those who sought to go their own way, rejecting both the idea of IMF help and ultimately of exchange rate flexibility (Malaysia), and secondly those who did not seek IMF aid but used policies similar to those promoted by the IMF in seeking to deal with the crisis, through their own best efforts and superior economic management (Hong Kong and Singapore).

Malaysia

In the case of Malaysia, the government not only had to combat the full force of the crisis, it also had to deal with a growing policy quarrel between Prime Minister Dr. Mahathir Mohamed and Deputy Prime Minister Anwar Ibrahim, the former railing against the market, blaming Western currency speculators for impoverishing his country and the region as a whole and saying that currency trading should be banned, the latter championing the free market and supporting the IMF's case of fiscal and monetary tightening. Mahathir fired his

Deputy Anwar, who was subsequently arrested and convicted on several charges. The Governor and Deputy Governor of the central bank, Bank Negara Malaysia, resigned and the following week, on September 1998, Malaysia imposed capital and exchange controls, fixing the *ringgit* at 3.80 to the dollar and banning the offshore spot and forward *ringgit* markets. As a result of this, domestic liquidity increased, allowing interest rates to be lowered, thus reducing the debt service burden on the domestic corporate base and banking system, an important consideration given that Malaysia's total debt to GDP at the time was around 160%. Malaysia is currently undergoing a strong growth recovery and GDP growth is anticipated at 4.8% in 1999 and 5.0% in 2000 after a 7.5% contraction in 1998.

SINGAPORE

The case of Singapore concerns one of fundamentally superior economic management. One of the most open trading nations in Asia, it was especially vulnerable to the collapse in inter-Asian regional trade which resulted from the Asian regional crisis. Well aware that competitive devaluations by its trading partners could result in a loss of competitiveness, the Singaporean authorities set about restoring that competitiveness through a series of microeconomic and budgetary measures, most notably including a 15% point cut in the employer contribution to the CPF, the national provident (pension) fund compulsory for domestic workers. Prior to the crisis, Singapore was already running a current account surplus of over 15% of the GDP so it had a substantial cushion to limit the damage to its currency. As a result of the downturn in domestic demand, that current account surplus almost reached 21% in 1998 and is expected it to be just over 17% in 1999. Outside of China, Singapore and Taiwan were the only countries which did not see their economies contract in 1998 in the emerging Asian region which we follow. Singapore saw growth of +0.3% and on current form this is likely to be followed by a growth of 6.0% in 1999 and 8.0% in 2000. How did this happen? The Singaporean authorities allowed greater flexibility in tracking the Singapore dollar against its basket of trading currencies, thereby implying a modest depreciation, but they explicitly did not allow a devaluation of the currency for the purpose of maintaining or expanding trade competitiveness. Thus, while the Singapore dollar was allowed to weaken slightly at the height of the crisis, from a high against the dollar in May 1995 of 1.3830 to a crisis low of 1.8160, the crisis-related depreciation of the Singapore dollar from 1997 through the end of 1998 was around 25%, comparing favourably with devaluations of 40-50% for the Thai *baht* and the Philippine *peso*, with the Indonesian *rupiah* losing an astounding 80% of its value at one point. The Singapore dollar could not but be swept along to an extent by the crisis, but the important point was that investor confidence in the handling of the economic and financial fundamentals of the country remained assured. While Singapore did not take the road of devaluation, it also avoided the policy U-turn by IMF programme countries which are now looking at budget deficits of around 6% of GDP for 1999. The Singaporean authorities allowed a budget deficit of just -0.3% of the GDP in 1998, followed by an estimated -1.5% in 1999 which is likely to be flat in the year 2000. Strong long-term fundamentals, a prudent policy mix and a clear focus on maintaining the overall cost competitiveness of the economy, through allowing the market mechanism for re-pricing the domestic property market and through cutting the employer cost base through the CPF contribution reduction, were the foundations for the city state's rock solid economic performance. Without any sense of false flattery whatsoever, the Singaporean economic and financial authorities are among the most impressive anywhere in terms of their skill in running the economy.

HONG KONG

While other Asian currencies were allowed to depreciate, to whatever degree, Hong Kong did not have that luxury, having adopted a currency board in October 1983 when the peg - for want of a better word, since it is not strictly speaking a currency "peg" - was fixed at 7.80 Hong Kong dollars to the U.S. dollar. What the Hong Kong authorities themselves call a linked exchange rate regime (i.e, a currency board) is designed to allow Hong Kong interest rates to adjust automatically to currency pressures via changes in domestic money supply, whereby the selling of Hong Kong dollars results in an equal reduction in the Hong Kong dollar money supply, thus causing interest rates to rise. Eventually, as the logic of the currency board system goes, domestic Hong Kong interest rates reach a level which attracts renewed investor interest in the Hong Kong dollar, causing purchases of that currency and subsequently an equal and opposite increase in the supply of Hong Kong dollars to the system, thus causing interest rates to fall back once more. In theory, the system is beautifully and elegantly simple. However, the practice of financial markets can be somewhat more violent. The date of October 23, 1997 was the first of several to be etched in the minds of those who watched the Hong Kong markets during the crisis. That day, the benchmark Hang Seng stock market index lost a stunning 1,211.47 points, at the time its largest one-day drop in history as speculators attacked both the currency and asset markets at the height of the first wave of the Asian crisis. As the Hong Kong dollar came under increasing attack, increasingly large amounts of Hong Kong dollars had to be withdrawn from the domestic money supply as required by the rules of the currency board. The Hong Kong Monetary Authority sat back and watched as the overnight borrowing rate skyrocketed to 300%. The combination of soaring interest rates and heavy foreign exchange intervention caused USD-HKD to hit an intraday low of 7.4800, compared to usual trading levels at the time of around 7.7450, as the Hong Kong dollar screamed higher against the U.S. dollar in the wake of panicked speculators desperately trying to get out of their short Hong Kong dollar positions. October 23, 1997 was a day of high drama, a day when investors throughout the territory gazed up at public stock market screens in horror as the Hang Seng was smashed, a day when the speculators thought they were winning and ended up very badly burned as sky-high interest rates caused their funding costs to soar, a day the HKMA was tested and not found wanting. It was not to be the last time that the HKMA was tested however, far from it, though the bruising which the speculators took on that day caused many to take quite some time before they returned to have another go.

Basically, the options open to the Hong Kong authorities came down to two: hold the peg or let it go. The authorities chose to hold it at all costs, in the face of significant criticism from financial and economic commentators (mostly outside Hong Kong, and who were thus not exposed to the result of a de-pegging!) and rightly so. As I argued at the time, a de-pegging or an adjustment/devaluation of the Hong Kong dollar would have been catastrophic for Hong Kong. Many at the time said that Hong Kong needed to devalue in order for it to regain trade competitiveness lost to its major competitors in the wake of the ASEAN and North Asian currency devaluations during the Asian currency crisis. This logic is deeply flawed. Returning to the strict definition of the exchange rate regime in Hong Kong, the Hong Kong dollar is not pegged as several ASEAN currencies were pegged to the dollar at the time (only for those pegs to be blown apart), but is instead linked to the U.S. dollar via a currency board, whereby the HKMA, the monetary authority of Hong Kong in lieu of a standard central bank, guarantees to sell dollars at a rate of 7.80 Hong Kong dollars to the market, backing that guarantee with its own foreign exchange reserves from the Exchange Fund.

The currency board survived its test in October 1997, just as it had many before that (and subsequently), and by the end of the first quarter slightly more favourable liquidity conditions had allowed a relaxation in domestic Hong Kong interest rates, causing the spread between the 3-month HIBOR rate and the Fed funds' target rate to finally dip back below pre-crisis levels. This was to be a temporary relief however for the Hong Kong markets and for the exchange rate system, which started to come under renewed attack in June and July of 1998. Local interest rates were forced sharply higher, while the stock market turned South, falling to a 1998 low of 6,544.79 from above 16,000 in 1997. At the time, speculators had discovered a way of "manipulating" the local markets as the HKMA would later charge, selling the Hang Seng futures, borrowing Hong Kong dollars and selling them short against the U.S. dollar, thus forcing interest rates higher. What they lost on their Hong Kong dollar borrowing, they more than made up for on their short Hang Seng futures' and short Hong Kong dollar positions, seemingly free money. A large scale attack on the Hong Kong dollar and Hong Kong asset markets took place in early August of 1998. The Hong Kong authorities, not surprisingly took exception to this given that the economy remained mired in deep recession and higher interest rates would exacerbate that. Trading in Hang Seng stock index futures exploded in early August, with gross open interest in the front end contract rising to 92,000 contracts from 70,000 in June. Eventually, the Hong Kong authorities decided to do something about this, with the Financial Secretary and the HKMA Chief Executive Joseph Yam giving approval for the HKMA desk to intervene in the stock market with the specific aim of eliminating the speculative presence. From August 14-28, the HKMA bought cash stocks and Hang Seng futures, with a total worth of around HKD110 bln, causing the Hang Seng to rebound back above the 10,000 level. Incredibly, the HKMA had taken on the markets and won - again - but this did not come without a deluge of criticism, both from within Hong Kong this time and externally that the authorities, by intervening in the market had effectively abandoned their free-market principles.

The HKMA followed this up in September by introducing a number of measures to boost the overall market liquidity, when measured it caused the Hong Kong dollar to halve almost instantly, further burning the speculators. The package of measures contained two major provisions: a convertibility undertaking to demonstrate the authorities' commitment to the currency board and a cushion of liquidity through a series of technical improvements to that currency board system. On the first, the HKMA provided a crystal clear undertaking to licensed banks to convert Hong Kong dollars in their clearing accounts into U.S. dollars at a fixed rate of HKD7.75 to the U.S. dollar. In addition, from April 1, 1999, that convertibility undertaking exchange rate of 7.7500 would change by 1 pip per calendar day, taking 500 calendar days to complete the move to 7.80. On the second provision, the HKMA made a commitment to increase systemic liquidity reducing the ability of speculators to manipulate the market, which was what the HKMA saw as levelling the playing field. More specifically, the HKMA suggested 6 specific measures:

1. Removing the bid rate of the Liquidity Adjustment Facility (LAF)., thus keeping more interbank funds in the system.
2. Replacing the LAF with a discount window with the base rate of that (formerly the LAF's offer rate) to be determined occasionally by the HKMA but in general by the market.
3. Removing the restriction on repeated borrowing of overnight Hong Kong dollar liquidity through repo transactions using Exchange Fund Bills and Notes.
4. New Exchange Fund paper to be issued only when there is an inflow of funds, ensuring that all EF paper is fully backed by foreign exchange reserves.
5. Introducing a schedule of discount rates applicable for different percentage thresholds of holdings of Exchange Fund paper by the licensed banks for the purpose of accessing the discount window.
6. Retaining the restriction on repeated borrowing in respect of repo transactions involving debt securities other than Exchange Fund paper.

Joseph Yam, the HKMA Chief Executive, said: "These measures aim at strengthening Hong Kong's currency board arrangements and achieving an even higher degree of transparency and disclosure. They will enhance the robustness of Hong Kong's monetary arrangement, characterized by the linked exchange rate system. They should also help to reduce excessive volatility in interest rates."[4]

The measures were aimed at significantly boosting systemic liquidity and at the same time increasing transparency of the currency board system, thus allowing the potential for the market itself to offset speculative interest. Despite further criticism of these measures and ongoing criticism of the stock market intervention, it is no exaggeration to say that this package of measures was brilliant. In addition to those stated aims, they eliminated much of the market concern regarding the HKMA's previous apparent policy of stating a convertibility rate of 7.80 to the dollar while actively intervening in the foreign exchange market at 7.7500, thus allowing the potential for arbitrage and putting into question its commitment to the currency board - if the HKMA believed in the strength and efficacy of the currency board system, why did it need to intervene at all instead of letting the mechanism work.

The HKMA's response to repeated attacks against the currency board system attracted praise from none other than the New York Fed President William McDonough for its steadfastness and resiliency in the face of the most trying of financial market conditions. Yet, while it seemed to have won a series of battles, the fundamental economic situation remained dire. After seeing its economy expand by an impressive 5.3% in 1997 - the height of the boom in local asset markets, in the run up to the Handover on July 1, 1997 - Hong Kong's economy contracted by 5.1% in 1998, a stunning reversal of 10.4% points. Unlike other Asian countries which saw their currency depreciate, deliberately or inadvertently as a result of the crisis, Hong Kong did not have that luxury given the currency board peg requirement. Equally, on the fiscal side, the HKSAR - Hong Kong Special Administrative Region of China - was restrained by the Basic Law from having significant fiscal deficits which would be deemed fundamentally imprudent. Hong Kong ran a budget deficit of -2.5% of the GDP in 1998 on the basis that this was an emergency situation, which is likely to have been followed by a deficit of -2.9% in 1999. Despite some degree of deficit spending and a cut in the national income tax, the main brunt of the adjustment fell on the three main pillars of the Hong Kong economy: property, financial services and tourism/retail trade. On the first issue, the government, which remains the sole owner of remaining plots of land due to the Colonial heritage of the place, ceased having new auctions to try and re-balance the supply/demand equation. The second issue, resulted in mass layoffs of bank staff as financial institutions sought to downsize to reflect greatly reduced demand for financial product, of whatever sort. On the third, tourism collapsed.

Fundamentally, this adjustment in the form of asset prices and demand was actually no bad thing, for Hong Kong by 1997 was an extremely expensive, un-competitive place, as reflected most clearly by house prices (which doubled from January-June 1997 alone). Hong Kong did not have the problems that Thailand, Indonesia and Korea had, namely of excessive short-term foreign currency debt and a shaky banking system. On the contrary, the HKMA was a very prudent and sound regulator of the banking system, ensuring the maintenance of bank capital adequacy ratios substantially in excess of the Bank of International Settlements (BIS) requirements. No, Hong Kong's problem was one simply of loss of price competitiveness, a loss which was shown up and greatly exacerbated by the Asian currency devaluations against the Hong Kong dollar as well as the U.S. dollar in the wake of the crisis given Hong Kong's need to maintain a fixed exchange rate commitment. The HKMA was right to maintain that commitment to the currency board system at the time, during the crisis given that the alternative would have courted a financial disaster potentially worse than Thailand given the proportion of the U.S. dollar and Hong Kong dollar assets in the system as a result of the currency board, and more specifically the fact that the domestic banking system's capital base was in Hong Kong dollars. If the peg had been let go at any time during the crisis, the resulting devaluation of the Hong Kong dollar could not have been limited and would have caused a proportional devaluation of the banking system's capital base. It would have caused the one thing it had not done to any degree up until that point, a loss of confidence in the domestic supervisory institutions and in the domestic banking system. There would have been mass panic, runs on banks. The banking system would have imploded, domestic interest rates would have skyrocketed rather than fallen as demand for Hong Kong dollars collapsed and the stock market and the economy would have gone into meltdown. It would have been the type and degree of financial catastrophe from which it would have taken Hong Kong decades to recover. During the crisis, there was absolutely no benefit to the

HKMA in letting the peg go, and every reason to maintain it. Those who called for its abandonment were talking utter nonsense. This does not mean to say that a currency board cannot be eventually replaced by another form of exchange rate regime. It is to say that if the currency board system had been seen to be defeated, it would have caused disaster, and not just for Hong Kong. All other currency boards in the world would have been instantly targeted. Argentina has much to thank Hong Kong for, and vice versa.

Going forward, Hong Kong may decide that a policy change is necessary given more suitable conditions and fundamentals, however what it did in 1997-98, maintaining the peg at all cost was exactly the right thing to do. Anything else would have been disgracefully irresponsible. The Hong Kong authorities also, justifiably, deserve much praise. What one can say however is that their policy response was not asymmetric. They intervened against what they saw as excessive and manipulative selling pressure against the Hong Kong dollar and its asset markets, but they were not so similarly zealous when those same asset markets were rallying excessively in 1996-97. Was this not also speculation? It is not a sufficient answer for the HKMA to say that they do not intervene in financial markets, since they plainly did do exactly that in August 1998. It would not have been beyond the remit of the monetary authority at the time to warn against the potential dangers of speculative gains, indeed it should have done so, though political factors ahead of the Handover might have made that somewhat difficult and a sensitive issue in practice.

Tinkering with the Micro-Economy

The last strategy response from the Asian countries which we will look at briefly - and subsequently in a later chapter in substantially more detail - is that of microeconomic reform and restructuring. In contrast to the Latin American debt crisis of 1995 which undoubtedly had major microeconomic effects, but whose roots were macroeconomic, the very root cause of the Asian crisis lay in the micro-economy. Consequently, a key strategy for dealing with the worst effects of the crisis and for reviving Asia's shattered and bruised economies had to deal with microeconomic management and reform. Here, one has to say that the record in 1997-98, while fine in theory, was poor in practice, in the implementation of that theory.

Some progress was made however. Since the onset of the Asian crisis, several Asian countries have sought to improve their regulatory frameworks for domestic financial institutions, forcing increases in bank CAR ratios and the improvement of standards on loan provisioning and loan classification.

In addition, the governments of Korea, Indonesia and Thailand sought to varying degrees to put in place an institutional and legal framework for the resolution of debt restructuring. Finally, all three countries increased foreign investor access to their markets, companies and banks through the raising of foreign investor ownership ceilings and the reduction or elimination of rules inhibiting such access. Korea, for example, fully liberalised foreign purchases of domestic Korean *won* bonds and abolished most ownership restrictions for foreign investors, key elements in the task of re-liquifying the Korean financial and economic system. In the financial sector, to recall, Thailand closed 56 finance companies, while Korea closed more than half of its merchant banks. In addition, it closed two commercial banks, re-capitalised them and sought to re-sell them to domestic and foreign investors. The governments of Korea and Thailand announced the issuance of domestic bonds worth up to 15% of the GDP, placing these with domestic financial institutions in order to put a floor under the balance sheet of their respective banking systems.

All sound measures and proof indicated that the efforts of the IMF and World Bank were not wasted and that progress was made at the micro-economic as well as the macroeconomic level. That said, one should not under-estimate the damage caused at the micro-economic level by the crisis and thus the remaining problem. The World Bank in its report "East Asia: The Road to Recovery", said that it was estimated that as a result of the crisis two-thirds of Indonesian firms suffered losses exceeding their equity, while for Korea this figure was two-fifths and for Thailand one quarter.[5] Higher interest rates, plunging capital bases, a collapse in available domestic bank credit as banking systems sought first to repair their own balance sheets combined to produce a ruinous result for many Asian corporations. In the go-go days of Asian economic growth, the fundamental weaknesses of many of these companies, including small capital and equity bases and over-leverage on cheap, in many cases government-induced credit, had been hidden by strong top line growth in the P&L.

Diminishing total returns was a warning prior to the crisis, a warning which went unheeded at all levels.

High debt-equity ratios was however the natural product of the Asian growth model, itself founded on consensus and co-operative rather than competitive economics. Asian governments had sought to expand deliberately the strategic export sectors. In order to do so, they provided, directly or through their banking systems, cheap, directed credit, subsidised loans and tax breaks. Insufficiently deep Asian equity and bond markets required that the Asian corporates rely for most of their external funding on bank loans. In the early 1990s, many Asian governments removed or reduced borrowing limits, particularly on foreign currency borrowing, but failed simultaneously to strengthen banking, corporate regulation and supervision. When I arrived in Asia at the start of 1996, before I joined the banking sector, many of its markets and economies felt like a Gold rush precisely because there was insufficient control or supervision of bank lending or corporate borrowing. It was the "Wild East" in that just about anything went. Cheap credit was available and deals were done whatever it took. Corporate governance played a part also in that corporate borrowing was in many cases hugely excessive relative to its potential for driving the bottom line. As a result, a substantial part of corporate profit went into paying interest costs, thus making corporations especially vulnerable to domestic interest rate rises. For example, by 1997, according to the World Bank, more than two thirds of all profits of listed Thai companies went to cover the interest costs.

In addition, excessively cosy relationships between domestic bank loan officers and many corporations led to increased loans to firms with high debt leverage and low profitability. Political pressure from the top to make loans to favoured or strategic companies had an eventual cost and in 1997 and 1998 that cost was high - and remains high to this day. As stated in **Asia Falling**, it is all about incentive. Banks had little incentive for ensuring that their loans were creditworthy, while corporations had little incentive to ensure that their loans were needed in the first place since they would get them anyway. The market pricing mechanism was thus significantly distorted. What we have seen subsequently is not only the result of that but effectively an attempt by "the market" to achieve a greater degree of pricing mechanism equilibrium. In the 1960s and 1970s, many Asian countries privatised banks and corporations, however in many cases they retained a heavy hand in their financial running. As an economist, it is my profound view that the state is inherently inefficient from a profit perspective in running companies and banks, a condition brought about by the fact that profit is not the only or in some cases even the major motive. Interlocking relationships between the government, banks and corporations thus reduced the ability of the market mechanism to function, thus inexorably leading to ever diminishing returns and the consequent need for ever increasing credit just to maintain those returns. "Cronyism" was a factor behind the Asian crisis. To anyone with any common sense, this is merely stating the obvious, but to some apparently it has to be said. Granted, that same cronyism or contact- or consensus-capitalism depending on how one terms it was also a key plank of the Asian growth story for at least two decades, but such practices, lacking the discipline of a free market which focuses only on the bottom line eventually led to major price distortion, such distortions inevitably being corrected, albeit after a substantial period of time and at the expense of a regional crash.

Inadequate domestic asset markets and more specifically the infrastructure of those asset markets, namely zealous and INDEPENDENT regulators and deep and broad institutional investor bases were also a key reason for the lack of true market discipline which pervaded in Asia in the 1990s. For instance, in 1996, the mutual fund industry represented under 10% of the total Stock Exchange of Thailand (SET) trading. Outside of Singapore, many Asian countries had weak or minimal pension fund industries. Finally, the very organisational structure had a part to play in the eventual Asian crisis, characterised most commonly by a diversified conglomerate structure whose shares were closely held by a family. Given the lack of development of the Asian equity markets and the lack of minority shareholder rights, these owners again did not have sufficient incentive to make their corporations efficient. They simply did not have to.

The result of all this was that the crisis caused wholesale bankruptcy in countries which had these fundamental microeconomic flaws. Indonesia was easily the hardest hit, followed by Korea and Thailand. The extent of the damage reached systemic proportions in all IMF programme member countries. Solving this crisis at the microeconomic level always necessitated a comprehensive and co-operative strategy involving international creditors, domestic banks and corporations, domestic governments and the influence of multilateral organisations to prod proceedings along in the right direction. Using the incentive rule, such strategies only work if they have to, if they are forced to. This implies the breaking up of those cosy relationships between banks, corporations and governments. There is a key lesson from the Japan crisis (1991-and still counting) in this. Bank restructuring in particular works most effectively if it is enforced by the government, creditors or shareholders, rather than at the agreement of cosy agreements. This was a key reason why the Japanese government attempts at bank restructuring - however belated, however pitiful - have so far failed to achieve what most in the West see as the desired result - a profitable, healthy bank. Instead of this, Japan has gradually been nationalising its financial system, a strategy which is doomed to ever diminishing returns and ultimate failure. When faced with the painful choice between propping up institutions (and those cosy relationships) or biting the bullet and letting such institutions go or be forcibly restructured, no matter what the short term cost to prices or market confidence, Japan chose the easy way out.

It has yet to be confirmed that Thailand, Korea and Indonesia have avoided this route. If they have not, that will have dire consequences for the medium- and long-term growth prospects of their economies. The alternative to the approach of bank-led restructuring is theoretically and has been practically that of government-led restructuring. Under this model, the government creates an asset management company to reduce and restructure bank non-performing loans, taking over and restructuring bad debts and replacing these assets with bond issues, thus the banking system is re-capitalised. While governments may prefer voluntary negotiations between bank creditors and corporate debtors, without appropriate balancing mechanisms in order to avoid social structure damage, this is rarely the most appropriate way of achieving an efficient result. What seems clear is that there must be an element of enforceability of this restructuring by the authorities and equally a degree of submission to market pricing discipline. On the latter, this means, whatever price the market currently supports is the price you get for your distressed assets, not the price you or your government might want.

However, those distressed assets need domestic as well as foreign buyers. More has to be done to democratise the Asian equity markets, increasing the rights of minority shareholders, developing strong mutual and pension fund industries which in turn can help enforce corporate and bank restructuring - or throw out directors and CEOs through the creation of emergency shareholder meetings - a source of much humour in Japan for some time and look at the cost of that. Disclosure and accounting standards have to be improved (or in some cases created). Remember, things don't improve if they don't have to improve. The message to Asia is a clear, if an uncomfortable one: the Asian capitalist model does not work anymore. It has passed its sell by date. This is not to say that Asia should necessarily and automatically adopt a U.S. version. It is to say that Asian governments and financial authorities should create true market places, which might or might not mimic their U.S. counterparts, but which focus on creating free and fair trade, strong regulatory and supervisory standards and the institutional investor structure to support deep and liquid asset markets. The pricing mechanism used must be the market rather than the relationship. Why? Not because that is the U.S. model (it is questionable whether or not it is in fact given trade subsidies which both the U.S. and Europe provide), but because it is the most efficient model, providing the soundest base for long-term sustainable growth. That, surely, must be the aim.

The emphasis on the market pricing mechanism must not be at the expense of ignoring the importance of creating a sufficient legal framework, a crucial element in any country's infrastructure, as important as ports and roads, as electricity, housing and education. In the case of a debt and currency crisis, the first priority in this regard must be to provide an adequate bankruptcy law framework to encourage new investors to pick through the rubble of distressed assets. Only when this occurs will there be sufficient incentive not to become distressed in the first place. In the wake of what appears to be strong recoveries in Asia, this may no longer seem relevant, but it most assuredly is. Without sufficient microeconomic reform and restructuring, those recoveries will most assuredly prove fleeting, the result of temporary fiscal and monetary stimulus which when removed in order to avoid renewed inflation results in a sharp pullback in domestic demand.

Generally speaking, there are three types of resolving bankruptcy or insolvency: liquidation, rescue or agreed restructuring or "work out" involving informal relationships outside of the court's mandate. Both liquidation and rescue necessitate the presence and active involvement of the formal court procedure, the first leading most likely to a sale of assets to a third party (the company and the court being the first two parties), the second involving the administered rescue of a company as a viable and going concern through public infusion or in the private sector case most likely debt-equity swaps. The dependency in Thailand, Korea and Indonesia on the Asian model of consensus rather than market capitalism led to an initial emphasis on informal work outs after the crisis, despite the emphasis by the IMF on the strengthening of the institutional infrastructure framework. Issues such as "loss of face" and the necessity to maintain business and banking relationships have proved to be strong obstacles to the initial creation and then the enforcement of efficient bankruptcy laws. However, it is wrong to say that culture is an inevitable obstacle to this process. The Singapore bankruptcy code, shaped by the UK 1985 Insolvency Act is a case in point, involving supposed Western legal enforcement with an Asian emphasis on compromise and negotiation, a potential model for others in the region to follow. Extending that example, it is no coincidence whatsoever that Singapore has an exceptionally strong corporate legal framework and zealous and independent regulatory bodies, and at one and the same time its corporate and banking systems are relatively low geared - as befits PROFIT necessity - and have survived the Asian crisis for the most part healthy and intact. There are no doubt strong relationships between banks and corporations in Singapore, but they are not allowed to be the founding premise for debt creation.

Outside of Singapore, in crisis countries where the relationship became the essence of the pricing mechanism, rather than the market, is where the Asian model eventually broke down when it was forced to compete with the unfettered forces of the global free-market system. The Asian model does not have to be scrapped wholesale, but the driving force and the incentive for economic growth have to be altered in favour of the market. Strong relationships can and should still exist. That need not change, but they cannot be the primary motivating force behind economic expansion. Not anymore. The alternative is to reject the global system and turn inwards, but that is not a realistic option for any but the foolhardy. The "emerged" nations chose that alternative in the 1930s, in favour of trade and capital market protectionism. The Great depression was the result.

Going forward, Asia, now more than ever, will need access to great amounts of liquidity. In the short term it might get that from asset managers seeking short-term returns. However, to rely on those is to ignore many of the key lessons of the crisis, not least that over-reliance on short-term capital flows is a perilous policy choice - and that is exactly what is, a policy choice. There is an alternative, and that is to create a more viable platform for foreign direct investment in the cases of some, institutional infrastructure for others, re-capitalising their financial systems not only with money but with the legal and supervisory framework to encourage investors to the view that the crisis will not re-occur.

So much for what has not happened at the level of microeconomic reform, what is needed, what is to come - or not. This is not to take away from the fact that 1999 saw a dramatic recovery in Asian economies, one which surprised many. The length of that recovery will, as we have seen, depend crucially on the extent of microeconomic reforms which Asian countries attempt to achieve. That said, IF such reforms are imposed, it is a recovery which has some chance of continuing into 2001 and beyond, depending of course on how the external environment, not least in the U.S., pans out. The next chapter looks at this issue of Asian economic recovery, how it was created, the recovery's first symptoms and why macroeconomic dynamics suggest it will continue at least in the short term.

CHAPTER 3

THE RECOVERY – SET TO CONTINUE?

If 1998 was a year of excruciating pain for most Asian economies - which undoubtedly it was - then 1999 has been altogether a different story, one which has repeatedly and publicly been dubbed the year of Asian recovery by the world's media. Even those Asian economists who were reluctant to forecast a supposed "V-shaped" recovery from that dire year of 1998 were gradually forced to admit gathering signs of economic expansion. From early 1999, it looked as if we could see a revival due to the Keynes-ianist policies adopted in the wake of the IMF's policy U-turn of allowing significant monetary and fiscal easing.

In truth, the first signs had appeared in the last quarter of 1998. In Thailand and Korea, where the crisis had begun, exports had collapsed and imports were continuing to contract by some 30% year-over-year through the end of the third quarter reflecting an equal collapse in domestic demand. In Indonesia, domestic prices were still rising, but elsewhere they were falling, further confirmation of that slide in demand. However, in the fourth quarter of 1998, we started to see a marked reduction in the year/year contraction of imports in Thailand, Korea, the Philippines and even Indonesia. If the first sign of financial market stabilisation was the collapse of imports and the consequent, dramatic turnaround in national trade accounts, the first sign of *economic* stabilisation was paradoxically almost the complete opposite, that is the slowdown in import contraction if not the actual revival in imports.

The Revival of Imports Herald The Approaching Recovery

Some suggested this could lead to the collapse of the only support left for domestic currencies, namely the huge trade surpluses that were being generated as a result of that collapse in demand which had in turn led to sharply lower imports. Others attributed this to year-on-year basing effects, dismissing any prospect of recovery in the near term and pointing instead to the protracted downturn in Latin America, Mexico and Japan after their respective financial crises in 1982, 1995 and 1991. Yet, to us, this slowdown in the pace of import contraction represented something quite different, the first, faint flickering of recovery. In medical terms, it would have been the first up-beat on a heart monitor which had been flat-lining, faint, but still there. Proof at least that the patient was not going to die.

Demand remained deeply depressed by standard consumption indicators, unemployment continued to rise and economies for the most part continued to contract on a quarterly basis. These were, however, lagging indicators, for the most part reflective of the past, substantial inventory reduction and corporate downsizing. Some were sceptical of the reasons behind a gathering slowdown in the pace of import contraction in the likes of Thailand and Korea in particular, attributing the move the to J-curve effects whereby the devaluation of local currencies exaggerated the dollar value of imported goods. Yet, this slowdown in import contraction appeared to be also happening in volume as well as value terms, seriously questioning such a view. For the full year of 1998, imports contracted by a stunning 35.5% year-on-year in Korea and by almost 34% in Thailand after a 13.4% contraction in 1997, yet the first sign of improvement in this key indicator was seen in the fourth quarter of that year. If the collapse in imports was slowing down, that meant that at the very least the fall in demand was slowing, positive news in a regional environment where all prevailing news was dire to moderately bad.

That first sign of stabilisation in the IMF programme-countries such as Thailand and Korea were matched by the more efficient economies such as Singapore, which saw a GDP contraction in the fourth quarter of 1998 of -1.1% as against a contraction of -1.9% in the third quarter. While the feeling on the streets was one of utter misery as the full unemployment effects of the financial and economic crisis continued to be felt, particularly by those who had started off lower down on the ladder in any case, a gradual reduction in financial market pessimism took place in the final months of 1998 and the first quarter of 1999 as regards Asian economic prospects. Singapore actually saw positive growth in the first quarter of 1999 of +0.6% and other ASEAN countries saw their contractions continue to shrink. Suddenly, there was talk that since Thailand had been first into the Asian crisis, it would be the first out. Thai manufacturing production had clearly bottomed in May of 1998 (at a contraction rate of around -15% year-on-year), however this was rightly attributed initially to Thai companies re-directing production towards export markets which were still buoyant, as well as basing effects from the financial and economic collapse in 1997. By February of 1999, however, the Thai manufacturing production was actually in positive territory on a year-on-year basis, a degree of revival which could not simply be explained by exports, particularly as exports were still falling (they fell 4% year-on-year in the first quarter of 1999). Simultaneous to that, albeit after a lag, imports started to come back in earnest. After falling 11.6% in the fourth quarter of 1998, import growth in volume terms (and thus not distorted by foreign exchange considerations) actually rose over 5% in the first two months of 1999. Simultaneous to this process, the collapse in credit growth bottomed out and money supply growth data also regained positive territory in early 1999, the result of the massive fiscal and monetary stimulus which the Thai and other ASEAN governments undertook from the second half of 1998 onwards.

The Drag of Corporate De-Stocking Begins to Fade

A final factor was inventory reduction. In 1998, Asian companies across the spectrum had switched, re-routed or simply destroyed production in reaction to a collapse in regional consumer demand, the likes of which had never been seen before. To give some idea of this, in Korea, the 11th biggest economy in the world prior to the

Asian crisis, inventory de-stocking amounted to a stunning 7% of the GDP in 1998, a major factor behind the contraction. Yet would this economic stabilisation be sustainable, enough to result in a fully-fledged economic recovery whereby consumption indicators were actually rising?

The Korean industrial shipments-inventory only plateaued after reaching successive record highs for more than 6 months in March and April. Logic suggested this could be a good indicator that the stabilisation might well lead into a recovery and that recovery could well last for some time. If Korean companies were still de-stocking well into the first quarter of 1999, that meant they had not even begun the process of re-stocking those inventories. Just as the corporate de-stocking had exacerbated the initial recession, so re-stocking could accelerate the revival, particularly if it met with rising domestic demand - and that is exactly what happened, not only in Korea but at a regional level. For some the process was a lot faster because their corporations were either leaner to start with, or were focused on non-Asian export markets where the demand remained strong, such as the U.S.. For others, it took longer, but the process was essentially the same.

In terms of how the cycle worked, first the trade account turned around dramatically, producing massive surpluses due to the collapse in imports in late 1997 and most of 1998. Then that import contraction started to slow in the fourth quarter of 1998, while manufacturing, production and credit growth were bottoming, and inventory reduction was accelerating. The process picked up speed, producing actual positive growth in some cases (such as Singapore) in the first quarter of 1999, while others saw substantially reduced economic contractions. Anticipating this, the Asian stock markets went on a tear, After breaching the 300 level in the second half of 1998, the KOSPI, Korea's benchmark stock market index roared to around 650 in the first quarter of 1999, more than doubling in the process, before some profit taking finally occurred, a quite remarkable rally if it were not for the fact that it was copied by the stock markets of other Asian nations which had been badly hurt by the Asian crisis, in ASEAN and elsewhere. Still there were the sceptics, those who pointed with some considerable degree of justification to the mountain of bad debts in the IMF programme countries in particular, stating that such a high degree of non-performing loans would stop any such economic stabilisation, as seen earlier, becoming a fully-fledged, self-sustaining recovery. Paul Krugman who had so memorably questioned the very idea of the Asian Miracle in 1994, in a notable article entitled "Recovery: Don't Bet on it", similarly questioned the suggestion of recovery, stating that what "recovery" had been seen was in any case partial and perhaps more importantly Asia had emerged from what had been a potentially lethal virus still completely ignorant of how to avoid a resumption of it or other types of financial economic disease. [1]

One by One, The Foundations of The Asian Economic Recovery Were Put in Place

Yet right from January, 1999, there were solid grounds to believe that the foundations were in place for an economic recovery which at the least would last through the end of 1999 and more likely through 2000 as well. At the start of the year, investors had been largely focused on the timing of Asia's growth turnaround, however throughout the first and second quarters of 1999 it became increasingly obvious that that turnaround was upon us, largely for the reasons outlined earlier when looking at the first signs of stabilisation. Just about all the capital that could have, left the Asian crisis-hit markets and when that process had been completed, the natural process of import collapse followed by turnaround in the trade account, followed by currency stabilisation ensued. Massive fiscal and monetary stimulus, thanks to the IMF's policy U-turn put a floor under domestic demand, allowing monetary aggregates to recover. The slowdown in import contraction was the first sign that this was working. That was followed by the completion of corporate de-stocking and imports actually started to rise, not only year-on-year, which would have been greatly boosted by year earlier comparisons, but also month-on-month. Confidence has a way of feeding on itself, just as despair. The economy bottomed out, and the corporate re-stocking process began. In effect, the entire economy was being re-capitalised. The recovery in imports could potentially have meant that Asian trade surpluses would start to slow, and indeed in some cases that did occur, however that reduction was more than offset by external interest, namely from foreign stock and bond investors who could smell an opportunity in the recovery story that had now become widespread (if still questioned by some!).

The fundamental, macroeconomic conditions had been put in place to the extent that growth had gained significant momentum. By the second quarter of 1999, industrial production in the likes of Korea, Malaysia and Singapore was actually back above pre-crisis levels, surely confirmation if such were needed that this was no "dead cat bounce" in Asian economies, but something altogether more important and dramatic. What concerns remained thus shifted away from the timing of growth, to the sustainability of that growth pattern. The external environment was decidedly more favourable, and helped in large part by the three extraordinary rate cuts by the Federal Reserve in late 1998. Overall global growth prospects appeared to be improving as a result, though Japan at that stage was still mired in recession. Despite the latter, the increase in monetary expansion in Japan provided yet more capital for the Asian markets. In sum, the massive easing of both fiscal and monetary policy, following the stabilisation of the trade and current accounts, created a virtuous circle of rising growth, asset prices and consumer confidence, so much so that by the second quarter of 1999 classic consumption demand was providing the impetus for growth, an undeniable sign of recovery rather than stabilisation.

In many countries such as Korea, that rising demand was being met and added to by hasty corporate re-stocking of inventories to meet it. A further factor to consider was that some 40% of Asian exports went to Asia (ex-Japan). In this respect, exports to the three main, crisis-hit countries, Korea, Indonesia and Thailand had collapsed in 1998. Similarly, they responded vigorously in 1999. A few countries had dragged down the trade of the region as a whole in 1998, similarly a few caused the total trade to revive dramatically in 1999. Improved conditions for trade finance, the result of international efforts to allow for this and also the fall in global interest rates in the first quarter of 1999 helped Asian export growth to accelerate, both within Asia and outside. The first was almost more important given that it was this that produced the virtuous circle.

Risks to the Recovery

As the growth recovery gathered steam, it caused some to fret about the possible threat of inflation and a potential reversal of that easy monetary stance. However, the substantial degree of slack still left in the economy kept domestic price pressures extraordinarily muted considering the remarkable, vertical growth trajectory seen in many Asian countries. In somewhat more technical jargon, economic "slack" occurs when there is a positive economic output gap, suggesting that the actual output remains below the potential/trend output which is consistent with stable inflation. In other words, the economy is still operating below par. Indeed, it was not until the Federal Reserve started to take back its three interest rate cuts of 1998 in June of 1999 that Asian interest rates started to back up, reflective of the fact that the domestic Asian inflationary expectations remained extremely low.

At the time, there were two further risks to our outlook, the first that the *yen* would weaken substantially due to rising U.S.-Japan interest rate differentials and the persistently weak Japanese demand, particularly relative to that of the U.S., and the second that rising global growth would cause commodities to experience significant rallies which in turn would could cause major imported price pressures in a region which was predominantly a commodity importer rather than exporter. The first did not occur simply because the *yen* "failed" to weaken. Japanese growth in the first quarter of 1999 was an astounding 8.1% on a seasonally-adjusted annualised basis, surpassing some economic forecasts by a multiple. This should have been no surprise, since it too was the result of the keynesian-ist policies - a near-zero interest rate policy and truly humungous fiscal stimulus packages which would cause Japan to record a budget deficit in 1998 and 1999 of almost 7% of the GDP - a GDP which despite Japan's economic under-performance since 1991 and the bursting of the Japanese financial bubble remained second in size only to the U.S.. After the startlingly strong second quarter growth of over 8% on a Seasonally-Adjusted Annual Rate (SAAR) basis, Japan recorded decidedly more meagre growth of 0.4% in the third quarter, yet such was the market's reaction to the Q2 figure that it caused a fundamental reassessment by international investors of Japan's economic prospects. To be sure, some canny investors had got there ahead of time, however the Japan Q2 GDP number and a second factor, the raising of Japan's weighting within the Morgan Stanley Capital Indices of stock markets caused a general re-weighting of equity portfolios. Prior to this, investors had been "underweight" as regards exposure to the Japanese equity market, depressed by year after year of policy inaction and lack of progress, both at the micro- and the macro-economic levels.

Those two happenings in 1999 caused a re-evaluation of Japan's prospects. Like a ship changing course, it took some time for the international market to react to this, however the sheer weight of international equity investors raising their general rating on Japanese equities from "underweight" to "neutral", with the more bullish souls going cautiously "overweight" - cautiously because they had been disappointed so many times before - caused wave after wave of *yen* buying in order to purchase those stocks. With the dollar having topped out against the *yen* in May of 1999 at just under 125, these investors were not necessarily desperate to hedge given that the expectation was that the Japanese economy would accelerate relative to that of the U.S., particularly after June when the Fed started to take back its monetary easing of 1998. Readers may think that a currency should of necessity rise when the interest rates are increased. There is actually little evidence for this. Indeed, the complete opposite can be the case, particularly in currencies whose countries suffer from structural trade and current accounts and are thus dependent on capital inflows. In 1999, the U.S. is expected to have recorded a current account deficit of some USD300 billion. The U.S. dollar is the biggest "hot money" currency of them all. Consequently, when the Federal Reserve hikes interest rates, this can cause the U.S. stock and bond markets to fall, with the result that foreign investors - mainly from Japan - who fund the U.S. current account deficit through their purchases of U.S. assets to repatriate their holdings back into their own currency on the fear that those asset markets could cause further. In other words, a rate hike can actually cause a currency to fall. This is indeed what happened in the U.S. in 1994, when the U.S. witnessed its biggest bond market meltdown in history as the Fed was perceived as being behind the inflation curve and thus had to hike rates more and for longer than might otherwise have been the case. Equally, from the time of the Fed rate hike at the June meeting of the Federal Open Market Committee (known as the "FOMC" in market parlance), the dollar has headed in one direction against the *yen* - down, not just because Japan was perceived to be recovering, but because this was accompanied by U.S. monetary tightening which in turn caused a less favourable environment for U.S. assets in the short term, thus resulting in investor flight. Over the long term, such monetary tightening is the prudent course to take, the one which should maintain a sustainable level of non-inflationary growth. In the short term, it can cause havoc for both the country's currency and its asset markets.

So, the *yen* did not weaken, a relief undoubtedly for many Asian countries given that *yen* weakness from mid-1995-1997 (the result of the G7 policy of "orderly reversal of the dollar's decline" - see **Asia Falling**, Chapter 3) had been a key factor in the Asian crisis in the first place. Many of these countries competed against Japan in terms of exporting to third markets such as the U.S. and Europe. With the dollar rebounding from a record low of 79.75 in April 1995 to above 115 by January 1997, a recovery of some 44%, Japanese exporters were increasingly pricing their Asian competitors out of the market. In the second and third quarters of 1998, the *yen* fell back, with the dollar making a new recent high against the *yen* of around 147.60, a further 28% increase in its value from January 1997, this caused spill-over selling in Asian currencies as investors, warned by the example of the initial *yen* devaluation from 1995-97 and the effect that it had on the Asian currencies anticipated further Asian currency weakness by this time selling well ahead of a similar time lag. It was only with the help of the Federal Reserve and the Bank of Japan that market sentiment changed towards the dollar-*yen* exchange rate and thus as a result, the dollar started to pull back, that move being greatly accelerated in September and October as a result of the Federal Reserve's surprise three rate cuts. Once again, Asian currencies managed to find some relief, a greater degree of calm. By the first half of 1999, these Asian currencies were benefiting from the virtuous combination of capital and current account surpluses. In addition, Japan FINALLY appeared to be recovering. This would be positive for two reasons. First, that growth was likely to boost Asian exports to Japan on the back of rising Japanese domestic demand. Secondly, inflation was unlikely to show up in Japan any time soon, thus the Japanese interest rates were unlikely to rise much - though in truth fiscal concerns would cause higher interest rates at the back end and thus result in the dramatic steepening of the Japanese interest rate curve. Even if they did, the call rate was barely above zero, hence a move was unlikely to cause a major shift in Japanese capital flows, unless of course the Bank of Japan signalled that the move was part of a cyclical policy change. The BoJ did nothing of the sort. Indeed, it continued to stress concern about the sustainability of Japanese economic growth. In addition, the BoJ's foreign exchange desk undertook massive intervention in the foreign exchange markets to limit the recovery of the *yen* in an attempt to stop the domestic recovery - led, of course, by exports - from stalling. Despite this, the *yen* still strengthened. Indeed, Asian exporters watched with undisguised glee as the *yen* appreciated significantly on a trade-weighted basis from May 1999 onwards through October, thus boosting their own competitiveness against that of their Japanese competitors. By the third quarter of 1999, Korean exports, for instance, were expanded at a year-on-year rate of over 25%, not just because of their miserable performance the year before, but because the Korean *won* had depreciated significantly against the Japanese currency as a result of the general strengthening in the value of the *yen*.

The second potential threat to the Asian regional, economic recovery might have come from the rising commodity prices, exacerbating already existing inflation fears as a result of the recovery itself. With USD25 dollar oil, this was no small concern, particularly when one considered that the likes of Thailand and the Philippines imported more than 90% of their oil needs. To date, while the rising value of oil has in turn boosted the value of imports, that rising oil price has also been synonymous with improving global growth prospects. Producers and manufacturers have needed greater quantities of the stuff due to the rising domestic and external demand, thus the balance of risks for Asia in this factor has essentially to date been neutral, the one offsetting the other. In sum therefore, through the third quarter of 1999, general macroeconomic influences, both domestically and from global external factors, remained positive and the expectation was that they would stay positive for some time to come, at least through the year end and on into 2000.

Good News at the Microeconomic Level

There was further positive news, at the microeconomic level. Another major factor in the Asian crash, not only in the original Asian currency and debt crisis but also with regard to the subsequent recession of their economies was the collapse in semiconductor prices. Prior to the crisis, several Asian countries had long been criticised by analysts for their over-reliance on high volume, low technology, and low value-added production. Consequently, as a result of this as well as due to their natural desire to go higher up the value added chain as part of their natural economic development. By 1996, in this effort, electronics, including semiconductor chips, made up an average of 34% of the total exports of Singapore, Malaysia, Korea, the Philippines, Thailand, Taiwan and Hong Kong as a group. Prior to the crisis, manufacturers in Singapore made up to 40% of the world's disk drives, while one third of PC microprocessors were packaged in Malaysia. Encouraged by strong demand levels and good margins, Asian manufacturers who were not already in semiconductors had rushed to set up production facilities. Those which were already there significantly boosted production to offset this threat. Thus, by the start of 1996, Asia accounted for over 50% of world memory chip sales. Needless to say, this greatly increased the supply of computer chips on the world market and had a predictable effect on semiconductor prices, which began to slip back. New and innovative chips, along with consequent massive discounting on "old" chip models accelerated this process. At the same time, demand for PCs themselves was starting to shrink. For Asia, this was a fatal combination. PC sales had grown a stellar 25% in 1995. In 1996, this cooled to a "mere" 16% year-on-year, yet even this relatively modest slowdown was enough to trigger a chain reaction that was to have a major effect on Asian economies. The initial reaction by the disk drive and semiconductor manufacturers was to increase production further on the view that PC sales would pick up again. The pullback in semiconductor prices hit the bottom line and this had to be made up in volume terms. Asian manufacturers thus ramped up production, thus adding to what was already a rapidly expanding glut of excess capacity. What had been a modest pullback in semiconductor prices became a collapse, a complete meltdown. Semiconductor prices fell some 90% on average in 1996. For the Asian electronic manufacturers and exporters, it was a disaster. Given Asia's exposure to the world electronics' industry, this bit hard into exports, and indeed it was a crucial factor in the falloff in Asian exports in 1996 and 1997. Effectively, the profitability of a third of the exports of the countries mentioned above had been all but wiped out. Indeed, not only their profitability but their sales value. The crash in world semiconductor prices, precipitated by Asian manufacturing of greatly excess production relative to demand - not future demand but existing demand - preceded the crash in Asian currencies by little more than a year.

Granted, computer chips are not the whole story behind the Asian crisis or anything like it, but they certainly played a vital part in that crisis eventually taking place given the high proportion of Asian exports they represented. Examining a graph of the relationship between semiconductor sales and the currencies of Singapore, Taiwan, Malaysia and Korea (major manufacturers of semiconductors, then and now), we see a clear link between the two, albeit after a lag of around a year. This can be explained by the delayed effect the Asian currency devaluations had on export competitiveness, not least the competitiveness of their electronics' exports. By May, semiconductor sales, as measured by the Book-to-Bill Ratio (total global sales) had clearly bottomed and began a steep rise, only to fall away again by December of 1997, until bottoming at much lower levels in July 1998. In terms of the specifically Asian relationship to this, the reason was most certainly the greatly reduced ability of most Asian exporters to obtain export finance. In addition, at least initially, Asian countries saw little immediate benefit from the currency devaluations given the high import content of their export base - rising import costs offset the increased export competitiveness resulting from the falls in their own currencies. Eventually, however, as a result of the relaxation of the global market tensions in the wake of the three monetary easings by the Fed, such trade finance was more readily available and import costs had fallen back again due to the collapse in domestic demand. In addition, Asian currencies were by then stabilising. The combined effect was to accelerate Asian exports of semiconductors once more. As the graph shows. From the start of the year through to November, they continued to accelerate, a factor which should help Asian currencies going forward, into 2000.

(accompanying graph from Bloomberg, comparing the Singapore dollar, Taiwan dollar, Korean dollar and the Semiconductor global sales total produced by the Semiconductor Industry Association)

Asian Currencies vs Semiconductor Sales

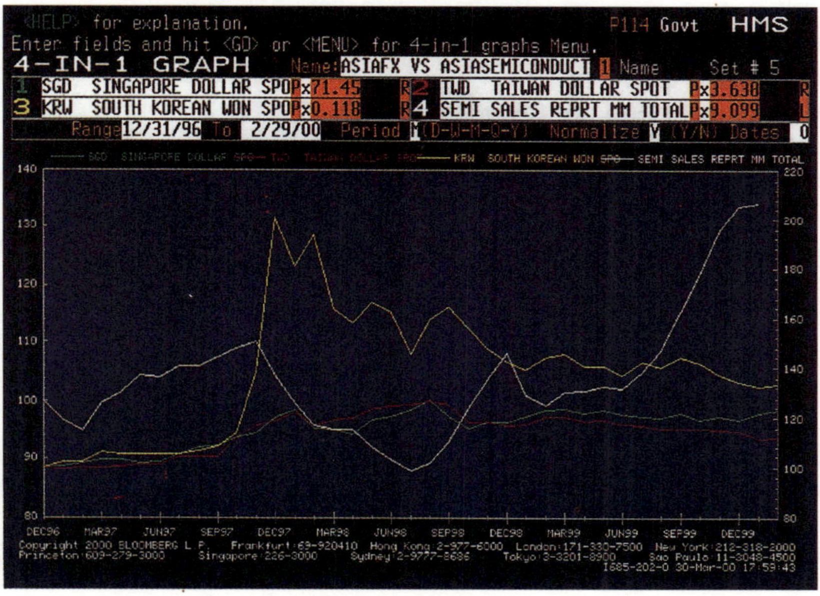

Source: Bloomberg

Some Microeconomic Concerns

Yet, not all was - or is - bullish on the microeconomic picture. The merits of a return to the strong growth pattern of years past in Asia is to be welcomed, but with some qualifications. For one thing, the sheer magnitude of structural dislocation from July 1997 when the Thai *baht* first devalued through the end of 1998 has surely reduced the sustainable long-term growth trajectory of many of these Asian economies. Without massive reduction in debt overhang of the corporate sector or further significant progress in banking sector re-capitalisation, the current growth risks were running out of steam. In addition, the structure of the Asian corporations also has a part to play given that going into the crisis is a significant proportion of these, notably but not exclusively in the IMF programme countries, were not corporations as we understand them, but family firms with little or no real or effective accountability, either to shareholders or creditors. Many of these went under, not only as a result of the crisis but surely as a result of the inevitable consequence of their own commercial decisions which had not in all cases been motivated with the best interests of the business in mind. Personal relations between family corporate owners and bank managers had in many cases led to excessive bank lending and corporate borrowing, both in local and foreign currency. The nature of economic relationships does affect the profitability of the economy, both at the micro- and the macro-economic level. Burdened by massive non-performing loans, it will remain quite some time before the Asian banking systems as a whole will simply be able let alone and will be willing to lend to their respective corporate sectors. Meanwhile, given that their personal fortunes were all but destroyed in the process of the crisis, many family firms would not be able to put up the collateral for such loans even if they were able to obtain them. This is not to say that the economy cannot heal at the microeconomic level as well, that such firms will eventually be re-capitalised or eliminated, thus re-capitalising the corporate base as a whole. Rather, it is to say that the process will take some time, several years if the Latin American crisis in 1982 is anything to go by.

Financial markets were reminded of this vulnerability in the third quarter of 1999. I said that monetary tightening by the Federal Reserve from June 1999 onwards was the reason which unsettled the Asian asset markets, causing domestic interest rates to back up and currencies to weaken. This was not the only reason however. For in that quarter, we saw the first really bad news of the year at the corporate and banking level. Up until then, the Asian markets had been booming, the result of the massive fiscal and monetary expansionist policies by governments and foreign investors rushing to buy Asian stocks as the recovery in the region gathered pace. Sceptics might suggest that this was merely a resumption of the excess investment that poured into Asia throughout the 1990s (up until 1997!) which had been another key factor in the Asian crisis, and such an argument has some undeniable validity. Asian corporate profits had started to improve by the second half of 1999 in a notable fashion - or losses to be reduced - but such an improvement was small relative to the degree of rise in many of these corresponding stocks. Such sceptics might well have asked what exactly had changed?! Had investors learned nothing?! In some cases, apparently not. Asian stock markets in the first half of 1999 had risen in most cases by 50-60%, riding on this tidal wave of liquidity (but not necessarily profitability). They were thus ripe for disappointment, particularly in an environment where global liquidity conditions were suddenly becoming more unfavourable as the Fed started to be less expansive and to take back its monetary easing of 1998. They were ripe for Daewoo in Korea, Bank Bali in Indonesia and Krung Thai Bank in Thailand. In many ways, these cases encapsulated the persistent microeconomic travails of these economies, a point not lost on global investors who promptly started to take profit on their holdings and repatriate those gains, given the added excuse of being prudent ahead of the impending Y2K concerns and liquidity from September 1999 onwards. These cases also showed the existing intransigence to reform from within Asian corporates, banks and even governments - and thus a task still lay ahead for those who were leading the reform effort. In addition, those cases were great drama for the world's press, easily-used analogies for the persistent of "crony capitalism", inciting headlines as to whether there had in fact been any reform in Asia. - an un-justified suggestion but one which nevertheless needed to be adequately defended against with the qualification that the reform process remained substantially unfinished.

■ Daewoo in Korea

The market realisation that Daewoo, the country's second largest *chaebol,* or conglomerate, was in trouble, struggling under a debt-to-equity ratio of almost 600% was a rude reminder to the Korean markets of the fundamental problems that remained. Daewoo had promised to sell off various units in order to raise cash and reduce debt, however its efforts at restructuring itself voluntarily were clearly inadequate. It took the Korean government to strong arm local banks into rolling over around USD15 billion of the company's debt. Investors reacted by pulling money out of trust and mutual funds related to this. Those funds in turn sold bonds in the open market in order to raise cash in order to pay for these redemptions. As a result, corporate and government bond prices plummeted under the weight of this concerted selling pressure, causing yields and interest rates to rise, thus exacerbating the cash flow and financing problems for the *chaebol* as a whole, let alone Daewoo. The government responded by setting up a market stabilisation fund with the vowed aim of buying up an unlimited amount of bonds in order to stabilise the Korean financial market conditions, and to a large extent it succeeded. Where it did not succeed was in eliminating the image of Korea's second largest *chaebol* nearly failing, an image that was not conceivable to most in Korea - until that reality struck. Daewoo had tried to stall for time by announcing a debt refinancing on July 19, however instead of calming the situation this led to a panic. While interest rates shot up, the stock market lost a stunning 11% in two days. On July 27, the government put control of the group's restructuring in the hands of its bankers. In retrospect, this was the first positive thing that had happened to the group in a long time. The collapse of the group led to its major units and affiliates being placed under a corporate workout programme. Under the debt workout programme, debt payments by 12 key units would be frozen for the following three months.

The KOSPI, the benchmark stock market index in Korea continued to get hit by a combination of investment trust fund selling to raise cash and general investor concern that other *chaebol*, notably the other top four could have similar problems. In this regard, the August 15, 1999 speech by President Kim Dae-jung, made somewhat pointedly on Liberation Day, was both a further attempt to put a floor under investor confidence and stop the panic, and a declaration of war against those who tried to resist the forces of reform and restructuring, a declaration of war on the 54th anniversary of South Korean independence from Japan against corporate inefficiency. President Kim's speech apparently took several days of drafting and the President himself toned up, made harsher the language. The message was clear. The drive for reform remained on course. The very next day, the government announced a sweeping restructuring of Daewoo, obliging it to reduce itself to 6 core units by the year end from the prevailing 25. The announcement was positive news and was received reasonably well, but the devil as always is in the detail.

A Western leveraged investor, looking back at what happened in the 1980s and 90s, through the process of junk bond-financed corporate acquisition restructuring and then the phase of "re-engineering" might say that what Korea really needed was a Michael Milken-type character, someone who could create a financing market which could in turn lead to the acquisition and ultimate dismemberment of many of these companies for the purpose of discovering, unlocking and realising the value buried under mountains of debt and excessive productive capacity relative to profit potential. The corporate system needed to be torn limb from limb and rebuilt, so this view went. While I have great sympathy with this view, that corporations ultimately have responsibility to both their employees and their shareholders and that if management does not do an adequate job of providing decent returns then it should be removed and the said company restructured in whatever way is best appropriate to provide those returns, this is needless to say in complete contradiction with the Asian model of capitalism. It pays no heed to relationships or the consensus, it is destruction for the purpose of creation. Such destruction is not tolerable to many Asian governments and businesses. The trick for them will be to provide an alternative which does still provide good returns, because those returns will be needed in order for investors to be attracted.

While President Kim's message was indeed a declaration of war against such corporate inefficiency, it is unlikely that it represented the intention to completely break apart the *chaebol* system. That would inevitably result in a major backlash against him and his government, not least by the *chaebol* themselves, but also by those made unemployed as a result, and Korean governments face elections where they can be thrown out by disgruntled voters whatever the merits of their reform plans. Rather, it was an attempt, once more at balance - the balance of trying to achieve sufficient corporate reform to change the fundamental nature of the system while seeking to avoid the worst excesses of such change. If he pulls it off, it will be a remarkable achievement - but that "if" remains in question as of this writing. Still, the fact that Daewoo is selling off assets and reducing capacity is positive news for the economy and the country as a whole - though it may not seem so to some in the short term. It means that companies will not automatically be bailed out, but could be dismantled. That in turn could influence and change the way Korean banks price loans to these companies - and that is long overdue.

Yet while Kim was not seeking to completely break up the system in order to cure it of its ills as some Western consultants or companies might have sought to do, there was no underestimating the importance of such a public case of corporate restructuring as Daewoo to his presidency. Success in restructuring Daewoo and providing a precedent for the *chaebol* reform, albeit as a last resort -

and thus an incentive to avoid that last resort - and he would truly be seen as the reforming President, the savour of Korean industry, the Korean economy, indeed the very nation itself. To fail would make him appear as yet another Korean President with a half finished agenda. It is no doubt with such thoughts in mind that he made that gloriously ferocious speech on August 15, 1999. The stakes were indeed high, and not just for the *chaebol.*

Perfectly symbolic of how those stakes were, of the titanic struggle that was taking place, was the announcement on November 1 that Kim Woo-choong, the founder and Chairman of Daewoo offered to resign, again an event completely unthinkable in times past, showing just how far Korea had come, as well as how far it had to go. Notably, the Korean stock market rallied over 5% after the news of the Daewoo Chairman's resignation offer. Change indeed was taking place. Such a removal represented a major loss for those who were trying to resist the forces of change and restructuring, a major victory for President Kim Dae-jung, and ultimately for the Korean economy in this global, competitive world which can no longer tolerate or afford artificially low financing rates, excessive capacity and a focus on sales over profit. Nowadays, the bottom line is indeed the bottom line and that is how it should be. The process is by no means complete, but significant progress has been made, progress that will eventually be reflected by a recovery in Korea's asset markets which were badly bruised in the third quarter of 1999 due to these concerns over Daewoo.

■ Bank Bali in Indonesia

Indonesia, preparing for its first democratic elections in November 1999, had its own drama, almost a soap opera involving allegedly misused funds, the IMF, auditors, ruling party members and high officials, a trail which some said might lead even to the highest offices. Up until the Bank Bali scandal, which also broke in the third quarter (it was not necessarily a good time for those who thought Asia was making real progress), the IMF and World Bank had been, with no small degree of self-congratulation, been praising the Asian recovery story. There was indeed a considerable amount to praise, only not as much as they thought. The emergence of the Bank Bali scandal was a further rude awakening, both to the IMF (which reacted with outrage), and international investors, almost as if both parties had never been duped before in Indonesia. Expectations and hopes that the restructuring effort to revitalise the Indonesian banking system, shattered in the crisis, was finally getting off the ground were crudely and nastily dashed with the revelation that Bank Bali had allegedly made a payment of USD70 million earmarked for bank restructuring to an official of the ruling Golkar Party for the possible purpose of helping Golkar's election chances. Bank Bali was seen not as an isolated issue, but as a symptom of a gangrene which remained in the system, and which had to be excised. The IMF and the World Bank promptly suspended loan payments to Indonesia, telling the government in no uncertain terms that the Bank Bali issue had to be resolved, and more specifically the full version of an audit by the PWC had to be released and the appropriate people punished before such loans would be resumed. The full release of that audit was not to be achieved until after the election, until after President Habibie and the Golkar were thrown out of office and President Wahid elected. The fact that its release did happen was positive. The fact it took so long was not, neither was the assumption that the Bank Bali case was by no means an isolated one.

■ Krung Thai in Thailand

Finally, in Thailand, there was the case of the Krung Thai Bank. PWC had a busy time of it, because they were also the ones who made a report allegedly claiming that problem loans accounted for up to 84% of Krung Thai's loan portfolio. This case had a further negative dimension as Krung Thai had been run by Sirin Nimmanahaeminda, the brother of Thailand's Finance Minister, Tarrin Nimmanahaeminda. Here too, the Krung Thai case was not important so much for its own aspects - though those were notable. No, in the context of the Asian recovery, it was again seen as being symptomatic of the lack of real reform at the microeconomic level, in Thailand and in Asia, and of the work yet to be done. The linking of Tarrin to the Krung Thai issue through the media and speculation of course did nothing to help investor sentiment, sickened as it was already by the examples of Daewoo and Bank Bali. On the contrary, it was a reminder of the small and incestuous nature of the Thai banking system, a reminder also of the persistently dire state of the Thai banking system towards the end of 1999, a system which still had non-performing loans amounting to around 46% of the total. Granted, this was paltry in comparison to the figure of around 75% in Indonesia, but it remained a systemic and structural obstacle to sustained economic growth. Indeed, it was and remains a threat to the recovery itself, not only in Thailand but also in Indonesia.

It is unfair to say that Asian governments, and more specifically the IMF programme countries have done nothing at the microeconomic level. Both Indonesia and Thailand created frameworks for both bank and debt restructuring, involving amendments to the law or new laws and legal bodies to push through that restructuring process. Key in this are asset management companies, entities which take bad loans off bank balance sheets, thus enabling the banking system as a whole to re-capitalise. Thailand's emphasis on voluntary or bank run AMCs looks flawed however. The U.S. Resolution Trust Corp was the first major example of such an institution, which obliged U.S. banks to part with their NPLs. In the context of Asia, Malaysia was one example of a crisis country that has significantly reduced systemic NPLs through the creation of government-run AMCs, Danaharta and Danamodel. Indonesia, for one has little or no history of following the rule of law rather than vested interests, hence what progress it has made in terms of creating a legal framework for bankruptcy resolution is in many cases not followed though on in practice. Similarly, in Thailand the bankruptcy framework in practice could take years for creditors to foreclose and grab assets from distressed debtors. Given the family nature of many Asian firms, the bias of sympathy remains in many cases with these companies given the stigma of a family losing its own company. As reluctant as one is to say this, such cultural aspects hinder rather than help the recovery process.

Yet, in the case of Indonesia which is most useful on the basis that many travel at the pace of the slowest, if only inadvertently, while progress in bankruptcy courts has yet to be substantial, the same cannot be said for IBRA, the Indonesian Banking Restructuring Agency. Given relatively draconian powers to seize assets by the government, it is IBRA rather than the bankruptcy court which will chart the future for the Indonesian banking system and thus its corporate sector. Indeed, such was the effort to make IBRA completely independent of political or financial influence that it has acted at times in decidedly authoritarian fashion, to the benefit of the banking system to be sure. Somewhat by accident, IBRA has become the reluctant manager of some USD80 billion of assets as a result of its mandate, exceeding as of October 1999 the entire capitalisation of the Jakarta Stock Exchange. The government's need for funds and the inability of the domestic investor base - such as it remains - to afford buying these assets is likely to mean that most are sold off to offshore investors. In terms of the re-capitalisation of the Indonesian financial system, this is positive news, as long as the IBRA accepts the prices bid for such assets. The task is not small. Credit rating agency Standard & Poor's Ratings has reportedly estimated the cost of banking system rehabilitation at over 70% of Indonesia's GDP, or around USD70 billion. IBRA's contribution to the state budget alone - in 1999 some USD2.5 billion - will mean forced sales of these assets, even better news. For once, the pricing mechanism of these assets will be working efficiently. Outside the banking sector, IBRA is due to sell stakes in some of the largest names in corporate Indonesia. While the pace of change may frustrate many, not least foreign bankers, there appears to be little question that it is happening.

MORE FUEL FOR THE FIRE?

The rallies in the Asian asset markets through the first half of 1999, up until such publicised cases as Daewoo, Bank Bali and the Krung Thai damaged sentiment, were not only due to investor anticipation of Asian regional and national recovery. It was also the result of the re-emergence of excess capital in the region, caused by the combination of the massive fiscal and monetary policy injections into the economy and the added bonus of offshore investors returning to bargain hunt. In practice, it represented the re-emergence of too much money chasing too few assets, particularly profitable ones, dragging up the bad along with the good. Such expansionist monetary and fiscal policies and the IMF loan disbursements caused some to question whether or not this was just more of the same; whether excess domestic and external investment (relative to savings) in Asia, whose collapse and flight had after all been behind the Asian crisis, were merely being replaced by the combination of fiscal and monetary expansion and IMF loan packages. The bottom line was that the fundamental dynamics had not changed, so ran this argument. It was still a case of too much money, whatever its origin, chasing too few assets, *more fuel for the fire.* As a Monetary Authority of

Singapore official remarked, there was a grave danger that Asia had learned nothing from its crisis.[2] What there was to learn was that the only way of effectively sterilising such investment and producing a solid, fundamental foundation for asset market valuations was in increasing rates of return at the bottom line. Only greater corporate and banking efficiency would provide the justification for investment and valuations. Here, whether at the micro- or macroeconomic levels, the crux of the issue is the idea of productivity, an area where the U.S. has excelled for the past five years at the very least. Tied in with the idea of productivity is the more specific issue of "Total Factor Productivity" (TFP), or rather what's left in growth after all the inputs are taken out. Debate continues to rage as to whether the Asian Miracle occurred against a backdrop of low or no TFP. Proponents for the idea that this was the very reason as to why the Asian Miracle was a myth presumably felt vindicated in the event of the Asian crisis. Yet counter arguments have been brought out, claiming that Asian TFP had in fact exceeded G7 levels and that consequently it had little to do with the cause of the crisis, which was focused rather on weak banking systems and excessive short-term borrowing of foreign currencies. It is not for here to expand on this theme. We shall exhaust this subject later in book, in Chapter 8, when we examine Asia's long-term strengths and weaknesses. Suffice to say that corporate inefficiency in terms of profits relative to other areas of the world, emerged or emerging, would seem to have been a logical reason, albeit not the only one, for the bursting of a bubble which indeed happened to Asia in 1997. Going forward, the need for greater efficiency should not be underestimated, indeed if anything it will continue to increase. The time when Asia did not have to compete with other emerging market regions for global capital is now over. Consequently, it will be forced to achieve higher rates of return, one way or the other. Previously inadequate returns are not to state definitively that Asia lacked in TFP. The likes of Singapore and Taiwan provided substantial value added to their investments inputs, before and after the crisis. In addition, technological advances made in Asia over the last two decades suggest that the lack of TFP argument is at the very least incomplete.

THE QUESTION OF SUSTAINABILITY

Such concerns over investment and TFP -- or the lack thereof -- undoubtedly have profound importance for Asia's future. However, within this argument, it is important to remember that whatever the case, Asia rebounded exceptionally strongly in 1999 and that recovery continues to this day. Going forward, the key question is of course how sustainable is this recovery. Within this, as the World Bank itself pointed out, the true medium- to long-term sustainability of the Asian macroeconomic growth is at the microeconomic level. In other words, shattered banking systems and damaged corporate sectors have not in all but the case of Indonesia held Asia back from torrid recovery, yet over the long term, as the example of Japan attests to most vividly, they will hold Asia back - and more - if left unmended. Sustainability lies in revitalising Asia's corporate and banking sectors.

Where some have outperformed, it is in their reduction of debt. The pace at which NPLs are reduced and new credit allowed to flow will be a leading driver of the pace of recovery in the years to come, indeed probably the key driver. A healthy degree of realism is needed with regard to this. As the World bank notes:

"To reverse the microeconomic origins of high interest rates-eroded corporate balance sheets, deflated collateral values, and banks' aversion to accept risk when they desperately need to rebuild capital-will require time and a healthier economy. This will probably take years rather than quarters."[3]

Asian governments may have to intervene more directly at the microeconomic level in order to ensure that the restructuring process remains on track, yet this risks getting Japan's disease which is the increasing nationalisation of the banking system. In this regard, the microeconomic restructuring of Asia does in fact bear strong similarity with that which took place in Latin America in the 1980s. In that case, the governments of Chile and Mexico revived lenders and depositors, restructured companies under new ownership and auctioned off distressed portfolios in order to preserve growing concerns. The problem and the opportunity is to balance the demands of the public sector, of government, with the requirements of market pricing and incentive. Without the latter, it is unlikely to work, not because of any lack of effort, but because it is simply much harder. When it is simply a case of the government trying to do it all without the benefit of market-induced discipline, the cause of restructuring can falter. This is hardly surprising since many of those conducting the restructuring were involved in the initial problems, or at the least know people, their friends, who were. Thus, to save a government from itself, to use the system itself to do part of the job requires providing incentives for both buyer and seller. The incentive for the seller is clear - there is no choice. As for the buyer, the incentive is a decent price. Initially, prices are artificially low, not just or even mainly because of an investor's desire to get absolute bargains, but because the investor community as a whole is understandably reluctant to accept low risk premia or high prices in the event of such a crisis. Transparency could help the process, yet another thing which Asian governments must push. A key measure which Asian governments could push for which would undoubtedly help them in the process of revitalising their economies is the liberalising and deregulation of the shareholder structure, bringing the requirements of directors and chairmen of local companies up to international standards and giving minority shareholders the ability to make mischief for corporate chieftains who they perceive as providing inadequate returns. This has been mentioned before, but it remains a crucial point, so it is mentioned again!

Success can be achieved, both at the microeconomic and macroeconomic levels. After the cataclysmic crisis of 1982 in Latin America, it took Chile "only" three years to complete what was a massive microeconomic restructuring, thus ensuring its longest, sustained period of growth this century, a remarkable turnaround and a model for Asia to emulate. Two out of the three Asian countries which first went into the crisis are now emerging with seemingly strong macroeconomic recoveries, albeit with substantial microeconomic problems still to solve and which will take several years to do so, the length of time depending entirely on their willingness to take tough decisions, to close and dismantle bankrupt companies, and sell their assets to any who will buy, to remove bank non-performing loans by force if necessary and encourage renewed lending growth, again providing incentives for that. Indonesia has just started its recovery phase. To many, even this statement would have seemed ridiculous. By the end of 1998, most of Indonesia's corporate sector was effectively bankrupt and its banking system had suffered runs and a meltdown in confidence. Yet, now it would appear that Indonesia has hit the bottom. It may not grow that much given the degree of its economic problems, but at least it has stopped falling. The story remains a relatively positive one for the rest of the ASEAN, notably Singapore, Malaysia and the Philippines, all of which are likely to outperform expectations for 1999.

THE IMF IS BULLISH (KEEN TO SHOW IT WAS RIGHT)

It was thus surely no surprise that the IMF's Managing Director (as he was then) Michel Camdessus took the opportunity on several occasions to sound a decidedly upbeat note about the region's prospects going into the second half of 1999. On May 20th, at the South East Asian Central Bank Governors' conference in Seoul, Camdessus, suggested that Asian prospects were clearly more positive due to a number of the domestic and external factors. He also - somewhat shrewdly - paid tribute to those in Asia, such as the governments, financial authorities, banks, companies and the populations themselves, who had withstood the crisis, for holding firm, maintaining their commitment to free trade (in theory, however imperfectly enacted in practice) and taking at the time difficult and distressing measures, including the laying off of millions of workers.

Camdessus attributed Asia's astounding recovery to continuing to focus on its long-term strengths, saying, "Few observers doubt Asia's potential to return to rapid growth. But I would suggest that what is in the making is not a return to the successful trends of the past but a new model of higher quality growth solidly rooted on the amazing strength of your Asian traditions and values...It will be rooted in an environment of fair and transparent competition on an even playing field and will be based on sound economic and financial institutions with a strong sense of social justice."[4]

Confirming that weak corporate governance was a serious flaw in many Asian economies prior to the crisis, and potentially a contributor to that crisis, Camdessus suggested that pressing ahead with corporate debt restructuring and work-outs was a major priority in order to provide a viable foundation for microeconomic recovery. Finally, he claimed that Asian countries were indeed finally addressing the crucial issue of financial sector weakness, though this work also had to be pushed forward through ensuring sound regulatory and supervisory structures - part of what I have called "institutional infrastructure".

Stanley Fischer, the IMF's First Deputy Managing Director, followed this up with an optimistic appraisal of the Asian recovery at the World Economic Forum on October 18, 1999, in a speech aptly titled "The Road to a Sustainable Recovery in Asia". Fischer suggested that the Asian region would grow 4.1% in 1999 and 4.3% in 2000 - note here that it all depends on one's definition of Asia, which countries one includes. That said, the trend is in line with the general estimate which is for growth of 5.9% in 1999 followed by 6.2% in 2000, helped by an improving external environment consisting of rising growth in Japan (most importantly) and the EU coupled with a moderate slowdown in the U.S.. To his credit, Dr. Fischer highlighted the risks which remained to the optimistic scenario. For one thing, Japan's recovery itself remained subject to risk, to potential reversal and an early resolution of its banking sector problems remained key. In addition, Asia had to enact even deeper structural reforms in order to be competitive and ensure long-term, sustainable, *productive* growth.

For its part, the World Bank pointed to the need for high quality growth going forward rather than just growth per se as being crucial to the sustainability of the recovery process. Given that this was a key point I made in **Asia Falling**, I cannot but agree. (see **Asia Falling**, Chapter 1: Growth at any Price). Asia's growth during the 1980s and 90s was in many cases high volume, high market share, low technology and low profitability. This model can no longer be afforded. The good news is that most Asian governments are only too aware of this fact. The bad news is that the transition will not be without considerable pain and it will take time. Full macro and microeconomic recovery could well take longer in terms of sustainable recovery in Asia than it did in Mexico and Argentina in 1994-95 due to the added problem of corporate insolvency and banking non-performing loans.

Yet on November 4, 1999, World Bank chief economist Joseph Stiglitz struck a decidedly upbeat note with regard to prospects for the sustainability of the recovery. Having achieved a considerable degree of controversy throughout 1999 for his ideological conflict with the IMF on how the Asian crisis should originally have been handled by the world's leading multilateral agencies (i.e. the IMF), he appeared to be in agreement with that institution by late 1999. On November 4, 1999, in an interview with the Far Eastern Economic Review, he suggested that the recovery was at hand and would be secured through Asia's "huge internal market". Stiglitz said that five years from 1999, the Asian region would have fully recovered.

"Asia will have created within itself this huge internal market which I think will be the key change. Whereas in the previous two to three decades, it has all been export-oriented towards the U.S. and Europe, those markets are becoming saturated. So the real growth is going to come from the internal demand in the region."[5]

Here I would also, totally agree. Asian countries have for the last two decades at least depended upon the "emerged world" and more specifically the U.S. and Europe to provide the source of demand for their exports, and thus the catalyst for the creation of those export-related industries. Last year, when I was on a trip around Asia, the head of a national industry association suggested that manufacturing production and capacity remained dependent on external demand. To my mind, this misses the point. Moreover, it is dangerous. To rely in such a way on external demand is to risk the consequences of that external demand suddenly declining for whatever specific reasons. This in turn would cause exports to that country to slow dramatically, negatively affecting the currency and asset markets of that country.

External Over-Reliance and the Need For Asia to Focus on Asian Demand

Asia as a whole remains overly dependent on U.S. demand for its exports, a clear example of what I called in **Asia Falling,** "external over-reliance". As U.S. officials have on occasion pointed out, the U.S. cannot be the importer of last resort indefinitely. With U.S. domestic demand remaining strong, rising imports will inevitably cause a further widening of the U.S. trade and current account balances until one of two things happen, the U.S. economy or the dollar "adjusts" (collapses) in order to close that external deficit once more. Tighter Fed monetary policy is likely to accelerate that adjustment process precisely because of the U.S.'s dependency on capital inflows resulting from its current account deficit. Asia cannot depend on U.S.

demand for its goods remaining strong indefinitely. In this regard, it can hope that Europe picks up some of the slack. As the U.S. is expected to slow down in 2000, the EU is expected to continue its gradual recovery. However, European demand is also not the whole answer, just as the U.S. demand cannot remain. Faced with the EU (and the prospect of its enlargement) and growing ties within NAFTA, Asia is faced with little choice but to accelerate the move to break down inter-Asian trade barriers, in order to provide the price and value competitiveness to compete externally with the rest of the world. It has to make domestic Asian demand the foundation of Asian growth, not just to secure this recovery but to ensure the growth of the region for the next two or three decades. Free trade still has some way to go in this regard, notably in places like Korea where domestic markets remain heavily regulated and protected. However, if the Asian leaders want to secure this recovery and provide that foundation, they will look to break down these barriers, providing much more opportunity and diversity in the economy and forcing previously strategic industries to compete. For many it will do them a lot of good - any entity which does not effectively have to compete becomes un-competitive, becomes fat and lazy precisely because there is no incentive to be anything else.

While Asia has a major manufacturing base - though much of that is actually Japanese - it could still do more to increase inter-Asian trade through the deregulation of trade barriers. Such a strategy would help accelerate Asia's move into retail trade and services, areas where up to now the U.S. and Japan continue to have some degree of comparative advantage. Such a process is unlikely to take the amount of time it took the U.S. and Europe to transform themselves, simply because the internet has revolutionised the distribution and speed of information delivery such that consumers know right away when prices are cheaper or more expensive in one country, one city from another. Here, ASEAN has a potential advantage, not only in terms of geographical proximity, but also similar economic structures, traditional ties and the very existence of the ASEAN to promote political and economic ties in any case. The Asian crisis, if anything, proves the necessity of accelerating the efforts of ASEAN, however limited they have been to date, to create a free trade area.

So much for the medium- to long-term. The key issue in 2000 remains whether or not the Asian recovery is sustainable. In our view it is at the general, regional and macroeconomic level. There remain a number of concerns however. For one thing, basing effects from the depressed state of Asian regional and economic activity in 1998 clearly played a part in the extent of the rebounds across Asia in 1999. In terms of a sustainable recovery, the key focus will not be the 1999 economic data in Asia, but that of this year, 2000. Not only will the 2000 economic data not show a favourable comparison for the Asian economies in the way that the comparison of 1998 to 1999 has done. The very fact that Asia rebounded so strongly in 1999 will mean an unfavourable comparison for 2000. It remains to be seen whether the market will be as charitable in 2000 towards these economies in terms of judging their asset prices as they were in 1999 when they seemed to forget such year-on-year basing effects. While the region's recovery may be sustainable, the path for Asian asset markets is likely to be a rocky one.

A further concern is that once the current phenomenon of massive fiscal and monetary injections have been withdrawn, partially or fully, the momentum behind the recovery could slow or even stop. A final concern is at the microeconomic level where the progress made to date remains inadequate relative to the demands of the 21rst Century and of the New Asia that could be. The pace of the development cycle continues to rise, its length to shorten. Faced with the information economy of the U.S. and progress, however incomplete in Europe, Asia does not have the luxury of many years to continue the process of transformation. Indeed, just as the internet companies of the day, countries are increasingly having to remake themselves. Despite the enormous pain caused and despite their faults the junk bond and re-engineering periods helped provide the foundation for the current, extraordinary U.S. growth cycle. It is not a question of whether or not Asia has to take the road of greater manufacturing efficiency, but by when, to what extent. In order to sustain the current recovery and create the New Asian Miracle, it will have to have to take many of the decisions it has up until now refused to take. In order to create, it will have to destroy. It is not a question of if, but of to what degree and how this will be fitted in to the political and economic ethos of consensus and harmony. The example of Singapore proves that there can indeed be a balance between these two codes. International standards in all aspects of manufacturing and service must be either created or applied more fully, and companies and banks must be made more efficient. In order to do that, jobs will have to be lost, people retrained. For this to happen, Asian governments must ensure that contacts between business, government and the market are not the driving force behind the economy - since the eventual inefficiency of this model has surely been proven and somewhat dramatically. Of course, Asian governments do not of necessity have to take this road. They can opt for the somewhat easier life, where the most painful microeconomic reforms are avoided so as to preserve such contract networks. If that is the road taken, then the loser will be the long-term health of the Asian regional economy. I say that with complete confidence because Japan is a shining example of what not to do, and indeed that is exactly what Japan did from 1991-1998 - avoid taking the tough decisions of forcing banks to give up their NPLs or close, avoid corporate restructuring and rationalisation, avoid the reduction of excess capacity, all in order to preserve networks. The rest, as they say, is history. Asia has a clear and shining example of what not to do - and it remains uncertain as to whether this present rebound in Japan will be enough to get it out of its 8-year economic slump.

In this regard, Korea appears to be a fine test case of where Asia is likely to go over the next decade (ignoring for now, its political and practical problems with its northern neighbour!). Nowhere, is the potential for social conflict (outside of China) so great, nowhere the progress made to date so substantial, nowhere the journey still to go so long. The example of the ASEAN is somewhat different because of their different economic structures and because they have the potential advantage of creating the ASEAN free trade area (AFTA) which they have said they would. Indeed, if the Asian crisis cannot accelerate that process, then nothing is likely to. However, Korea will be an example for individual Asian countries, whether they can indeed move on from the developing nation stage to the developed world. It is not by accident that the Chinese Premier Zhu Rongji chose the example of the *chaebol* for the development of the Chinese industrial base - though one could now argue that it is potentially an unfortunate example given what is happening to them now. Korea, unlike others, did make it into the OECD, did make it to the status of the 11th biggest economy in the world, a phenomenal feat given the devastation which was left after the 1950-53 Korean war. Yes, it fell back, collapsed under the weight of its own inefficiencies, its own economic weaknesses, as well as reacting to those of others, but at least it showed the potential of what might be for Asian nations.

Taiwan has not seen anything like the collapse which has taken place in Korea, but then again it is likely over time to be absorbed by China, one way or the other, democratically or not, politically or economically.

In addition, it has not seen anything like the incredible recovery that has been seen in Korea in 1999 and early 2000. Korea will be where the battle to get Asian nations into developed world status is won and lost. In this regard, there is much hope, but equally much concern. The job to achieve this is phenomenal, but the work has started. Korea is not the leader of the Asian recovering nations by accident. The Korean recovery is the topic of the next chapter, what is right and why it has recovered so strongly as a result, and what remains to be done (a frightening amount). It is the model pupil of the IMF's crisis rescue doctrine, but is that enough to sustain its recovery or will more radical measures have to be taken in order to keep its momentum going?

CHAPTER 4

THE LEADER – WHY KOREA IS LEADING THE RECOVERY

No image is more poignant, nor more apposite of the sheer determination of the Korean nation as a whole to face the economic and financial crisis of 1998 as a national threat than that of men and women bringing in gold and other jewellery to be melted down in order to help boost the depleted reserves of the Bank of Korea. Simultaneously, this showed the extent of the crisis, that individuals had to dig into their own pockets in order to help the authorities, and at the same time that Korea, if it had to go down, would go down fighting. In many situations of crisis and conflict, such determination can be the difference between winning and losing, between surviving and recovering or going down, from recession to depression.

Imagine the same situation occurring elsewhere, say in the U.S. for instance. People lining the streets, queuing up to hand over their money or their jewellery to the New York Fed on Liberty Street or the Federal Reserve Board on Constitution Avenue in Washington. Plenty of people have in times past queued outside the Fed, claiming that through interest rate hikes it has taken money involuntarily out of their pockets, but no-one has in recent memory volunteered to give it money! Such an act of generosity requires the existence of a state of such national crisis which harks either of a state of war or depression. Think of 1929 in the U.S. and then think of Korea, 1998. The two events do not necessarily share the same fundamental characteristics, but what they do share is the sense of panic, of utter desperation, of bankruptcy and unemployment. Where they part is in the response to that crisis. Korea in 1998 did admittedly have an advantage. It had the IMF, albeit after substantial national reluctance to accept an outside bailout of the country. The world of 1929, however, did not have a lender of last resort, as the IMF became, either directly or indirectly involved through the bailout programmes it put together, during the Asian and subsequently the Russian and Brazilian crises. Indeed, that was one of the main reasons why the depression lasted so long during the 1930s. There was a crisis of leadership. Korea, whatever its reluctance and perhaps feelings of shame that it had to be helped, did have that lender of last resort.

This does not detract in the slightest from the extraordinary response of the Koreans themselves to the crisis, a response which can only be compared to that against the unprovoked attack by North Korea in 1950. Let there be no misunderstanding, in economic terms, Korea in December of 1997 came within a whisker of "losing". Only the extraordinary determination of its President Kim Dae-jung and that of the Korean people themselves, along with the resolute support of the U.S. authorities and the IMF, and finally the brilliance of such individuals as Bill Rhodes, Robert Rubin and William McDonough saved the day. Such determination paid off. To be sure, determination is not by itself enough. In such times, humility is also needed, as is the willingness to learn from others, to accept help, to have the dedication to restructure and reform in the harshest of environments. That determination was symptomatic however of a resolve of the exceptional gains of the last 12 years, which had brought Korea membership of the OECD and made it the world's 11th largest economy and 12th largest trading nation. The short version of the story is that it was that kind of resolve, that kind of determination, albeit perhaps born of desperation, which produced the remarkable recovery we saw in Korea in 1999.

Indeed, the IMF Director of Asia Pacific Department Hubert Neiss in an article entitled "Public Sacrifice Serves as Driving Force for Recovery" which was reproduced by the "Korea Times", reflecting on what was then the anniversary of the outbreak of the crisis in Korea made special note of the ordinary Korean men and women who lined up to donate their gold jewellery to help fill the government's severely depleted empty foreign exchange reserves. "When I saw this, I was not only deeply moved, but also convinced that that Koreans had the determination to overcome this crisis, just as they had overcome other crises in history....If the right lessons from the recent unhappy experience will be drawn by everybody, Korea will emerge as a stronger economy, and the sacrifices of the Korean people will not have been in vain."[1]

By the time of the publication of this book, we should know that the Korean economy grew some 10% in 1999 after contracting almost 6% in 1998. Some sceptics have suggested that this was merely the result of a combination of massive fiscal and monetary injection, together with IMF loans and basing effects (year-on-year comparison to that 6% contraction). Others say that such macroeconomic recovery, whatever its extent, masks deep microeconomic fundamental flaws. Any serious response to the second suggestion requires substantial examination and debate, and indeed this chapter will focus on exactly this issue in considerable depth. First, however, on the issue of whether or not the Korean recovery was merely the result of artificial stimulus, the answer is a resounding "no!". Leaving aside the IMF, whose involvement was in any case dealt with in Chapter 2, let us examine precisely what policies the Korean authorities pursued and more specifically how and to what extent each has contributed to the Korean recovery. By doing this, we can hope to conclude how well the Korean economy might reform when and if such expansionist fiscal and monetary policies are withdrawn or even reversed.

THE BUILDING BLOCKS OF GROWTH

■ Stabilise the currency

As we have seen, before recovery could even be considered, the Korean *won* had to be stabilised using tight fiscal and monetary policy. Subsequent to the announcement of the IMF package, the Korean authorities who had previously said that on no account would the Korean *won* be allowed to fall below the 1,000 level to the dollar watched helplessly as the *won* came within a whisker of 2,000, falling to an all-time low of 1,985. Under the diktat of the IMF, the Korean authorities sought to stabilise the financial situation through strict monetary and fiscal discipline. On the monetary side, the Bank of

Korea's key intervention rate was raised to 35% as of the end of 1997, a level which crushed both creditors and debtors alike who had been used to cheap and abundant credit. As a result, short-term market interest rates rose to above 40% and the long-term interest rates rose to 29%. The interest rate curve was thus inverted, a traditional sign that the market is anticipating a recession. The next measure the Korean authorities took to stabilise the financial situation was to tighten the fiscal side further. In truth, the Korean government had traditionally kept the fiscal side relatively tight in any case. From 1991-1997, the government averaged a fiscal deficit of just 0.15% of the GDP. The combination of tight fiscal and monetary policy needless to say crushed the economy, but given the current account deficit and the run on the currency from which Korea was suffering that was unfortunately what was required. As we have seen, all the capital that could flee did. What was left was the natural mechanism of re-balancing, the ship that was tipping over righted itself but only because so many were thrown overboard.

■ Squash imported inflation

Given the high import content within the Korean economy, there were justifiable fears at the time that the depreciation in the Korean *won* from around 700 to 1985 against the dollar might cause imported inflation. As a result, the Bank of Korea let it be known, in its first decision following the revision of the Bank of Korea Act to make the central bank more independent, that it was targeting inflation rather than monetary aggregates and more specifically that it was targeting an inflation rate of 9% (plus or minus 1% point) for 1998, exactly double the rate seen in 1997. The BoK was helped in its task of keeping such imported inflationary pressures limited by both domestic and international factors. On the domestic side, the collapse of the real economy offset the import price effect from the Korean *won* devaluation. Equally, on the international side, low international prices of raw materials as global markets anticipated a global slowdown resulting from the Asian crisis. As a result, despite the fact that the Korean *won* devalued by about 50%, the Consumer Price Index for 1998 rose a mere 7.5%, a better result that the authorities could have hoped for despite their austere, stringent policy regime.

■ Put a floor under the banking system

Those who lay the blame for the current mess within the Korean banking system at the door of the Asian crisis -- the implication behind that being of course at the door of international investors -- are quite frankly fooling no-one. The Korean banking system was all but bankrupt going into the crisis, the result of two decades of government-directed credit policy and the nefarious results of that. Banks were obliged to lend to the top *chaebol* according to government mandate. Subsequently when that mandate became less official and more subtle, the banks still had no incentive to develop credit analysis techniques since they knew that the government would not let these conglomerates fail. An attempt by the banks to boost their profits through equity market purchases bought some time, but did nothing to stop the inevitable. The stock market downturn from January 1995 through the end of 1996 turned these profits into burning holes in the banks' balance sheets. In 1996, the gross profit margin of Thai banks was on the average double that of their Korean counterparts. If the Korean banking system had been a single bank and it had had to make full provision for all its loan and equity portfolio losses as of the 1996, it would have been declared insolvent. Foreign investor involvement had nothing to do with these problems. But for the fact that Korean balance sheets were somewhat opaque, one could have questioned the rationale of foreign investor involvement. If anything it was the belated realisation of this dire state of affairs that caused investor flight.

In short, the Korean banking system was a disaster waiting to be realised. The Asian crisis uncovered and exacerbated the extent of the disease, the gangrene within the system. It most certainly did not cause it. Given this appalling state of affairs, radical measures were needed to stabilise the banking system before any thought could be had of improving its profit ability. To this end, the first measure was the rollover agreement achieved by the IMF and internal creditors with Korean commercial banks of short-term foreign currency debt. The Korean authorities followed up this landmark deal which stopped the entire Korean financial system from imploding, with a decisive move of their own. Towards the end of May, 1998, the Ministry of Finance and the Economy announced a financial reform and restructuring package, including the issuance of government-backed bonds by KAMCO, the Korean Asset Management Corporation (a government agency created to buy up bad debts from the banks), totalling KRW25 trillion.

■ Start the restructuring process of the *chaebol*

Kim Dae-jung took office in December 1997 knowing full well that several Korean Presidents before him had sought to change the *chaebol* system and failed. They had had the best of intentions but in the end they had got nowhere. The system had beaten them. Kim did not exactly start from the best of negotiating positions. It was little exaggeration to say that he was roundly hated by the heads of the *chaebol*. In the 1987 and 1992 presidential elections he had stood - and lost - on a platform of social justice and workers' rights, hardly causes dear to the hearts of the patriarchal society which epitomised the *chaebol*. When he won the 1997 election, there can be little doubt that he was seen by Korea Inc as the enemy.

Kim did have one advantage though, albeit one which came at great cost to his country and its economy, namely the very fact that Korea was indeed in a state of national crisis and that crisis also affected the *chaebol* themselves. He was also a canny politician. He surprised many by appointing Kim Jong Pil of the opposition as his Prime Minister. A pragmatic if surprising step which at a stroke put the emphasis on consensus around the aim of national rebuilding. When Kim Dae-jung began his plan to reform the *chaebol* in early 1998, they were in a decidedly weakened state. The country had barely been saved from bankruptcy and much of that debt was down to the *chaebol* themselves. The top 5 *chaebol* accounted for over 50% of Korea's national output, while the top 30 accounted for around 85%, an outcome which could only have been the result of a deliberately cheap and directed credit policy. These were well known facts. It took no great leap of imagination then, on the part of the Korean population to take the view that the *chaebol* might have had something to do with their own misfortune resulting from the crisis in those early months of 1998. Well aware that he might not get another, more opportune chance, Kim pressed his advantage, seeking a restructuring framework from the heads of the main *chaebol* groups. While these were equally aware of the unfavourable economic climate - painfully so - a climate which obliged them to at least talk with this new upstart President, it seems likely that they thought they could get away with the same half-hearted reforms that had been attempted under past administrations. Act keen and he'll eventually go away like the others, seems to have been the underlying credo. In this, they were to underestimate greatly the determination of Kim Dae-jung and those bureaucrats and politicians who followed him. The *chaebol* thus agreed to Kim's plan of "the 5 principles of corporate restructuring" as listed in the Capital Structure Improvement Programme expecting to avoid most of the key elements which might seek to change the status quo, a status quo which they continued to think appropriate despite the crisis ongoing outside their guilded chambers. These 5 principles -- which were to be followed and enforced by the government most clinically -- were as follows:

1. enhance transparency of corporate management
2. remove cross affiliate guarantees (to be completed by March 2000)
3. improve financial structures
4. focus on core businesses rather than diversification
5. increase accountability among ruling shareholders and management

■ Cut interest rates once inflationary pressures have been defeated

In the first quarter of 1998, the CPI averaged 9%. Subsequently, this fell to 8.2% for the second quarter, 7.0% for the third and 6.0% for the fourth, resulting in the 7.5% figure for the full year of 1998. By December of that year, the monthly rate had fallen to 4.0% year-on-year, thus it was anticipated by the Bank of Korea that inflation would recede further. As a result, they targeted an inflation rate of 3%, plus or minus 1% point for 1999 as against 9% for 1998. Interest rates had however begun to fall substantially before that. Just as the original currency weakness, which let us not forget, came on the back of substantial trade and current account deficits, had resulted in interest rate tensions, the collapse of import demand resulted in the elimination of that current account deficit, which in turn buoyed the currency, allowing interest rates to fall. For 1997, Korea recorded a current account deficit of some USD8.7 billion. The first signs of recovery in the trade and current account were already visible however given that the country experienced a current account surplus for the fourth quarter of USD3.96 billion, as against deficits of USD7.35 billion, USD2.72 billion and USD2.05 billion in the first, second and third quarters respectively. The extent of the coming turnaround in the current account balance was first manifested in the first quarter of 1998 when Korea recorded a hitherto inconceivable surplus of some USD10.83 billion. For the full year of 1999, the current account surplus was USD40.04 billion, the largest surplus ever recorded in Korea's history. Clearly such a massive current account surplus was symptomatic of the collapse of import demand. That collapse stifled price pressure at the street level simply because there was now an excess of inventory and no demand. In terms of the financial markets, the turnaround in the current account balance reflected the righting of a ship which was about to tip over, the natural healing mechanism of an economy faced with an unsustainably high external imbalance. It provided fundamental support for the Korean *won* towards the first quarter of 1998 and into the second quarter, allowing the Korean authorities the leeway to relax official monetary policy. What ensued was a significant rally in the local Korean bond market.

Trend of key Korean interest rates (end of period figures)

	11/97	12/97	3/98	6/98	9/98	12/98	1/99	2/99	3/99	4/99	5/99
O/N call rate	12.1	31.3	22.1	14.4	7.1	6.5	6.0	5.0	4.9	4.8	4.7
91-day CP yields	17.8	40.8	23.3	17.0	10.8	8.1	7.3	7.1	7.0	6.1	6.5
3-year corp bond yields	15.1	29.0	18.3	16.0	11.9	8.0	8.1	8.7	7.8	7.7	8.4
3-year Treasury bond yields	--	--	--	--	11.5	7.0	7.1	7.0	6.6	6.7	6.7

Source: Bank of Korea

Note that this decline in interest rates and the consequent rally in the Korean stock and bond markets was not at all due to an improved growth outlook. On the contrary. It was a reflection of the improved liquidity conditions resulting from the defeat of inflation and the collapse of domestic demand. Thus, one could say that on purely fundamental grounds the rally in Korean bonds was justified whereas that of the stock market at this time was not, certainly not relative to earnings' projections. Korea was by no means the exception in this regard. Most of Asia which was initially hit by the crisis in 1997 similarly experienced a liquidity-driven rally in asset prices in the first half of 1998. If you remember in Chapter 1, this is what we termed Phase II of the "Classic IV-Phase Emerging Market Crisis". Lower interest rates and more importantly the normalisation of the interest rate curve, whereby the O/N rate eventually fell below 3-year yields allowed both the corporate and banking sectors to borrow at decreasing rates throughout 1998. Gradually, as the inflation data continued to be reported, not only did price pressure diminish but just as importantly - perhaps even more importantly - so did inflation expectations. For the first half of 1999, the CPI rate averaged just +0.65% was compared not only with the 7.5% rate for the full year of 1998 but also the Bank of Korea's own inflation target for 1999 of 3%, plus or minus a 1% point. Throughout 1999, Bank of Korea on occasion threatened that the cycle of low interest rates would soon come to an end. Given the degree of slack still in the economy, this seemed at the time an excessively hawkish policy to take. In reality, it surely reflected a desire on the part of the central bank to serve notice to the market well in advance of its intention to tighten monetary policy at some future stage. In addition, it was a useful way of occasionally, and when it deemed necessary, reining in the boom in Korean asset markets which was seen through the end of the first half of 1999 - that rally being on the basis of sound fundamental grounds rather than merely driven by increased liquidity.

In various speeches and comments to bankers and the press at large, Bank of Korea officials made their case very clear. Their priority was not growth per se but "to emerge completely from the valley of crisis and to shift the economy onto a sustainable growth track".[2] To this end, strengthening the base of demand through lower interest rates was clearly a help but by itself it was not enough. Bank of Korea had to make sure that going forward the Korean economy's growth did not come at the expense of price stability, either through consumer or asset price inflation. This marked a clear divergence, not only from past policies in Korea but also with the previous policy orthodoxy. Long-term sustainable growth would be achieved through macro- and micro-economic reform and inflation targeting; altogether a different policy ideology, but an improvement nevertheless from the previous policy orthodoxy which only targeted monetary aggregates and ignored asset price inflation. The Bank of Korea would not make this same mistake again. Not only that. Going forward, it would focus on the quality of growth, rather than just the quantity of growth which had undoubtedly been the focus during the late 1980s and early 1990s. To economists looking for signs of real fundamental improvement, not only in the economy but in the economy's outlook, this was music to the ears. As noted, the Bank of Korea occasionally throughout 1999 fired warning shots across the bows of the market, suggesting that monetary tightening might be imminent, however the very fact that it had to do so was surely proof of the success of its monetary easing throughout 1998 and the first months of 1999 which had seen the call rate fall from a high of 35% to trough out around the 5% mark.

■ Loosen fiscal policy

While the Bank of Korea was eagerly cutting interest rates, the Ministry of Finance and the Economy was given the green light by the IMF to set about loosening the fiscal straightjacket from the second half of 1998 onwards. As noted earlier, Korea had been very far from a profligate spender during its growth period or indeed even before. According to the IMF, the Korean budget deficit averaged -0.5% a year from 1970-1998. That figure included the -4% deficit which the IMF allowed for Korea in 1998, a hitherto inconceivable fiscal performance from a Korean administration. Given the size of the Korean economy, the economic contraction in 1998 notwithstanding, this was a massive fiscal expansion. Indeed, the combination of such substantial fiscal and monetary easing, coupled with IMF loans were the key driving forces behind the speed and strength of the recovery we saw in 1999. The increase in the budget deficit, as substantial as it was, was not a fundamental concern for the economy given the massive current account surplus which had been built up and was financed by government bond issuance. The fiscal expansion dealt with a combination of tax cuts and increased spending. In particular, both the Korean government and the IMF sought to increase spending with a specific focus on creating a social safety net for those victims of the restructuring process. In the August 1998 supplementary budget, the government announced a 30% increase in social safety net spending, an 8% increase in social overhead capital spending and a 25% increase in net lending. On the consumer side, the government made a 30% reduction in special consumption tax rates on consumer durables and cars.

Fiscal policy in 1999 was aimed at cementing the gains made in the economy in late 1998, stabilising demand and encouraging a revival of consumption. The government, as it had done initially in 1998 aimed for a budget deficit target of -5% of the GDP. Spending was front-loaded in the first half of 1999 in order to help sustain the recovery. For 2000, the government has agreed a draft state budget of -3.5% of the GDP, though in reality we are likely to see a smaller deficit than that given the stronger growth profile which Korea is currently showing. Note that the April elections in Korea are likely to influence financial markets - and many other things, no doubt! - so this -3.5% budget deficit target should be taken only as a guide. There is a risk that it could be higher as the government seeks to increase spending ahead of the election. That said, given Korea's traditional fiscal prudence, excess spending could be perceived as imprudent, particularly as the government intends to return to a balanced budget by 2004. A breakdown of the 2000 state budget as approved on September 21, 1999 compared with the 1999 budget is as follows:

(Trillions of *won*)

	2000	% change	1999
Education investment	18,578.9	9.3	17,003.0
Labour Cost of gov offcls	16,265.4	12.9	14,405.4
Defence, security	15,610.8	4.6	14,919.1
Infrastructure spending	14,042.3	4.7	13,408.8
Farming, fishing, village aid	8,914.3	4.3	8,543.1
Fin Ref, National Debt int.	8,556.4	24.8	6,855.9
Social welfare expansion	5,662.4	11.9	5,059.8
Info-tech support	4,554.4	13.5	4,013.8
Environmental	2,799.1	20.4	2,325.0
Venture capital, mid-sized cos	2,289.2	15.8	1,976.8
Cultural, tourism industry	931.5	40.1	664.7
Total	**98,204.7**	**10.1**	**89,175.4**

Source: Official Data

Despite the considerable effort which the Korean government and the IMF have undertaken through expanded fiscal and monetary policy in order to boost the economy, there have however been a large number of victims, through the unemployed, the homeless, the downsized and the rationalised. The fact that the unemployment rate rose from 2.6% in 1997 to 6.8% in 1998 and to 8.4% in the first quarter of 1999, peaking around that level on a quarterly basis showed that there was clearly a need for such stimulus, not only from an economic but also a social perspective. In a land traditionally wracked by sporadic bouts of social unrest - democracy in Korea having been a recent experiment, with what one might call a tempestuous childhood in the early 1990s - rising unemployment represented a political and social as well as an economic threat, one that proved a challenge even to the likes of Kim Dae-jung. After all, this unemployment did not only come about as a result of Korean companies going bankrupt due to the direct effects of the crisis. It also happened because of Kim's reform drive. There was bound to be a confrontation between organised labour and the government and indeed a confrontation there was.

RESISTANCE FROM THE UNIONS...

To understand the importance of that confrontation and subsequent relations between the Korean government, big business and the unions, one has to go back on how organised labour developed in Korea and more importantly what it had gone through just to survive under the military dictatorship which preceded that experiment in democracy from 1987. In the 1980s, it was quite normal for workers to be harassed to discourage any attempt at the creation of free and independent unions. Indeed, in the 1980s, the union movement was hammered by the regime's "purification" campaign which was an attempt to cut off the head of the hydra. As in all such cases, it did nothing of the kind. People can be brutalised or even killed but ideas live on. Thus, when such organised labour movements as existed were confronted with President Roh Tae-woo's experiment with democracy, it went to their heads. Freed from the repression of the iron fist, unions staged strikes across the nation. Several *chaebol* were the subject of repeated union strikes, during the late 1980s and early 1990s, notably Hyundai. The unions had not only found their voice, but the ability to air it, and more importantly the willingness to use their muscle to influence business and government. It would have been an irresistible temptation for most groups. For those who had suffered in the 1980s under the military regimes, it was not only that. It was revenge. For Korea's quarter century of stellar growth, there had been a sacrifice and that sacrifice had been the workers themselves. Now it was the labour's turn to hit back. The chaos that followed, involving riots, running battles in the streets, calls for general strikes and factories brought to a halt divided the Korean union movement. To generalise greatly, it divided them between those who saw every reason to continue such mayhem, for a multitude of reasons, and those who viewed such actions as extreme, preferring to take a more centrist approach to negotiation with business and government if they could.

When the crisis happened in Korea in late 1997, relations between the unions and the *chaebol* remained in a fragile state. Consequently, the demands by the government for corporate and banking restructuring produced outrage among the unions and the workers they were supposed to serve. As if the Korean workforce had not suffered enough on the alter of growth. Now, that growth had faltered, it was supposed to pay the price here too! For many this was simply too much, the straw that broke the camel's back. National strikes were threatened. In Korea, this was not a threat to be taken lightly.

However, here, Kim Dae-jung had a crucial advantage compared to his predecessors or indeed many of his colleagues in government. For long, he had campaigned for social justice and for workers' rights. Indeed, he had made himself such an enemy of the *chaebol* specifically and of the existing power structure more generally that he was clearly someone who stood for something other than mere wealth for wealth's sake, clearly someone who might be trusted. Kim sought about using this advantage, forming a tripartite body between the unions, the *chaebol* and the government to come to a common agreement from which no party could back out without losing face. To cut a long story short, he got the *chaebol* to agree to a restructuring programme, which would inevitably mean significant job layoffs, and he got the unions to agree to a government proposal whereby the Labour Act would be revised to allow for layoffs in the first place. In return for this, he agreed that the government would create a social safety net, a form of unemployment insurance - which would be paid jointly by the government and the *chaebol* - to provide specifically for those made unemployed by the restructuring process. So Kim created a social compact with big business and the unions which would hopefully alleviate or lessen the pain which the Korean economy would undoubtedly feel at the microeconomic level. To give some idea of the sums we are talking about, the government budgeted for a social safety net, including unemployment insurance of some 2.5% of the GDP, a substantial sum.

The unions were - for now - mollified. The more realistic among them realised that there was little alternative to going along with the tripartite social compact. For them to reject it, and come out on the streets would benefit no-one, including most notably themselves. Korea had to be as one if it were to escape the crisis. This is not to underestimate the extent of the pain that Korea was to experience, seen most visibly in the form of rising unemployment. Korea experienced levels of unemployment not seen for decades, not seen in fact since the post-war years. To some, it must have seemed as if all the efforts of the boom years had gone for nought, as if all those sacrifices had been wasted. Thus, while Kim had achieved an agreement with the unions, it was still a fragile agreement, one which was put to the test several times. In seasonally adjusted terms, the unemployment rate peaked in October 1998 at a rate of 8.5%, while in non-seasonally adjusted basis it peaked in February 1999 at 8.7%. Remember, that this was against a "normal" rate of 1.5-2.0%. In absolute terms, unemployment rose from 0.93 million in January 1998 to a peak of 1.79 million in February 1999. By September 1999, with the economic engine having ignited and the recovery progressing rapidly, that figure was down to around 1.05 million. Note that much of the rise in the number of the unemployed was not necessarily due to mass layoffs at the *chaebol*, which the unions fared and were all too prepared to respond to through strike action, but at small- and medium-sized companies which did not have adequate access to financing or support - or, somewhat ironically, the unions - and thus had no choice but to sack their unfortunate workers to reduce their cost base.

As a result of the tripartite agreement, however, Kim was given some breathing room throughout 1998 after achieving this agreement. Looking ahead, there is clearly a danger that confrontation with the unions could resurface as the economy recovers. More specifically, there appear to have been some cases where individual *chaebol* were reticent to make their contributions to unemployment insurance, either because they simply did not want to or because they were unable to given the strain of their existing cost base. The unions thus in specific cases had a valid claim that they and their workers were (again) paying more than their share of the costs of the restructuring process and to date seeing little of the gain. Wage claims are likely to be a key issue in 2000 and 2001 (more so than usual!) given this apparent disparity. Whatever gains Kim has made in his dealings with the unions, particularly in limiting strike action which would have otherwise risked the complete collapse of the Korean economy, there remains some risks going forward. Resistance to change comes not only from the unions however. It also emanates from the *chaebol* themselves, some of whom see little point in restructuring (it is truly incredible that such people are ever allowed the responsibility of management in such a case!), others who continue to try to actively resist the movement of change in order to maintain the status quo. They do not seem to realise that the status quo is a document which has been torn up, whether they like it or not. A document which had positives and negatives for all concerned but a document which nevertheless is no longer in existence. This is not to say that there will be some who seek to resist the course of history. There are "luddites" everywhere. The more inspired and visionary among them will seek to change, both radically and rapidly in order to meet the new demands with which they are faced. Those who seek to remain will be bypassed, one way or another. The longer they fight, the more damage will be done to the Korean economy.

...AND FROM THE *CHAEBOL*

We shall look at the progress (or lack thereof) of corporate restructuring later on in this chapter, an issue which is of course somewhat subjective. What is not, what is indisputable is that there has at varying times and to varying degrees been resistance to the restructuring and reform movement from within the *chaebol* themselves. As noted earlier, many of these corporate behemoths initially viewed the reform process under Kim Dae-jung with the same cynical eye as previous attempts at reform. Slow the process down, more it in detail and eventually the reforms will tire, get frustrated and go away - and leave us to continue with the way we have been doing things for the last 20 years. This undoubtedly seems to have been the subliminal message behind the superficially acquiescent tone of agreement to the initial talks with the unions and the government. This was a major misjudgement however. Kim had waited a long time to reform the Korean economy. While there would undoubtedly have to be comprises made, deals done in the interest of the goal, of the target, he would not be shaken off from that target so easily. Perhaps there were those within the *chaebol* management structure who realised the extent of that misjudgement beforehand. After his speech on Liberation Day, however, there was no further misunderstanding. The battle lines were drawn. Some of the *chaebol* seem to have hoped that the reform process would slow or stop as the economy recovered and perhaps more importantly as the April 2000 general elections approached. This was not to be. Rather, the reverse was to happen.

While Kim and his Finance Minister Lee Kang Bong-kyun made sure to say that they were not aiming to dismantle the *chaebol*, they equally focused on making the general business environment a touch hotter, more competitive for these dinosaurs. Things were never to be the same again. Hyundai Group was investigated on charges of tampering with stock prices. Samsung Group faced an inquiry by the Financial Supervisory Service into its financial affiliates. Looking at the industrial sector as a whole, the FSS was trying to crack down on the use by conglomerates of their financial affiliates, such as securities and investment trust firms, of financial funding excess to their business needs. Given that excess financing had been a major reason why the *chaebol* had built up excess capacity, the government was attempting to make sure - not unreasonably - that this excess of cheap capital relative to need did not reoccur. The intention was not to single out Samsung for investigation. On the contrary. Everyone would be given fair treatment. Indeed, Samsung was one of the better examples of a *chaebol* looking to reduce its debt-to-equity ratio. To this end, Samsung not only relied on a rising stock market, but actually repaid some KRW5.4 trillion in debt during the first half of 1999. Some have gone along with the restructuring process and from a long-term viewpoint these seem the most likely to prosper. Others continue to resist. The next major level of resistance could however be at the political level. Disappointed by the zeal of the government in corporate restructuring, these resistant *chaebol* could look to the opposition Grand National Party to save them from saving themselves. Recent remarks by the GNP that they were against any "irrational" reform of *chaebol* groups drew understandable attention, not least within the *chaebol* themselves. That said, the *chaebol* are no longer a united front, whether one is considering the top 5 or a broader perspective. There is little doubt however that some *chaebol* are likely to band together to support financially the opposition forces against Kim at the April 2000 elections. It would be a tragedy for Korea if those opposing the corporate and banking restructuring process, restructuring which is so needed if Korea's goal of first-world status is to be realised fully, were to win that election, whoever wins at the individual level. This is not to sound overly gloomy. All great aims require substantial, effort and sacrifice. Taking the easy option of stopping at the half-way mark might seem appropriate to some, whether to alleviate the degree of economic pain or for purposes of self-preservation, but the costs of that option will be exceptionally high. It would be nothing short of keeping Korea in an emerging markets status, rather than the status its achievements deserve - including those of the *chaebol* themselves. Indeed, it is in the interests of the *chaebol* themselves that they do not take that easy option. So much for what remains to be done. In the last two years, Korea has achieved a remarkable amount. Indeed, the degree of economic recovery has stunned the IMF let alone bank analysts.

WHY KOREA IS LEADING THE ASIAN RECOVERY

There is a reason that Korea is leading the Asian region out of recession, that its economy grew a stunning 10% in 1999. These things do not happen by accident. One could take the determination of the Korean people as a reason, and undoubtedly it is. Without such determination, the policies put in place by the government and overseen by the IMF would not have been implemented with such unrelenting zeal. Yet, this clearly is not the full answer, as appealing as it is. There are other, more clinical reasons, most notably the fact that Korea cut debt. It had two debt problems, one domestic and one external. Though the domestic debt problem undoubtedly influenced the massive devaluation of the *won* in 1997, it was the external debt problem which was the main cause of this, particularly the short-term external debt problem. With the insistence of the IMF, the Korean government set about cutting its short-term external debt with a vengeance. Note whatever the efforts of the governments of Thailand and Indonesia, fellow members of the IMF bailout programme, it was in Korea where the government really took a knife to debt.

Total External Liabilities (USD billion)

	Dec 1997	Dec 1998	Feb 1999	Mar 1999	change from Dec 1997
Total	158.1	149.4	145.4	145.5	-12.6
Long term	94.9	118.5	114.9	113.7	+18.8
Short term	63.2	30.8	30.5	31.9	-31.3
Public sector	22.3	36.5	34.1	34.2	+11.9
Financial institutions	89.6	71.9	70.0	69.5	-20.1
Domestic corporations	46.2	41.0	41.4	41.8	-4.4

Source: Bank of Korea

Granted, to a major extent the rollover agreed by the IMF, the Korean banks and international banks at the start of 1998 was a major catalyst for this debt reduction. In addition, the Bank of Korea, well aware of the dramatic turnaround in the trade and current account balances as a result of the economic collapse and the upward pressure that this was putting on the Korean *won*, called on Korean banks to step up repayment and loan loss provisions for their external debts. Given the size of these debts, this was a major force in limiting the strength of the Korean *won* throughout 1999. Indeed, but for that resultant demand from the Korean banks to buy dollars in order to repay or provision for these debts, it can safely be said that the dollar would have plunged against the *won* to around 1,100 or lower. To a corporation which was efficient, well managed and tightly run, this would not have presented a problem. To some of the *chaebol*, gorged and obese on their diet of cheap credit for two decades, a higher *won* against the dollar and more importantly the *yen* was a major threat against their export competitiveness. The authorities obliged by limiting the ability of their currency to rally and on occasion causing it to weaken, most notably when the *yen* weakened. Corporations elsewhere in the world are not provided of this excuse, nor this help - nor should they be.

Meanwhile, the monthly trade and current account surpluses which Korea was churning out - amounting to a current account surplus of USD40 billion in 1998, lest we forget - were providing the Bank of Korea with the cushion it needed, first to repay the IMF loans and secondly to defend against further crises or financial or economic threats. From a mere USD8.9 billion as of the end of December 1997, usable foreign exchange reserves (excluding foreign deposits which cannot be called on easily or speedily) rose to USD50.1 billion as of January, 1999 and were USD65.5 billion as of September of that year. In 1997, the true weakness of the reserves' position had been somewhat hidden by including deposits abroad at Korean banks, however needless to say these were not easily called upon. The difference between total reserves and usable reserves which had been around USD15 billion towards the end of 1997 was USD3.5 billion as of January 1999. By September, Bank of Korea was no longer publishing two figures, explaining this by saying that it was too small (around USD200 million) to consider worth reporting. So the Bank of Korea obliged Korean banks to bring home foreign deposits which were owed to the central bank. Bank of Korea also obliged the banks to repay loans to it. In turn, the central bank repaid its own loans to the IMF. By mid-September, 1999, Korea had repaid some USD12.3 billion of the Supplemental Reserve Facility it received from the IMF, reducing its liabilities to USD6.2 billion, the only country in the region to have repaid any of its IMF debt by that time. By August 1999, Korea's total external debt had fallen to USD142.6 billion, while net external liabilities had plunged to a mere USD1.1 billion.

Korea not only cut external debt but also domestic debt. While the official non-performing loan data for Korea were nowhere near the levels of Indonesia or Thailand, systemic non-performing loans were still estimated at around 30% of the total. Clearly, the corporate and bank restructuring effort had much to do with the reduction in that total. The government effectively nationalised two commercial banks, Seoul Bank and Korea First Bank, restructured them and then sought buyers, while it forced the closure of several merchant banks. It then entrusted the job of reducing systemic non-performing loans to KAMCO, the Korean Asset Management Corporation. While, as ever there remains much work to be done, the results have been impressive. By the end of September, 1999, non-performing loans at 17 Korean banks were down to KRW19.033 trillion, or 6.2% of the total loans. NPLs were down some 27% from end-June that year when they had represented 8.7% of the total.

Korea's markets had long been even more protected than those of Japan. The government sought to raise the foreign investment ceiling, simultaneous to its corporate and banking restructuring efforts, realising that capital investment would be needed to complete the national restructuring process, not just multilateral loans or fiscal and monetary easing. Initial results from this effort were disappointing for the simple reason that the Korean parties involved refused to accept the market price. Eventually, however, albeit belatedly and with considerable reluctance, the realisation dawned that lower prices would have to be asked for if sales were to be achieved with foreign investors. The result of this was extraordinary. For the first 10 months of 1999, Korea attracted some USD10.3 billion in foreign direct investment. This was roughly the same amount of the FDI as Korea had accumulated from 1962-1992. Kim Dae-jung's first meeting with George Soros shortly after his election victory at the end of 1997 had signalled a dramatic change in many ways, not least Korea's official policy towards foreign investment. From then on, despite some obstacles, it was welcome. A number of high-profile deals caught the headlines, notably the purchase by the Dutch company Philips Electronics NV of half of LG Electronics' flat-screen business for just over USD1.5 billion and the acquisition of 51% of Korea First Bank by Newbridge Capital, a U.S. investment firm.

Further efforts at the re-liquification of the Korean economy were to follow. A major problem which had hindered the export sector of other countries in the Asian region in taking advantage of the massive devaluations of their currencies had been the lack of ability to obtain trade credit. The perception of greatly increased credit risk following the initial credit rating downgradings of Korea, Thailand and Indonesia by the major rating agencies caused a tightening of in some cases a complete elimination of trade financing lines to companies. In the case of Korea, the larger corporations, the *chaebol*, had an advantage in that affiliates could borrow from each other - although the government efforts to eliminate cross guarantees and excess borrowing were and remain an obstacle to that. Small- and medium-size companies did not have this advantage, and indeed it was for this precise reason that many went to the wall. As part of its fiscal relaxation effort, the government specifically sought to give temporary credit assistance to the SME sector to the tune of USD3.3 billion for maturities of up to one year.

In addition, the government stepped up its privatisation effort which originally planned to privatise some 11 state-owned enterprises and their subsidiaries. The National Textbook Company, Korea Technology Banking Corporation, and Namhae Chemical Corporation were sold off, as was a 5.8% stake in POSCO which reduced the government stake in that company to 20.8%. The government also plans the full privatisation of four other state-owned companies -- Korea Ginseng and Tobacco, Korea Gas, Daehan Oil Pipeline, and Korea District Heating over the next three years - in addition to the sale of Hanvit Bank which issued GDRs and the 5% stake sale in KEPCO. Korea Telecom has also been publicly listed and the government is to reduce its share in the company to 33.4 percent by the year 2000.

Korea has also gone further than most in creating what I have termed "institutional infrastructure". That is, it has set about creating the framework for prudently supervised and regulated, deep and transparent asset markets - most notably a domestic bond market- which can efficiently reallocate Korea's high savings' rate where the money is needed most and at a market-determined price. The alternative, as we saw before the onset of the Asian crisis was inadequate capital markets in Asia which caused domestic corporations to rely excessively on bank lending, in many cases from domestic banks with whom they had an excessively cosy relationship. The result was massively excess debt relative to needs, and a huge bank exposure to these companies. There rest is of course history. In order to have sufficient institutional infrastructure, you need three key elements: a large domestic institutional investor base (pension, mutual and life insurance funds), prudent and independent regulators (an independent central bank as a starting point, followed by a specific regulator for the stock market and also one specifically for the banking system, all to have complete independence from government fiat or whim), and finally deep and transparent capital markets (stock and bond markets).

To this end, the government submitted legislation to create mutual funds. In addition, it allowed the issuance of asset-backed securities and also finally allowed the entry of foreign investors into the domestic Korean *won* bond markets. Finally, the government further deregulated the Korean *won* foreign exchange market in April of 1999. Among the measures it introduced, it allowed Korean banks to participate in the offshore non-deliverable forward market, thus all but eliminating the price and yield difference between onshore forwards and offshore NDFs. Full foreign exchange market deregulation is expected in 2001 at the latest.

While the results of all this have indeed been impressive, not to say extraordinary, it is clearly not enough to say that. In order to get a full picture of just what happened in Korea in 1999 and what is still happening one has again to return to the data, albeit with some explanation. The table on the next page shows the performance of the Korean economy in the third quarter of 1999.

Growth Rates by Kind of Economic Activity and Component of Expenditure[1)]
(at 1995 constant prices)
unit : %

	1998p					1999p			
	1/4	2/4	3/4	1/4~3/4	Year	1/4	2/4	3/4	1/4~3/4
Gross Domestic Product	-3.6	-7.2	-7.1	-6.0	-5.8	4.5	9.9	12.3	9.0
Agriculture, forestry & fishing	6.2	-3.5	-7.0	-3.8	-6.3	-7.4	5.3	4.2	2.8
Manufacturing	-4.6	-10.4	-9.1	-8.1	-7.2	10.3	20.4	26.8	19.2
Electricity, gas & water	4.5	0.3	-4.1	0.2	-0.5	2.8	7.1	6.1	5.3
Construction	-3.9	-6.6	-10.1	-7.2	-9.0	-14.8	-7.8	-10.0	-10.5
Services	-4.5	-7.4	-6.2	-6.0	-5.4	6.5	10.4	12.4	9.8
Final consumption expenditure	-8.4	-9.7	-8.9	-9.0	-8.2	5.0	7.3	8.4	6.9
(Private)	-9.9	-11.2	-10.4	-10.5	-9.6	6.2	9.1	10.3	8.5
(Government)	1.3	-0.7	-0.6	0.0	-0.1	-1.7	-2.3	-1.3	-1.7
Gross fixed capital formation	-20.6	-23.7	-22.2	-22.2	-21.1	-4.3	4.9	6.9	2.8
(Construction)	-5.9	-7.8	-12.0	-8.8	-10.2	-13.7	-8.5	-10.0	-10.5
(Machinery & equipment)	-38.3	-46.1	-39.3	-41.4	-38.5	12.9	37.2	48.0	32.2
Exports of goods & services	25.7	13.2	8.0	15.1	13.3	10.3	15.1	22.2	15.9
(Merchandise)	27.1	16.5	9.5	17.2	15.6	11.9	18.3	25.3	18.5
Imports of goods & services	-27.2	-25.5	-25.9	-26.2	-22.0	27.0	26.9	32.0	28.6
(Merchandise)	-27.7	-27.3	-28.7	-27.9	-24.6	26.4	30.8	40.0	32.4

Source : Bank of Korea

Notes:
1) Percentage change over previous year
2) p: preliminary

The 12.3% expansion of the economy in the third quarter was broad-based, with four out of the five key sectors of the economy showing growth. Undoubtedly, however, it was led by manufacturing, and thus implicitly by the *chaebol*. The dramatic rebound in manufacturing production - most notably in semiconductors, computers, cars and industrial machinery - came about due to a recovery in domestic demand for these products and persistently strong external demand in key third markets such as the U.S. and Europe, coupled with the rise of the *yen* relative to the Korean *won* which made Korean exports ultra-competitive versus their key Japanese competitors. In addition, it came about due to the region-wide recovery in Asia, not least in Japan itself, from the start of 1999.

Looking at the individual sectors of the economy, private consumption started its recovery in the first quarter of 1999. Undoubtedly, a large part of this was due to basing effects given the extent of the contraction in the first quarter of 1998, in the wake of the Korean *won* devaluation and the initial phase of the economic collapse which followed that of the financial sector. However, private consumption spending increased through the second and third quarters of 1999, suggesting that the authorities' efforts to boost demand were having real benefit and result at street level. The recovery in imports in the first quarter of 1999 was also, as we noted earlier, further evidence of that recovery in demand. Though they are not the whole story, positive basing effects undoubtedly helped boost the 1999 economic figures in Korea. For 2000, the basing effect will be reversed given the very high base comparison of 1999 data. That said, our bank believes strongly in the recovery of Korea and we continue to anticipate growth of around 9% for this year, based on a persistently strong private sector and external demand. Where basing effects and slightly less relaxed fiscal and monetary policy will perhaps restrain growth, corporate re-stocking and the recoveries in Japan and Europe will sustain it.

RISKS TO THAT RECOVERY

That said, despite the extraordinary progress that has been made, and the fact that the Korean economy grew some 10% in 1999, one should remember that the degree of contraction in 1998 and the amount of damage done to the economy shows that this recovery remains quite fragile. Don't get me wrong. I am not saying that I do not believe in this recovery which is ongoing in Korea. What I am saying is that one should not take it for granted. Many of Korea's problems have been solved, but by no means all of them. The Korean authorities would be the first to say that now is not the time for vigilance to be reduced. The example of Daewoo surely proves that. There are other risks to a continuation of the recovery in Korea, notably in the banking system and also on the political side, but first let us look at Daewoo, not only for its own merits but for what it represents, as a symptom of what remains within the *chaebol* structure, what work remains to be done in order to make Korea Inc work in a long-term, sustainable way rather than the bloated, self-indulgent way which helped in providing Korea's boom years but which must now be discarded as an economic and a corporate philosophy in this hyper-competitive world in which we live, a world which judges only according to one criterium: profit.

■ The lesson of Daewoo; the *chaebol* are still not doing enough

If there was anyone who believed that the *chaebol* were doing enough to restructure, the discovery in mid-July of major financial problems at Daewoo Group and the subsequent announcement on August 16 that Daewoo could not meet its debts of some KRW57.5 trillion, an announcement which was to be followed by the stunning decision of creditors to seek the dismantling of the group, surely dismayed such optimists. Yet, there were grounds for both optimism and pessimism in the subsequent events at Daewoo. On the negative side, it clearly showed that there were some *chaebol* who were still not doing enough to restructure (to put it charitably). From the end of 1998 through the end of June 1999, Daewoo Group's debt-to-equity ratio actually increased to some 588.2% from 526.5%, this at a time when the Korean stock market was roaring (which should reduce the ratio given that it increases the equity valuation component by which the debt is divided) and at a time when the other four of the top five *chaebol* saw their ratios decrease substantially. If Daewoo's eventual collapse was a long time coming given such incredible debt levels, this was a small comfort to the other *chaebol*, whatever the progress they had made. The fact that it was allowed to collapse, that the government not only allowed it to be put under a corporate workout programme but actively encouraged that, and allowed the dismantling of what had once been thought a great company was a clear warning to all the *chaebol* that the government was very serious about the issue of corporate restructuring.

Indeed, in the wake of the Daewoo collapse, Hyundai Group came under no doubt unwanted scrutiny as local and foreign media noted that its debt level had risen from KRW61.5 trillion as of the end of 1998 to KRW64.9 trillion by the end of June 1999. Its debt-to-equity ratio fell during that period from 449.3% to 340.8%, however this was still well short of the government's target of 200% by the year-end of 1999. Hyundai's first half 1999 P&L performance also caused concern in the market. The importance of restructuring the corporate sector to avoid further collapses such as Daewoo where possible became more obvious when in November of 1999 the Korean government had to go to considerable lengths to avoid a crisis in the trust fund sector which faced redemptions on Daewoo bonds, having to provide a financial market stabilisation fund, with initial capital of KRW20 trillion, which promised to buy an unlimited amount of bonds from the funds. While the issues for the top 5 *chaebol* may not necessarily be the same as those of say the top 64, or even Korea's industrial sector as a whole, it is useful to look at their performance as a guide of what has been done, and what has yet to be done.

Financial structure of the top 5 *chaebol* (Trillions of *won*)

		Hyundai	Daewoo	Samsung	LG	SK
Debts	End-1998	61.5	59.9	44.7	36.4	22.5
	End-June 1999	64.9	61.8	39.3	35.2	21.4
	Difference	+3.4	+1.9	-5.4	-1.2	-1.1
Debt-to-equity ratio	End 1998	449.3%	526.5	275.7	341.0	354.9
	End-June 1999	340.8%	588.2	192.5	246.5	227.3
	Difference	-108.5%	+61.7	-83.2	-94.5	-127.6

Source: Korean Industry Data

For Korean industry as a whole, going forward, it is probably a reasonable assumption that outperformance in terms of both profit and share price will be achieved not only by reduction of the debt-to-equity ratio per se, however important this is, but by reduction of the absolute level of debt. While some progress had been made in this regard, it would seem to be inadequate if Korea Inc is to be measured against its international competitors. Furthermore, it would appear that more progress needs to be made in terms of reducing excess capacity, both in terms of manufactured capacity and ultimately the workforce.

While some Korean officials still argue vehemently that Korea does not in fact suffer from spare capacity and allegedly never did - presumably ignoring debt-to-equity ratios and operating profit margins which would probably lead to the sacking of the management in most OECD countries, the club which Korea still presumably wants to remain within and certainly which it classifies itself by - is an inexcusably incorrect argument. These same officials argue that Korean industry remains dependent on external demand. In other words, should external demand falter, some of these companies could be in deep trouble. That would seem to be the message. Yet, these are not small companies which are only exporting one or more product lines. On the contrary, the biggest of these are global conglomerates. The very fact that they *cannot* depend on their domestic markets, shows up a number of things. For one thing, it suggests that either these companies are too large or the Korean economy is too small. I would argue that both are the case. Regarding the latter, the potential of the Korean economy would be infinitely greater if it were fully opened up to competition, both domestic and foreign. Some of these officials have complained that the *chaebol* remain hamstrung from improving their lot given government restrictions on equity raising and mergers and acquisitions. Such measures should merely be viewed as the natural extension of those being attempted by the government to develop Korea's capital markets. If spare capacity is not a problem, then let these behemoths feel the full force of the winds of competition in raising capital and see how they fair. No longer should cheap capital be available on tap. That helps no end in the end, neither the *chaebol* nor the banks. The *chaebol* remain vulnerable to a decline in external demand precisely because they continue to rely on price, and thus the exchange rate. Indeed, they appear to be relying more on this than on the competitive advantages of their own businesses.

Diversity has brought with it many successes, but it has certainly not resulted in optimisation of returns. That said, given how closed Korea's markets were, it never had to. If one is to take the Korean government at their word, the Korean capital markets of the future will be a different beast to those which have existed up to now. For quite some time, Korea's stock market has been inadequately transparent and the home to retail and corporate punters. In other words, it has been a betting shop rather than a liquid market where corporations can be fairly priced and receive capital adequate to their needs. That will change. For it to change, the government needs to scrap what restrictions remain on raising equity and on mergers and acquisitions and needs to reinforce minority shareholder rights and the powers and responsibilities of the regulators concerned. Most people do not improve in any field if they do not have to, if they do not have some incentive to do so (whatever that incentive is, be it financial or simply their own pride). Corporations are no different. Open up the capital markets of Korea and such officials who claim that the *chaebol* do not have to change will soon be singing a different tune. This is not to detract from those *chaebol* who have made real progress, notably the ones who cut their absolute debt levels. It is to say however that such progress is not enough. The idea of throwing open the domestic capital markets continues to face major obstacles, not least from both commercial and political interest groups whose interests are hurt by such deregulation. However, it is refreshing to hear none other than the Bank of Korea say that "we all recognise that the restructuring of the economy must be according to market principles if it is to be sustainable". Quite so, and most of all if "victory" is to be declared by and for the Korean people themselves.

■ Korea's shaky banking system

As we noted earlier, Korea's banking system was bankrupt in all but name going into the Asian crisis. That crisis was merely a couple of nails in the coffin. Since being made independent however, the Bank of Korea and its new colleague the Financial Supervisory Commission have set about the task of restructuring the banking system with considerable gusto. As of November 1999, some 5 commercial banks, 19 merchant banks, 6 securities' companies and 5 insurance companies were closed down. A further 9 banks were obliged to merge, to form 4 successor banks. As a result, the number of banks was reduced to 23 from 33. In order to recapitalise the banking system, the Korean government has so spent some KRW64 trillion.

Yet while substantial progress has unquestionably been made, there remain major concerns, not least the increasing government presence in the Korean banking industry. While this was inevitable given the industry's need for government support in the wake of the crisis - or even before - it is not necessarily the best way of achieving the best long-term returns for the industry, as the example of Japan has demonstrated most painfully throughout the 1990s. As of November 1999, of the 17 commercial banks, the government owned two of the three largest - Chohung and Seoul - having privatised Hanvit, and was a majority shareholder in three others - Housing & Commercial, Kookmin and Korea Exchange Bank. For years, the Korean government, whatever manifestation that it has taken, has treated the banking industry as a tool of national monetary policy. It will take some time for that instinct to be expunged fully. This was demonstrated most clearly when the government obliged the banks to provide the funding for the KRW20 trillion financial market stabilisation fund. While Korea's markets managed to stabilise in the wake of that move, Korean banks still face major risks on their exposure to the bonds they own as a result of contributing to that fund, particularly when Korean official interest rates start heading higher as they inevitably will do.

In any case, one should be asking the question as to whether the setting up of a financial market stabilisation fund is appropriate at all. This is not to say that the answer to that question is definitely no. It is to say rather that the question must be asked. Why should the investment trust corporations be bailed out. In this case, it was because of their enormous exposure to Daewoo. And whose fault was that? The banks made their own mistakes in abundance. Why should they have to pay for those of the investment trusts as well? In addition, this is quite a different operation from the IMF bailout programme whose constituent policies were aimed at allowing the economy's own automatic stabilisers to work in a time of crisis. In this case, the stabilisation fund's purpose appeared to be to prop up bond prices. For any such operation, the justification appears decidedly weaker. The Korean government will of course claim that the operation was necessary in order to avoid a crisis and a run at the investment trusts given the specific case of the collapse of Daewoo. Perhaps so, and perhaps such extraordinary measures were necessary. This is not however the first market stabilisation fund which the authorities have created. Markets are meant to go down as well as up. For a market to fall is not necessarily a bad thing. Of course, it might be to those investors who get hurt in the fall, but that is the risk of investment. The Korean government's commitment to allowing prices to fall is yet to be sufficiently proven.

The banking system is still shaky enough without this unwanted exposure to the investment trusts. Seeking to oblige the government by applying a more rigorous decision-making process towards the granting of new loans (for some, it was no doubt the first time any such rigour has been used), the banks do not yet have the appropriate credit analysis skills or technology to perform this feat at a time when the banks are also being asked to lend more to SME companies whose balance sheets are frequently even more opaque than those of the *chaebol*. In the first 9 months of 1999, bank lending to SME companies was around KRW10 trillion, almost 15 times what it was for the whole of 1998. Clearly, this is great news for the SME sector which has for long suffered from the discrimination of banks preferring to lend to their friends in the *chaebol*, but it is only equally good news for the banks if SME companies are made to follow the same sort of improved corporate governance and accounting standard principles as the *chaebol* are currently being obliged to follow. Without this, non-performing loans are likely to start rising again at the banks, even without further *chaebol* collapses. By December, we should have seen confirmation of this when the banks make provision for doubtful loans as well as those which are already classified NPL. The combination of stricter provision requirements and rising bad loans is already reducing bank profits. The 17 commercial banks recorded losses of almost KRW2.5 trillion in the third quarter of 1999 as against profits of just over KRW3 trillion in the first half. Those losses could well increase when the debt restructuring schemes for Daewoo's 12 core companies are finalised. Just for Daewoo alone, the banks may have to set aside a further KRW10 trillion in loan loss provisions by the end of 2000.

While the efforts of the Financial Supervisory Commission in establishing prudential regulation in the banking system and boosting bank Capital Adequacy Ratios (CAR) above the BIS standard of 8% are only to be commended - and seen as brave if one is to believe the reports suggesting that that the FSC head Lee Hun-jai received threats - such increased loan loss provisions and reduced equity could well take the CARs of many banks back below the 8% level, thus making them vulnerable once more to further financial disturbance and potentially in need of further government support. The FSC initially aimed to have all banks develop adequate credit analysis techniques by the end-1999. This was, needless to say, an ambitious goal. For the industry as a whole, the task of changing the mindset, and not just in credit analysis, is likely to take longer. The good news is that the dramatic recovery in the Korean economy this year shows that it can be done if the will is there.

Looking at the economy as a whole, in 1998 and the first half of 1999, the Korean authorities put in the "hardware" of the Korean economic and financial recovery, installing a new regulatory framework for both the *chaebol* and the banks, having first stabilised the financial system. For the rest of 1999 and on into 2000, the goal must be to develop and install the "software" for the economy and the financial system, a new type of software based on market principles rather than the old, developmental, patrician style. This will be no easy task. Indeed, one could say that it is a task with which Japan, the second largest economy in the world, has been wrestling for much of the 1990s. If Korea is to succeed in its goal of matching or even passing Japan, of achieving true first world status, then it is a task in which Korea cannot afford to fail. The best way to make it succeed, it seems to me would be to get the market itself to help ensure that success by specifically changing appropriate regulations to encourage an incentive for its success. For instance, the government has encouraged minority shareholders by reducing the stake needed to bring a motion at a company's annual meeting to only 0.01% of total equity and has also now ensured that publicly-traded companies are obliged to appoint a quarter of their directors from outside. These are good first steps. Setting up a Korean junk bond market and scrapping the restrictions on mergers and acquisitions would really get the ball rolling. If anyone can make this work, whatever the obstacles and whatever the enormous change of mindset required, it is the Koreans. That's the good news. The bad news is that the threats to the recovery are not only economic. They are also political.

■ A week in Korean politics can be a very long time

While Kim Dae-jung's presidency does not come into electoral question until the year 2002, the country faces parliamentary general elections in April this year. The ruling coalition of the National Congress for New Politics (NCNP) under Kim and the United Liberal Democrats (ULD), which only managed to secure a National Assembly majority in September 1998, should do reasonably well given the economic recovery, certainly well enough to maintain if not to extend that majority, but there remain risks to this rosy scenario.

For one, the basis of the coalition between the NCNP and the ULD appears to be on increasingly shaky ground. The coalition was always in any case a marriage of convenience, one cemented in the December 1997 presidential election campaign given Kim's promise to make ULD leader Kim Jong-pil Prime Minister. The ideological differences between the NCNP and the ULD remain significant. The ULD, when it joined the coalition, had demanded a cabinet-type structure rather than a strong executive presidency. Kim Dae-jung appeared to agree to this, only to subsequently say that the cabinet structure had to be delayed given the economic emergency. While this explanation may well seem justified under the circumstances, without reviving the actual idea of a strong cabinet structure this is little consolation to the ULD. The NCNP has benefited of late from defections from the opposition Grand National Party, however were the ULD to threaten to defect itself from the coalition, this in turn would pose a major danger to the NCNP. In any case, the *chaebol* who argue that the government is hypocritical to demand reform of the corporate sector without reforming themselves have an excellent point. Korean politics needs reform badly. A relatively recent democracy, it needs substantial strengthening of the democratic political process. Political parties up until recently tended to centre around individuals rather than ideas. This represents a weakness rather than a strength, since the very essence of democracy is based upon the idea of accountability to a set of principles, rather than to any particular person or group.

In addition, if the President wants the heads of the *chaebol* to be accountable to their workers, then he should start with increasing the accountability of the office of the presidency. Rather than weakening his own position, this would represent a very clear and strong signal to the country as a whole. Not least, it would call the bluff of those *chaebol* chieftains who presently say that political reform is inadequate. They would no longer have that excuse not to reform themselves. In the meantime, there is still potential for some within the *chaebol* to seek revenge on Kim Dae-jung by attempting to finance a GNP win over Kim's NCNP-ULD coalition. Attempts will no doubt be made to lure the ULD away from its coalition with the NCNP.

Another key issue in Korean politics remains that of North Korea, which as ever has the potential to be critical for South Korea. President Kim Dae-jung's "sunshine" policy towards North Korea appears to have been better received, however North Korea remains extremely unpredictable, not to say dangerous as its test firing of a ballistic missile over Japan proved beyond any doubt. It remains to be seen whether or not Pyongyang wants to play a role in the April elections with its southern neighbour. It is doubtful whether any such influence would be positive.

Some Recommendations

Despite the progress made to date, Korea has to go further in reforming its political, economic and financial structures if its long-cherished goal of first-world status is to be achieved on a sustainable basis. South Korea surly has an appointment with destiny and that appointment will be with North Korea, in one form or another. Not having believed that I would ever see the unification of Germany in my lifetime, I would now say that the eventual re-unification of Korea is an inevitability. Perhaps I will be as wrong on Korea as I was on Germany. Much will clearly depend on that unpredictable North. However, while South Korea cannot prepare North Korea for that eventual unification, it can prepare itself. Just as was the case with West Germany, unification with North Korea, assuming that is done through economics and democracy rather than through war, would represent a massive shock to the South Korean economy. The best way of coping with that is to build a flexible economy, which has numerous layers and balances, providing a wide variety of job- and wealth-creation channels. An economy which depends solely on external demand, as some would have it, is clearly not fit for the task. Unification may indeed be some way off. Years or even decades. It should however be a consideration from the point of view of the development of the Korean economy and financial markets, an incentive for the present Korean government to accelerate and still further the reform and restructuring process in order to make preparations. Ahead of such a momentous event, such preparations need to be made merely to carry on the progress that has been made towards the eventual goal of first world economic status. Tentatively and with no small degree of humility, I make the following suggestions as to how this process might be aided.

■ Full deregulation of Korea's capital markets

The Korean authorities have made great strides in liberalising and deregulating the foreign exchange market, most notably through the regulatory revisions put into place on April 1, 1999, however there remain restrictions on the amount of Korean *won* foreign investors can borrow - which is exactly the reason that there remains a slight differential between the onshore and offshore forward markets. In addition, Korean companies are obliged to deal with banks located in Korea, rather than the bank which produces the best price, wherever it might be located. Finally, Korean companies have for long been dissuaded by the relevant bureaucratic organs from using foreign exchange options. Used appropriately, these can mitigate against and manage risk rather than increase it. One could well argue that the paucity of appropriate and available hedging instruments ahead of the Asian crisis was a factor in accelerating that crisis. The government has said that it plans the full deregulation of the foreign exchange market in 2001 and this is to be commended, the delay presumably allowing more time for the Korean economy and financial system to recover from its collapse in late 1997. Those who argue it should remain restricted given the possibility of speculation against the Korean *won* by foreigners presumably exclude the possibility that these same foreigners might actually buy Korean *won* due to prudent macro- and micro-economic policies. The lesson of these types of financial crises, both in the emerged and the emerging markets, is that they usually start with a lack of checks and balances. Put crudely, someone has to be there to blow the whistle, someone has to be a watchdog. A further lesson is that whatever the best efforts of individuals, the market is usually a more effective and a better arbiter in the long run. Investors, of whatever sort, sometimes seem illogical and on occasion do appear to behave in an illogical fashion, but such periods are in the grand scheme of things being relatively infrequent. The authorities are there to mitigate against the worst excesses of such irrational behaviour, but usually are not needed. The aim is for the market to be able to right itself.

Consequently, with Korea now having the appropriate regulatory bodies to police it when necessary, the Korean *won* foreign exchange market should be free and open. A similar case could be made for the Korean *won* domestic bond markets. Here too, the government has made much progress, recently allowing foreign investors entry. For long, however, the Korean capital markets, such as they were, have been dominated by the *chaebol* and a few select banks. They need to be set free. In order to achieve that, they need to have a more diversified investor base, both in terms of domestic and foreign investors, and a more diversified set of issuers. The SME sector needs to be encouraged to tap the Korean capital markets more and banks, again both foreign and domestic, need to be encouraged to target this sector for issuance. This would help make capital market pricing more egalitarian, less focused on special relationships which as we have seen eventually distort the entire market structure. In this regard, Korean SME companies can help themselves greatly by providing greater balance sheet transparency. Once this is achieved, and if they are allowed to, foreign banks can help develop a capital market for sub-investment grade companies, which would undoubtedly allow them a cheaper source of funding than bank lending.

■ Competitive channels of finance

In short, companies and banks need to have channels of funding which compete with each other. Until recently, this was inconceivable give the nature of Korean capitalism, which was government-directed, and bank-executed for the benefit ultimately of the *chaebol* and for a time the Korean economy as a whole. Korea needs an end to guided capitalism and instead needs to accelerate its embrace of market capitalism for it is this that will bring it its goal of sustained first-world status. Looking ahead, Korea Inc needs to be built not only along the lines of the *chaebol.* These provide the industrial bedrock of the Korean economy, but they will not have sufficient incentive to be innovative unless they face mounting competition from within as well as from without. The reform efforts by Korea's bureaucrats of the *chaebol* have so far met with limited success, in large part because the *chaebol* have not been impelled to reform. True, some have made considerable efforts at reform, others somewhat more token efforts while the example of the collapse of Daewoo is surely a timely reminder of the resistance which remains the whole idea of reform. Yet, these *chaebol* have never had to reform in the sense that they have never been faced with extinction if they did not. That is until the government allowed Daewoo to collapse. This was an excellent lesson for the Korean industry. My hope is that it will be continued. If competition regulation is thrown open at home, and import tariffs scrapped for good measure, this would be a major step forward. Then there would be a greater incentive for the *chaebol* to reform. To be sure, some of this reform would be painful. To date, the major *chaebol* have escaped by one means or another the major de-manning process which must surely come if such companies are to become efficient. That delay may well only increase the need for workforce reduction in the end. In good times, fundamental weaknesses are masked. The lesson of 1997 is that they are not masked forever.

It is in small business, however, where Korea Inc will find its economic future, from which the well-spring of innovation will come, just as it has been for the U.S. and where it is increasingly the case for the UK and Japan. Korean small businesses have suffered during the crisis much more than their larger cousins, in large part because they did not have access to friendly domestic bank managers. In 1998, according to the Korean Small Business Association, some 23,000 businesses went bankrupt. While creating a small business is of necessity a risky undertaking, the environment and the ability for doing so needs to be encouraged, using tax incentives and small business-lending schemes. There has never been a level playing field in Korea where small companies had equal access to finance, at least in theory, relative to the *chaebol*. If Korea's capital markets are opened up, are set free, that will change, and for the better, both for the small businesses and for the *chaebol* themselves. Korea will in any case need a diversified economy going forward, one which not only focuses on the traditional heavy industries or mimics the technological creations of others, but which develops and creates its own high technology bases through the process of enhanced domestic competition.

Of course, this is all very well in theory. In practice, it is likely to take years for all this to be achieved. One example shows the change that will be required in the mindset concerns of the automotive industry where until recently all Koreans who dared buy a foreign car faced the threat of a tax audit, a clear disincentive to even the most tax observant. While North Korea is known among many things for its ideology of "juche" or self-reliance, it would appear that South Korea's economic boom for the last two decades up until the crisis in

1997 has also been characterised by this. Yet this hermit-like approach, this excessive dependency on self reliance, while perhaps admirable, is surely outdated. If Korea is to become a true global economic power, as is surely its aim, not only has its economy to embrace the global marketplace, but so do its government and its people. Most assuredly, they will be made welcome, for the contribution they can make is substantial - and the benefits they could reap as a consequence equally substantial.

KOREA GOING FORWARD

When one hears of the public listing of internet companies in Korea, whatever one's concerns might be of the state of internet stocks as a whole, one is encouraged and hopeful for Korea's economic future. If there is such a thing as a new economy or even a new economic age - and as Alan Greenspan might put it that remains to be proven - it is surely founded on the idea of a diversified economy. The West developed the concept of the information economy in large part because they were forced to, precisely because they lost much of their competitive advantage in heavy manufacturing to the likes of Korea. The U.S. and to a certain extent Europe, though the latter remains to all intents and purposes a protected market, had to diversify, has had to find new economic engines faced with this competitive threat. Korea, for now, is one of the beneficiaries of this process, however as the crisis proved, such price advantage can be a fleeting thing. It is certainly not something which can be relied on for any length of time. It is for precisely this reason that Korea Inc needs to look to new technologies, not only to try to compete with the West but in order to offset the future price competitive threat against its existing industries from other emerging markets. For instance, Korean shipyards remain extremely competitive at present, indeed some of the most competitive in the world. If China devalued the *yuan* (not that I believe they will, but just let's suppose), they would face a very different, and much more hostile world. To put it bluntly, they might be priced out of the market by their Chinese competitors. Diversification of the economy is also needed to cope with the further job destruction that is needed within the *chaebol*. To date, the major *chaebol* have largely escaped the substantial job reductions that will be necessary for going forward in order to make them sufficiently competitive. This cannot go on indefinitely. Eventually, there will come a day of reckoning. Korea needs to develop and create service industries in order to cope from the fallout of this process. In addition, it needs to create the educational infrastructure where such workers can be retrained.

While the prediction of political events is a perilous occupation, and one which I certainly do not intend to get into, I take the view that the April 2000 general elections and the 2002 presidential elections will result in the continuation of the reform process for the simple reason that all sides have had it explained to them that there is little realistic alternative. Going back to the old ways of guided capitalism is simply not an option anymore. Foreign investors, far from taking over Korea as some Koreans might have feared, instead encourage a much more dynamic type of Korean capitalism to be created, one far less vulnerable to financial and economic collapse. Let us not forget that it was the old, guided-style of Korean capitalism which caused the collapse in 1997, dragged down under the inevitable weight of its own contradictions, as one economist might put it. What will emerge from this crisis will surely be a Korea which inspires others, not least by its economic and financial flexibility, as well as its determination to succeed whatever the odds, whatever the cost. Late last year, I went on a customer trip to Seoul, among other places. What was immediately striking was its apparent vibrancy. The shops were full, the roads clogged with traffic (inadequate infrastructure!), the hotel I stayed in jammed with foreign business and banking groups. This is all very well as long as the lessons have been learned.

Personally, I think they have, precisely because those lessons were so painful. The progress made to date in restructuring and reforming the *chaebol* and the banks may seem inadequate to some, superficial to others. Clearly, I would agree that there remains a massive amount of work to be done in this regard. The job is most likely only half done at best. Where Korea has succeeded however, whatever the limitations on its gains elsewhere, has been in reducing debt and thus allowing for new credit growth. Raised credit ratings have helped, but credit ratings have been raised elsewhere in the region and not necessarily resulted in higher credit growth - or indeed any credit growth! Debt reduction is key. The result in Korea has been a reduction of the corporate credit crunch and new loans being made. While other Asian countries have recovered, this is the real reason Korea is leading Asia out of the recession and into recovery. If Korea continues to reduce debt, hopefully at an accelerated rate, it should continue to lead that recovery.

Going into the initial stages of the Asian crisis, it was expected, or rather hoped for, that Japan would lead Asia back to recovery. Indeed, that Japan's recovery at home could be a lesson for Asia, one to emulate and follow just as Asia had followed Japan's economic boom in the 1970s and 80s. Rather the opposite appears to have happened. While the Japanese authorities have been extraordinarily generous in providing financial help to Asia in its time of need through the Miyazawa Initiative and other loan programmes, making loans totalling USD72 billion as of this writing, Japan's progress in sorting out its own financial and economic mess remains mixed. Indeed, rather than take a lesson from Japan, Asia, particularly in the form of Korea has given Japan a lesson, notably in how fast one should respond to domestic debt problems in order to keep them manageable. Japanese financial and manufacturing capital were however instrumental in the developing of the Asian Miracle in the first place. For the Asian regional recovery to be sustainable, Asia needs Japan's own recovery to be sustainable. It is to the subject of Japan, the lessons it has learned and those that it has yet to learn - while the likes of Korea pass it by - the state of the economy and of how it remains chained and restricted relative to its potential though change is happening, that we turn to next. The potential for Japan, even compared to its economic achievements up until, its own crisis at the start of the 1990s, remains immense. Indeed, if you can't get excited by the potential that awaits in Japan, you probably don't have a pulse!

CHAPTER 5

THE LESSON – JAPAN AND ASIA

The collapse of the Asian Miracle in 1997 and the subsequent revival in 1999 of the Asian economies clearly does not tell the whole story. We are only one year into the recovery, and as we have noted there remains much work to be done. This recovery remains fragile, whatever its apparent size and strength according to the data. Yet, even now, in the first quarter of 2000, there are some lessons which we can extract from the Asian recovery, both for Asia itself, and for others, most notably Japan.

LESSONS OF THE ASIAN CRISIS

■ For Asia

For Asia alone, there are a number of lessons, not least that sound, long-term economic policies actually matter. This is not to say that Asia did not get many of such policies right for two decades, thus producing the Asian "Miracle" in the first place. It is to say rather, that to a certain extent it was a victim of its own success. Rising growth rates in individual Asian countries and rising intra-Asian trade resulted in accelerated regional growth, attracting ever greater amounts of foreign capital. That foreign capital both masked and caused, albeit inadvertently in most cases, fundamental weaknesses within Asia at the microeconomic level. In addition, it simply swamped Asia's fledgling capital markets, which were unable to cope. As a result, asset prices were chased higher, not for sound fundamental reasons, but because it was simply a case of too much money chasing too few assets. Classic inflation theory was at work, albeit in asset prices rather than consumer goods. Excess capital was allocated in an increasingly inefficient way and targeted towards increasingly speculative ventures. The result was widening current account deficits and mounting debt burdens. The rest, we of course know. Despite the recovery we are now seeing, the severity of the collapse in 1997 has caused serious pause for thought among Asian economic planners and strategists. The results of such consideration usually fall into one of two camps:

1. Foreign investors are to blame
2. The economic model upon which the Asian Miracle was founded is itself flawed

In the first camp, we have those who simply like to blame foreigners, either because it is politically expedient to do so or because it is ideologically or racially pleasing. One should never underestimate the will of people to blame others, to find scapegoats. Rather more seriously, we also find in this camp those who argue that foreign investors were indeed partly or largely to blame, particularly for the severity of the Asian crisis and the extent of the damage done. Having reaped the benefits of the Asian Miracle through rising stock prices and rising returns from FDI, knowing fully well the degree of corruption and lack of transparency in many of these countries, these same investors turned tail and ran when the going got rough, so runs this argument. Capital flight not only was a symptom of the crisis, but actually caused or at the very least greatly exacerbated the crisis. While having some appeal, I would say that though this argument is critically flawed, it most certainly has to be addressed.

Why is this argument flawed? First, let us look at its merits. There is little doubt that foreign investors, as well as foreign banks, going out to Asia in the late 1980s and 1990s had a reasonable idea that despite the merits of the Asian Miracle, there were also some flaws, notably a lack of corporate transparency and high levels of corruption in some countries, in particular Indonesia and Thailand. To many, no doubt, this was something you lived with. Indeed, from a superior, Western perspective, what more could you expect in the third world? Re-titling the third world or lesser developed world as the emerging markets may have made the description more politically acceptable or correct, but it has done nothing to reduce the perception of superiority and inferiority for some. Readers should be very clear that this is not my view, but they should be well aware that it remains the view of some in the West. There is little doubt that for many Westerners, the rise of Asia was an excuse to travel and engage in activities which they would not normally partake of back home. Wanchai in Hong Kong and the Pat Pong in Bangkok surely bear ample witness to this. Why should investors be any different? The view that the rules of home do not necessarily apply abroad is simply human nature. While one might think that investors should behave differently to such human traits, they don't necessarily do so.

When I arrived in Hong Kong at the start of 1996, it is no exaggeration to say that its stock market resembled a casino. I had no interest in partaking of this gambling den at the time (or since). I was much more interested in writing about and analysing the region, and travelling throughout it. Foreign fund managers who came to Hong Kong, or to other countries in Asia did not necessarily have the luxury of this choice. Rather, they had asset quotas and allocations to fill. Faced in the Asian region as a whole with a relative lack of corporate or banking transparency, artificially low interest rates, high credit growth and higher levels of corruption, they were ultimately given the choice or trying to maintain the investment selection standards of back home (and thus limiting their purchases severely), avoiding the area entirely, or plunging in and hoping for the best. The attractions of this last choice were that markets in Asia were already rising. For some, it would seem, temptation overtook the instinct for sound judgement. Needless, to say, this analogy is somewhat simplistic. Many Western investors would subsequently argue that they were lied to as to the merits of their investments. Perhaps so, but it is actually unimportant with regard to this argument. What was clear was that the Asian asset markets for the most part - here I would exclude Singapore - were relatively opaque by Western standards and thus foreign investors knew that, and more to the point knew that that represented some degree or risk. What degree was un-quantifiable, granted, but the risk was there. Consequently, it was a risk they took on, willingly or not, when they entered such markets.

Yet, according to this argument, the same Western investors who took such risks, realising the fact, should have stayed the course when the going got tough, when Asia markets started heading lower. Here lies the crux of the matter. My immediate response to this is: why should they? These investors are not there of necessity to benefit the country they are investing in. Such investment may well benefit that country, but that is not the main reason for the investment in the first place, which is rather more simply to make money. In any case, to argue that foreign investors should not have fled is to ignore another fact: that many of the domestic investors were actually among the first to flee. Just taking the Thai *baht* foreign exchange market as an example, foreign corporations were most certainly not the first to run when the *baht* started coming under pressure. For the most part, they were involved in foreign direct investment projects and thus simply could not flee so easily or so quickly. Foreign investors have a mixed record, with some having started to reduce their investments in Thailand by the start of 1997, while other celebrated cases showed that they were - to their cost - continuing to invest into the Thai stock market right up until the *baht* devalued, and in some cases right after that. While there is unfortunately little data available with regards to the direction of transactions in the Thai foreign exchange market, anecdotal evidence - which will have to be relied on for the lack of other methods - suggested that Thai corporations were among the first to sell their own currency in those first few months of 1997. The sceptical among you may then ask why did so many Thai companies subsequently either go bankrupt or lose massive amounts of money in foreign exchange losses. There are two reasons for this. Firstly, I said that some Thai corporations were among the first sellers of the *baht*. The Thai corporate sector is like those elsewhere in so much as it is not a homogenous, individual corporation, but instead is made up of many, quite different parts, reacting to different economic signals and behaving quite differently. Secondly, by the time the *baht* had devalued such was the size of the Thai foreign-currency corporate debt that at a national level Thai foreign currency debt amounted to almost USD100 billion in 1997, or over 60% of the GDP. The sheer scale of the amount of un-hedged debt and the relatively small size of the Thai *baht* foreign exchange market meant that most were unable to hedge a substantial part of their foreign currency debt before the *baht* devalued, before it was effectively too late to do so. To say that foreign investors should have stayed under such circumstances, should not have fled, is simply to ask the unreasonable. A better comment might have been that many should never have been there in the first place, but that is quite a different matter.

The second idea resulting from post-Asian crisis consideration, namely that the Asian Miracle model of economic development is itself flawed also deserves cross-examination. In the wake of the Asian crisis, it is equally understandable that such an idea might come about. For many in Asia, the Asian crisis meant losing their business, their life's savings. Under such circumstances, clearly something had "gone wrong". If one is not to blame the "farang" or "qweilo", then one might well consider that the economic model which the government or the region had been operating had become or was always, flawed. It was a key point of **"Asia Falling"** and also one made earlier in this book that the model was indeed flawed in so much as Asia produced the right macroeconomic policies to attract massive amounts of foreign capital, but did so well ahead of creating any framework in order to cope with that capital influx. A key lesson of the Asian crisis is that the region possessed inadequate "institutional infrastructure". That is, it did not have deep and liquid asset markets, and strong and independent regulators to police those asset markets (including the domestic banks that operated within them) and finally a strong domestic institutional investor base. Those countries which did not suffer major structural damage from the Asian crisis, such as Singapore, did indeed have such institutional infrastructure.

The model has further flaws, yet all centre around a single idea: it is out-dated in its present form. Asia has used its economic model of higher investment and savings to produce high growth. The cost of that has been falling productivity and quantity rather than quality. In addition, lack of corporate transparency and regulation has clearly had a price and that price has been steep. As we saw in the last chapter on Korea, there are happily some powerful people in Asia who are determined to redress this imbalance, most importantly for Asia's future development and for the Asian peoples themselves. The model of development which produced the Asian Miracle also produced what I have termed external over-reliance. It is not enough for Korean companies to be dependent on external demand, nor is it sufficient for Asian exports as a whole to hope that the U.S. demand will remain strong. Inevitably, the U.S. import demand will falter. By that time, Asia had better have found answers to the question of how it diversifies its exports. While the recoveries of Japan and the European Union should help offset the effects of the anticipated U.S. slowdown which is to come this year, in 2000, Asia should start at home, should look to itself to find the alternative to the U.S. demand, by tearing down the intra-Asian trade barriers and by producing an Asian Free Trade Area, as the leaders of the ASEAN have indeed promised.

A further fact which Asia should have discovered as a result of the Asian crisis, which is also included in the category of external over-reliance, is that it remains overly dependent on foreign technology. Before the crisis, for the most part, much of ASEAN was simply an assembly plant for foreign multinational corporations; granted, an exaggeration, but not much of one. While Western companies might like to think that Asia is dependent on Western technology, it is to Japan that Asia remains truly dependent. Such is the manufacturing base that Japan has built in Asia over the last two decades that it now forms much of the manufacturing base of individual Asian countries. For instance, in auto manufacturing alone, Japanese manufacturing affiliates make 95% of the total production in Thailand, Indonesia and the Philippines. Such plans are thus dependent on Japanese high technology for advancement, and such technology is guarded jealously at home in Japan, and revealed sparingly. A lesson for Asia is that when companies create "global natural monopolies" in specific product lines, such lines being increasingly based on high technology as global competition increases, the effects of financial and economic crises are greatly mitigated. Such global natural monopolies in product lines are themselves based on technological rather than price advantage and are thus less vulnerable to unfavourable price swings and reduction in demand. Korea and Taiwan are ahead of the game in Asia in terms of developing their own high technology bases, but they too are overly dependent on Japan, particularly in terms of manufactured computer and high technology parts.

A final lesson might be that the Japanese model upon which parts of Asia have based their manufacturing expansion is also out-dated in its present form. The Japanese model of economic expansion seeks to do away with what it deems excessive competition ("*kato kyoso*") and instead relies on triangular co-operation between government, business and labour. Labour, supply and distribution networks are created in order to cement this harmonious co-operation. When there is a downturn in demand for a company's products, staff are shunted off to cheaper factories or even countries. The model is flawed in that it relies on acquiescent shareholders to accept inadequate returns. It also relies on acquiescent consumers to pay for these companies having excessive overheads. Given the extent of economic under-performance in Japan during the 1990s, it is questionable how long this model will last in its present form. Unlike some, I do not say that it will be completely ditched for the Western model. Rather, in order to survive, those who propagate the current model in Japan will do as they have always done - learn what they can and what they have to from others and use that to improve their own. The same is likely to be the case for Asia. There is a third way between the Western form of capitalism and that of Japan which is founded on networks and consensus capitalism, and that is simply a merger of the two. The two are not necessarily in direct opposition. Networks can survive and prosper and be accountable as well.

That said, the lesson from Korea is that a combination of debt reduction and increased competition is the quickest and most effective way of dealing with Asia's current problems. Government intervention has done much to stabilise the financial and economic crisis in Korea and subsequently to bring about the recovery. The major reason as to why the Korean economy is booming however, while the recoveries elsewhere appear less strong is that Korea has cut debt; perhaps not enough, but it is has started the process. With Korea's bureaucrats having made a good start, and having created the appropriate regulators and supervisors, it should now throw open its domestic capital markets to finish the job.

■ For Japan

This is not only a lesson for Asia, but more specifically for Japan. For the last decade, Japan, the second most important economy in the world has been labouring under a mountainous - and increasing - debt burden, the result of the bursting of its asset bubble in the 1980s. Rather than tackle that debt burden proactively, and thus produce unwanted results such as bank and company closures, unemployment and popular anger, Japan's famed bureaucrats have dithered, occasionally allowing themselves to be persuaded to do something though never enough and never when it was required. Tomes have been written about the Ministry of Finance and also the Ministry of International Trade and Industry which has for long been demonised in some Western circles and readers can be assured (not to say relieved) that this work will not attempt to repeat those works or cover the same ground in any way. Rather, it is to say that it is hardly surprising that we saw such relative inaction from the ministries. They were hardly likely to tear down a structure that they themselves had built and which they continue to oversee. Yet, while the stubbornness of these ministries in question remains not in doubt, the acquiescence of the Japanese public is increasingly so - and about time too! For too long, the Japanese consumer has been robbed blind by inflated prices. For too long, the Japanese investor has been unable to discover the true worth of his or her investment due to the inadequacy of Japanese supervisory and regulatory standards in the stock market. It would seem that for long Japanese individuals have been mollified in this regard, told that they possess the highest standards of living in the world. In real life terms, this was an outright lie. The ongoing boom in the U.S. has finally confirmed that in statistical terms.

One wonders how long the Japanese public and the Japanese investors are going to put up with this? Citizens of Japan awake! The people of Japan have suffered for long because of the inadequacy of the polity and of the bureaucracy. Indeed, they have suffered for too long. It is high time that changed. The key lesson from the Asian crisis and from the recovery in the likes of Korea is that that can change. Yet in order to see how, in order to determine what lessons Japan can take specifically from the Asian crisis in order to restore itself to full economic health and to sustained economic recovery, one has to examine the current situation in Japan.

Japan: A situation report

The Japanese economy roared in the first quarter of 1999, showing a seasonally adjusted annualised rate (SAAR) a growth of some 8.1%. On a year-on-year basis, this represented a decidedly more meagre growth rate of only 0.1%, however relative to the -2.9% year-on-year contraction for the whole of 1998, it still represented a major improvement. This view that the economy had bottomed appeared to be confirmed by further examination of the 1999 first quarter data. Domestic demand, which had been crushed in the wake of the 1997 consumption tax hiked to 5% from 3%, the engine's spark plug which had been silent for that mournful year of 1998 in Japanese economic history fire, finally ignited. On a SAAR basis, domestic demand rose some 9.7% in the first quarter of 1999. Private consumption, business investment and housing investment rose 5.1%, 12.9% and 4.9% respectively. However, the real story was public investment, which exploded, rising some 47.9% on a SAAR basis due to massive fiscal stimulus carried out by the Japanese government. The economy's second quarter performance was somewhat more modest. Growth was a revised 0.9% (SAAR), however at least it was in positive territory. Domestic demand was 0.8%, private consumption still quite impressive at 3.4% and housing investment at a remarkable 82.0%. However, again the real story was in public investment, which saw a 15.1% contraction in the second quarter as the effects of fiscal stimulus were withdrawn.

This might be a cause for concern were it not for the fact that we as a bank firmly believe in this recovery which is now being seen in Japan. Granted, there have been many false recoveries before in Japan in the 1990s in the wake of the bursting of that country's financial bubble in 1990-1991. Compared to an average annual growth rate of 4.0% during 1981-1990, Japan has grown by an average of a mere 1.2% if one includes forecasts for both 1999 and 2000 and this is including the anticipated recovery. During the 1990s, Japan saw an annual growth rate of 1.0% or less from 1992-1994 and after a 5.0% growth in 1996 the rate of economic expansion fell to 1.4% as a result of the consumption tax and then to a 2.9% contraction in 1998, surely the low point of Japan's economic performance that decade. However, we believe this recovery because there are finally signs that consumption is coming back and that it is likely to stay. It has taken a long time - too long - to get to this stage and it has taken extraordinary measures in the form of the Bank of Japan's zero interest rate policy and the government's massive fiscal stimulus packages which are likely to result in a budget deficit to the GDP of around 7% but the engine of consumption finally seems to have restarted. Why is it different this time? To me, the answer is that Japan in late 1997 itself nearly faced a financial disaster. The Asian crisis caused dramatic instability within the Japanese financial system given its significant loan exposure to Asia, reduced stock portfolio profits on bank balance sheets as the Nikkei 225 fell, resulting in valuation losses to Japanese exporters in Asia and a worsened outlook for Japanese trade. In short, it was the best thing that ever happened to Japan.

Japan needed a crisis

Many commentators examining Japan's problems have said that what Japan needed was a really good crisis to give the necessary impetus for it to revive itself from its malaise. I have considerable sympathy with this view. On the occasions that I went to Japan in the 1990s, I never once felt that a crisis was at hand. Yet from 1955-1975, Japan had seen growth exceeding 10% a year and as we saw above its growth rate for 1981-1990 was still strong at 4.0%. Relative to Japan's historical economic performance since the war, the country was indeed in crisis, it just needed someone to tell it that! Readers will be crushed to learn that I did not volunteer for this job. Rather I watched and waited, like everyone else. Soon enough, the crisis emerged itself. It was exactly what Japan needed, though at the time it caused much concern and distress. The Asian crisis was both a lesson and a catastrophe for the Japanese banking industry as well as its manufacturing base. In the second half of 1997, corporate Japan woke up to the sickening prospect of its cherished profit rebound, driven largely by Asian-based manufacturing plants, being threatened. Throughout the late 1980s and 1990s, corporate Japan had built a substantial manufacturing presence in Asia, in part to take advantage of a greatly reduced cost base relative to Japan, an important consideration in particular when the *yen* was rising. In truth, it was also a carefully orchestrated strategy to avoid trade friction with the U.S., diverting a not insignificant part of the Japanese trade surplus with the U.S. away from Japan and to Asia. The collapse in Asian demand and skyrocketing costs due to imported inflation resulting from the Asia currency devaluations somewhat derailed that plan. Meanwhile, Japanese banks, which had spent the previous 7 years trying to write off gradually their massive bad loans, the result of credit profligacy during the go-go 80s, were suddenly faced with a new and significant threat to the health of their loan books. For 7 years, Japanese authorities, principally but not solely the Ministry of Finance, had delayed, fudged and dissembled, hoping that somehow they and the financial system could emerge without having to admit that a crisis situation existed. Huge public works' programmes were tried, followed by "moral-suasion" and even an active market intervention through the use of the postal savings' fund to boost the stock market and thus alleviate losing bank and life insurer stock portfolio positions.

None of that had worked. It had been a case of merely tinkering with the problem of bad debts, putting a band-aid on a weeping sore rather than excising it with a scalpel. That was fine for a while. Indeed, up until June, 1997 it was thought in some circles, both foreign and domestic, that the Japanese financial system had turned the corner and banks and financial institutions were on the mend, the result of further bad debt write-offs and reductions. Overtly, the sore had healed. Internally, however, the sepsis had spread, infecting the financial system, becoming a gangrene within the economy as a whole. Asia's currency, banking and economic crises brought that reality sharply into focus. As investors - and governments and central bankers, somewhat belatedly - concentrated increasingly on such weighty issues as asset quality and foreign exchange risk within loan exposure, the failing health of Japan's financial system was brought to light. The Ministry of Finance could no longer hide the problems. Indeed, its role as the defender of the banking system was threatened. With the collapse of Yamaichi Securities, Sanyo Securities and Hokkaido-Takushoku Bank towards the end of 1997, the years of self deception were finally at an end. Up until then, banks and companies had pretended to restructure and the Ministry of Finance had done what they could to hide the worst of the bad debts and to oblige continued political support for their policies, in terms of the banks, the budget and the taxation system. The sight of Shohei Nozawa, President of Yamaichi Securities, weeping before the world's cameras as his company was forced to close was deeply shocking to the Japanese public, not least because it had been allowed to happen, because the Ministry of Finance and the Japanese government had actually allowed Yamaichi to fail rather than to support it further. For the banking industry itself, even more shocking was the failure of Hokkaido-Takushoku, one of the 20 major banks in Japan which were thought to be fully supported by the Ministry of Finance. The failure of Hokkaido-Takushoku did not happen because the Ministry of Finance simply stood aside and let it happen. It occurred in spite of vigorous attempts by the Ministry of Finance to stop it. The failure of Hokkaido-Takushoku (or "Takugin" as it was known) was a major defeat for Japan and as a result a major victory for Japan. The following week, on November 24th, Yamaichi collapsed. Nozawa-san blamed himself for the company's failure. Whatever the case, the authorities, the Ministry of Finance and the Bank of Japan were to blame. For years, they had swept under the carpet the fact that Yamaichi had hidden losses and debt problems. For years, they did nothing to solve that situation. The banking and security company failures in late 1997 were the result of that foolish policy.

In late November and early December of 1997, the Bank of Japan was forced to intervene heavily in the money market to offset the very real threat of a credit crunch, the result of market unwillingness to lend to any financial institution with even a hint of problems, adding massive amounts of reserves to the system, or failing to drain reserves in order to stabilise the unsecured call loan rate around its then target level at 0.50%. As a result of the failure of Takugin and Yamaichi Securities, the market as a whole started charging a "Japan premium" to lend dollars to Japanese banks over and above the standard market rate. For some, this was merely an inconvenience, for others painful, for still others life threatening. In the end, the authorities bridged the gap but only on the condition that the banks disclosed their bad loans and wrote off significant portions of those bad loans for the year to March 1998. Wary of a public backlash against new public funds to support the banking system but all too well aware of the financial threat which the banking system now posed in its present form, the government injected some Y7.4 trillion of public funds in order to stabilise the system.

Big Bang

The authorities managed to stabilise the Japanese financial crisis of late 1997, however the subsequent downgrading of Japan by a credit rating agency, while producing howls of outrage in political and bureaucratic quarters, demonstrated the persistent seriousness of the situation. It was clear that gradual reform was not enough. What was needed was radical reform, what was needed was shock therapy - Japan Inc wired up to electrodes. The Hashimoto government, as ill-fated as it was did have one good idea and that idea was financial market liberalisation, or "Big Bang", the first stage of which took place on April 1, 1998, with the revision of the Foreign Exchange Law, allowing Japanese retail investment with foreign bank branches in Japan and with foreign banks abroad. Ministry of Finance officials had expected a gradual increase in Japanese retail exposure to foreign banks and security houses. What actually happened was a flood. In times past, this might have caused the authorities, both the politicians and the bureaucrats, to try and back-pedal on the reform process or even try to reverse it. With the government's pledge to deregulate and liberalise the Japanese financial system by April 2001, they no longer have that luxury. In addition, the financial crisis of late 1997 has shown that there is no alternative. Japan cannot simply go on propping up the financial system. Even Japan, with its financial resources, simply cannot afford to do so for much longer. Radical reform, and/or shock therapy, is the only *option* left. There is an old saying: you only change when not changing becomes more painful or difficult than changing. This adage is certainly the case for Japan. It is a shame that it came to that, but in a very real sense thank God it did. The alternative was the continuation of a slow descent into bankruptcy and ruin for the *entire nation.*

A number of forces are obliging Japan's banking sector to become more competitive. For a start, many of the banking sector's customers have left. The deregulation of Japan's domestic bond markets, as inadequate as that deregulation remains, has led to many of Japan's leading companies deriving all their surplus funds (that is, funds surplus to cash flow) from the capital markets. Japan has always been a dual economy in the sense of a world class first economy of exporters and a second class economy of domestic businesses that were propped up by domestic lending and by the keiretsu-system of business groups. What we are seeing in Japan is the increasing obviousness of this dual economic system. A light has been shone into the dark and some very unsettling things have been found in bank and corporate balance sheets. Believe it or not, this is actually good news. For one thing, if the light remained off, you would never know what was there. For another, when the light uncovers these things, you are faced with a choice. You can choose either to deal with the problem or not to deal with the problem, but what you can no longer do is to pretend that it does not exist.

Faced with the apparent dropping of Ministry of Finance support for the banking system, banks are now obliged to deal with these problems. In doing so, more often than not, they are forcing their customers, in many cases this second economy, to restructure. In addition, foreign competition is being introduced into the Japanese financial system with several banks making purchases in Japan. The collapsed and nationalised Long-Term Credit Bank of Japan was sold off to a U.S. fund manager Ripplewood Holdings which could restructure and re-list it within five years. The biggest incentive for the banks to restructure however is the April 2001 deadline itself. Up until then, the government guarantee for all banking system deposits will remain in place. After that date, a system called "pay off" will replace it, covering only the first Y10 million on each deposit. This will introduce real competition to the Japanese banking industry, which is why the banking industry is squealing so loud to have the deadline delayed. So far, admirably, the government has stuck to its guns.

Changes in accounting standards also represent radical reform for Japanese banks and businesses. Just as in Asia ex-Japan where consolidated accounting was relatively unknown prior to the crisis, so there is now in Japan a major push for a complete revision of the accounting rules, according to internationally-accepted standards. The lack of consolidated accounts in Japan allowed companies to hide losses in affiliates or even to distribute the parent company staff to these affiliates in tough times. However, starting with the current fiscal year, the results of which we shall see from April onwards, Japanese businesses will have to consolidate their financial accounts. The results will be interesting to say the least. For the first time for many, they will represent a true and fair valuation of the company concerned. Companies will also have to market-to-market the value of securities on their books, rather than account for them according to book value.

Open for business

Much of what we are seeing in Japan today is the result of the opening up of Japan's markets both from within and without. Granted, many could and do argue that the opening process remains too slow and is by no means incomplete, indeed it has just started. That said, there is now no question that the process has started and not just in the banking industry. In 1997, Japanese companies had foreign direct investments amounting to 6.5% of Japan's GDP.

Conversely, foreign companies had FDI in Japan amounting to only 0.6% of the GDP. Since the crisis, however, there have been a number of notable, high profile investments made in Japan by foreign companies such as GE Capital, Bosch and Cable & Wireless. In March of 1999, the French car company Renault announced that it was to buy a 37% stake in Japan's Nissan. Previously, such an acquisition of a Japanese company, albeit of a minority stake, would have been unthinkable. Indeed, it would simply not have been allowed. The structure itself within Japan would not have allowed the acquisition to take place. Consequently, that acquisition is surely symptomatic, both of the seriousness of the situation which faces Japan, and also of the scale of change which is currently taking place. Foreign companies continue to face major obstacles in penetrating Japan's markets, not least the system of non-tariff trade barriers which Japan has in place. In addition, the distribution network between producers, wholesalers, retailers and suppliers will take some time to break down. However, to say that the process has finally begun is itself a radical act. Finally, it is also a credible one. Even foreign companies only manage to achieve a relatively small market share in Japan, the very fact that their goods are cheaper and of a similar or better quality to those sold in Japan can cause a significant change in terms of the domestic market pricing. For instance, in 1992 a major U.S. computer company entered the Japanese domestic computer market with a line of discounted computers. While the company was not quite able to achieve a 5% market share, the result of its entry to Japan was that the Japanese domestic market price for that line of computers fell by over 30%. Unless Japan goes back on the reform process, things will never be the same again. The second economy of mediocre domestic businesses by world standards cannot tolerate such a collapse in prices and therefore margins. Even the most profitable companies within the first economy will have to restructure faced with such competition. The very existence of entrepreneurs in Japan today shows that something radical indeed is happening. Japan has watched as U.S. growth powered by information technology, is producing an ever widening gap with Japan. We are starting to see the first signs of Japanese people starting to do something about that gap. The goal of many school leavers is no longer to be a "salaryman" but to start one's own company. The sexual revolution going on in Japan, where women are finally getting a chance to work rather than being forced to stay at home is contributing to that process. Japan is finally waking up to the fact that it has massive amounts of untapped human capital.

Talking about a revolution

Increased competition and a new entrepreneurial spirit is surely good news, but there is a danger in getting too excited. The extent of economic restructuring needed in Japan is massive. According to an OECD report, only in three manufacturing sectors in Japan were these more productive than their U.S. counterparts (transportation equipment, electrical machinery and basic metal products). The rest were some way behind. To cite an example, Japan's food processing industry is only a third as productive as that in the U.S.. Over-manning and un-competitive supply and distribution practices have resulted in ridiculously high prices by international standards. For instance, the cost of a beer in Roppongi when I was last there, was Y2,000 or about USD18. Now, how more ridiculous can you get?! Seriously, as we noted before, Japanese consumers have been ripped off for years. Yes, they have had available some of the best product lines and some of the best technology - for in many areas Japanese technology is second to none, including that of the U.S. - but at an extremely high price, the result of the alliance between government, big businesses and bureaucrats. To mollify them somewhat, Japanese consumers were told that they had the highest standards of living in the world and in moments of candour that high prices were the result of lifetime employment. Whether or not that was true, it certainly is not now. The classic story of the salaryman going to work, only there is no work because he has been sacked, and sitting on a park bench all day rather than go home and admit that, is one which resonates widely in Japan, particularly when many have committed suicide rather than admit. The end of lifetime employment has not been a revolution, rather a creeping state of evolution where it is no longer affordable. There is a quid pro quo for this new lack of lifetime unemployment. It is and will be lower prices and better and more consumer choice. Perhaps, we are witnessing a revolution after all.

Macroeconomic implications

We should not get too ahead of ourselves, but that said what is going on in Japan is of profound importance and not for Japan alone. It will certainly have major implications for Japan's economy; perhaps, just in time given Japan's financial crisis of 1997. The opening up of Japan, and more particularly of the Japanese consumer market will have profound significance for the Japanese trade and current account balances. Roughly speaking, from 1950-75, Japan ran a policy of approximately balanced trade whereby in order to export it had to import. This was followed by a new policy from 1975 onwards where it focused on producing ever larger trade surpluses, where exports and trade surplus represented an increasing portion of the total national economic growth. While this benefited the exporters, it had three negative effects for the Japanese economy.

Firstly, it resulted in the strengthening of the *yen*. From the break-up of fixed foreign exchange rates when the *yen* was some 360 to the dollar, the *yen* has undergone a period of systematic and consistent strengthening, barring the occasional period of dramatic but temporary weakness. Economists talk gaily of capital flows exceeding trade flows by 10-1, thereby dismissing the argument that higher trade surpluses equate to a higher currency over the long term, yet capital flows are erratic and can follow trade flows, particularly when there is anticipation of fundamental improvement in the country concerned. From 360 to the dollar, the *yen* peaked at a mere 79.75 to the dollar in April 1995. From there, it fell back again due to the G7 policy or seeking an "orderly reversal" of the dollar's weakness, reaching a medium-term low of 147.60 in August of 1998 before recovering dramatically, rebounding some 30 *yen* or so in two days. The bottom line is that trade flows do matter. For this reason, the dollar has historically (1971-1999) been a weak currency, while the *yen* has been a strong currency. A significantly firmer *yen* over a sustained period of time results in a tightening of overall monetary conditions. Given that the *yen* firmed by a multiple of around 4.5 over this period, it is no surprise, leaving other factors aside that the Bank of Japan had to cut interest rates. Just taking the 1990s, Japan's short-term interest rate, as measured by 3-month Certificates of Deposit, fell from 7.0% in 1991 to 0.1% as of late 1999. A large part of that decline was merely to offset the rise in the value of the *yen*. The alternative is for the economy to take the brunt of the required adjustment, which it has also done.

Secondly, given that the *yen* has been rising over this period, this has made Japanese exporters cut their export prices in order to continue to compete abroad. Given that Japanese companies had a system of lifetime employment, what they could not do was to cut jobs. Thus, they reduced their intake and sought other measures, relying increasingly on offshore production facilities in lower-cost locations in Asia, particularly in the ASEAN. At home in Japan, they could not cut jobs but what they could do was to restrict wage growth or even to cut wages. Thus, throughout this period, wage growth continued to fall behind productivity growth. This should be good news for companies and in the short term it is because it produces higher profit margins and higher profits. Over the long term, if sustained, it can be catastrophic. Why? Because what is wage growth after all? Surely it is the ability to consume relative to inflation. If the difference between the amount one can consume (productivity) and the ability to consume (wages) is getting increasingly large, eventually there will come a point where consumers can no longer afford to consume. It is a simple equation of supply and demand. We also saw this in Japan' housing market, where supply was severely restricted because of lack of available land as well as earthquake considerations while demand continued to rise. The eventual result was that the land under the Imperial Palace in Tokyo was supposedly worth more before the bursting of Japan's financial bubble in 1991 than the entire Californian real estate market. Note that it is not actually important whether or not this comparison is statistically correct. What is important is that one can even consider such a comparison in the first place! In terms of apartments, a reasonable but not a particularly nice one usually went for somewhere around Y500 million. To most families, this was or became impossible to finance. The only way they could do this was to take out 35- or 50-year mortgages. When the bubble burst as interest rates went up in Japan, this was catastrophic for such home owners. In sum, wage growth is the ability to consume, or demand. If productivity, that is supply, outstrips demand on a sustained basis for long enough the gap between the two becomes too large to fill by marginal or debt-financed demand. The result is a crash. That is what we saw in Japan from 1990-91 onwards.

Thirdly, rising trade surpluses in Japan made the country dependent on external demand. Though trade was not a significant portion of the Japanese economy, by 1990 it was around 12% and remains so today. Thus, the U.S. recession in 1991 when the U.S. economy actually contracted 0.9% was particularly painful, as was the Asian crisis. By the time of the Asian crisis, Asia was receiving some 45% of Japanese exports. Rising trade surpluses are like the second factor noted above a good thing in the short term but over the long term they make the country dependent on external demand and thus vulnerable to a sudden fall in that external demand.

They are also symptomatic of an imbalance in the economy. In Japan, to this day, they suggest that there is a major imbalance between the amount of investment going into exports relative to that going into the domestic economy. This surely confirms both the fact that Japan continues to have trade barriers, both tariff and non-tariff, and the existence, if such confirmation were needed, of the dual economy in Japan. The opening up of Japan's markets, whether it is through deregulation or foreign investment will not only increase the foreign presence in Japan, something like the United States' Trade Representative office has been demanding for two decades, it will also boost domestic demand. Plus, it will cause Japan's trade surplus to shrink. Japan's trade surpluses have actually done Japan as a whole no favours. They should not be mourned. Japan's trade and current account surpluses are likely to be attacked from another angle as well, over the long term. Another way to define the current account balance, aside from looking at trade data, is simply savings minus investment. In 1991, Japan's savings' rate (including private and public savings) was 32.8% of the GDP while its investment rate was 30.2% of the GDP. In 1998, its savings rate had fallen to 29.7%, however its investment rate had fallen further, to 26.5%. Not coincidentally, Japan had a current account deficit in 1998 of 3.2%, which also equals 29.7 minus 26.5. Japan's current account surplus is going to fall in 1999 and 2000 to around 2.7% of the GDP. However, looking further out, in my view if such deregulation and liberalisation as planned by the government is actually implemented, Japan's savings' rate, at least in terms of private savings, will continue to fall and at a faster rate than investment. Deregulation in Japan will in a sense merely accelerate what is already happening. As Japan continues through its modernisation phase - in historical terms, and relative to the last 100 years of its history - it is likely to see the same break down of the family unit as has happened in the U.S. and Europe, albeit perhaps not to the extent. The process is already happening. This has profound implications for the national savings' rate. On the one hand, the new generation appear to be decidedly keener to spend rather than to save relative to their parents and certainly to their grandparents. In addition, the elderly have less incentive to save more to specifically pass on such wealth since the family has moved out. The elderly may be saving more for themselves but they are undoubtedly saving less for others. A reduced savings' rate will, all else being equal lead to a reduced current account surplus. This is not going to happen immediately. Few things happen that way in Japan; but happen it will. At least in economic terms, this is no bad thing. Japan needs a more balanced trade policy badly.

While the deregulation process appears on track, albeit grudgingly in some quarters, it could still do with a helping hand. One way that can be done, as we saw above is to reduce the trade surplus which should in turn boost domestic demand. A further, more specific way is to increase the amount of affordable housing. Japan suffers from a deficit of available land and housing. It is surely one of the most obvious things you notice when you go to Tokyo. Here you are, in one of the great cities of the world and it is like an ant-hill, so packed are the buildings next to each other, so congested, and so densely structured. One author recently suggested that what Japan should try is to build skyscrapers, high rise blocks in which to house people. Right idea, wrong execution. Tokyo, let us not forget, stands over five tectonic plates and is a frequent location for major earthquakes, not the best place to have skyscrapers. There is no question though that Japan does need more housing. The government would do well to use part of the money from its fiscal packages to build more apartments and houses rather than waste it on roads or the like. When people buy a new house, they need to fill it with consumer goods. In order to do that, they have to consume!

There are other implications of the changes that are ongoing in Japan. It is little exaggeration to say that Japan is a nation of tax cheats. But it is also a little surprising given how high taxes are in Japan. Eventually, one by one, countries are realising an unpleasant fact: the more you tax people, the more they try to hide their money, and the more they try to squirrel it away in numbered accounts, away from the grasp of the dreaded tax man. It is simply human nature. It has nothing whatsoever to do with what you happen to believe, whether you believe that tax is theft or rather that it is necessary to redistribute wealth from the greedy to the poor. It is simply what happens. Thus, in order to increase tax revenues, you have to *cut* taxes. I hasten to add that I do not claim any originality for this argument. I find it incredible that one has to repeat it, that there remain those who still believe fervently in keeping taxes high. In Japan, the authorities are concerned about the state of public finances, where the budget deficit is likely to be almost 7% of the GDP for both 1999 and 2000. Consequently, they loath to cut taxes, but that is exactly what they should do if they want to *increase* the amount of tax revenue received. The best example of this at work, despite its obvious economic differences, is Hong Kong where the standard income tax rate is 15%. The penalties for tax evasion are high, but then there is little incentive to evade tax so few do it. Consequently, year after year, with the exception of the Asian crisis years, Hong Kong has run not only balanced budgets but budget surpluses. A city state of some 6 million people or so is clearly a different proposition to Japan where Tokyo alone has over 10 million people. The principle is the same however. Thankfully, it appears at least in some quarters that the authorities are looking at this issue and (finally) coming up with the right answer. Recently, the highest income tax rate was cut to 50% from 65%. If one assumes that the highest earners are more able to evade tax than those lower down, this should result in a major contribution to the budget over the long term.

Japan's authorities are obviously concerned about the budget deficit for the specific reason that Japan is getting older. The "greying" of Japan is due to accelerate from some time around 2010, whereupon this phenomenon will put an increasingly large strain on public finances and in particular social security and pension payments. In order to finance the ensuing need for rising social welfare pay outs and falling tax base - unless Japan goes completely radical and scraps its social security system which is extremely unlikely - the Ministry of Finance faces the task of cutting deep into the budget deficit, in fact making it into a surplus. While tax cuts if managed prudently could contribute to this process, clearly this by itself will not be enough. The government will at some stage also have to start cutting back on spending. Clearly, to do that before the economic recovery which is just starting in Japan is self-sustainable. This is why it is so important that the government and the financial authorities tear down the barriers to consumption as speedily as possible. Ultimately, deregulation will be the crucial platform for improving the budget. Further, deregulation is crucial in freeing up the Japanese financial sector to produce better and higher returns - to offset the higher obligations they will face in the years to come. Deregulation is the key, whether in finance, real estate or manufacturing. Yet there remains the threat, given authority intransigence to lose control of their freedoms, that other economic sectors will only deregulate when they, like the finance sector, face a crisis. Certainly, despite the merits of doing so, they will not give up without a fight if history is anything to go by. In my view, the process has started and is irreversible. Japan has effectively been in a state of crisis for the last decade without realising it. It is just starting to wake up to that fact, just starting to do something about it.

A more resurgent Japan will be a source of increasing imports for the U.S. and Europe, but also Asia. Between 1985-1993, Asia's trade deficit with Japan increased from USD9.3 billion to USD54.2 billion, despite the fact that Asia was running increasing trade surpluses with the West. In 1998, Asia ran massive trade and current account surpluses due to the fact that their economies collapsed. In 1999, those trade surpluses have started to contract as domestic economies recovered. Offsetting this, increased Japanese demand will mean rising Asian exports to Japan. When one thinks that roughly 70% of Asian exports to Japan are by Japanese corporate affiliates located in Asia, it seems certain that this will contribute to supporting Asia's trade surpluses as a whole and more importantly that it will cut into the Asian trade deficits with Japan. That said, over the long term, Asia remains dependent on Japanese parts and technology which is why it has had the trade deficits in the first place. If it wants to get rid of those deficits, it will have to build its own technological base to rival that of the Japanese.

The situation in Japan appears to be improving and barring a major earthquake - Japan, as the Japanese know well, is due for one for the reason that they are supposed to come every 70-80 years - or fallout from the Y2K problem, I remain very bullish on economic prospects for the Japanese economy. Major change is going on in Japan. It is not happening at the pace with which we associate change in the West, but it is happening and that is itself a major step forward. However, Japan still has major problems to face during this restructuring and recovery period. A key lesson from the example of Korea is that economic recovery is helped by cutting debt. Japan could do well to learn this lesson given the debt problem it has. The Hashimoto government estimated that private bad debt amounted to some USD580 billion. Officially, Japan's public debt is around USD4.5 trillion, or around one year of the country's GNP. Unofficially, if one includes the Fiscal and Loan Investment Programme and other such bodies, its public debt could amount to USD10 trillion or more than two year's worth of GNP, a worrying total indeed. When you think that Japan's foreign exchange reserves are large at USD273 billion, think again of this figure.

At the corporate level, it is clear that the high gearing (debt/equity) ratios seen in Korea and elsewhere in Asia were merely symptomatic of what had been going on in Japan for some time, when one considers the fact that many Japanese companies have debt/equity ratios of around 400%. While high gearing ratios might have been appropriate in the developmentalist stage of capitalism, they are most certainly not in this new, ultra-competitive age, where the bottom line rather than the top is the only concern. For years, Japanese corporations have been protected from such considerations as accounts have not been consolidated and minority shareholders were either bullied or were allowed no say in the matter. This is increasingly no longer the case. Those who are more responsive to shareholder interests first will benefit first. Here too, the process will take some time, but it has started and it is irreversible. Like the Japanese consumer, the Japanese shareholder has been robbed blind for too long. Increasing signs that minority shareholders are actually taking company directors to court for not upholding the best interests of the shareholders is excellent news in this regard, however horrifying it must be to some in Japan. For too long, Japan's corporations have not been accountable to the people who actually owned them, and that includes the minority shareholders. The very process of increased accountability will necessitate directors trying to achieve higher rates of return for their companies which should help with the process of reducing corporate debt. Japanese banks and corporations could do worse than look to Asia to see how they have coped with the debt problem. In particular, the example of Korea is striking. There is an alternative to Japan's creeping nationalisation of its banking industry and that is the restructuring of its banking system through public injection of funds, followed by re-capitalisation through equity issues. Similarly, in the corporate sector, Japan still has excessive capacity relative to domestic demand. Japan should take a leaf out of Korea's book and look to break down the barriers which stop mergers and acquisitions. One way or another, increased competition from entrepreneurs and small and medium-sized companies will force Japan's corporate behemoths to restructure. Those who don't try to fight the process, but instead go along with it will come out on top.

Japan also has a lesson for Asia however. While restructuring the balance sheet and more specifically reducing debt is of course crucial, both at the national and corporate level, it also matters what you produce. While the world watches in wonder at the information technology advances in the U.S., many of these advances and many of these companies are dependent on parts made in Japan - and only made in Japan. Japan has what I would term technology monopolies in a number of industrial areas in electronics, machine tools and parts, engineering, automotive production, avionics and robotics to name but a few. Thus, despite the worst effects of the crisis which made importing of Japanese components prohibitively expensive due to the devaluation of Asian currencies against the *yen* these Asian countries had little choice but to continue to import key Japanese parts and products of their own export engines were to continue to fire. This is even true of such technologically advanced countries as Korea and Taiwan, let alone those which are principally ex-export or assembly locations for foreign multinationals. This technological advantage is crucial because it has supported key Japanese industries during bad times at home. The lesson for Asia should be clear, not just in terms of ridding itself of dependency to Japan but also to develop its own technology base and to create the foundation for a balanced, first-world economy. This is not to say that this will be easy. Japanese manufacturers have applied an extremely strategic approach to investing and producing in Asia. Rather than just using it as a low-cost centre, they have sought to maximise output efficiencies by placing production facilities in each Asian country which has a specific production comparative advantage. By making the domestic economy dependent on their capital and production, they frustrate domestic attempts at competition. This is by no means an accident. It is a deliberate policy. Equally, while lower value technologies are exported from Japan to take advantage of cost advantage, high value technologies remain in Japan. Going forward, Asian countries will have to focus less on completely balanced budgets and more on high technology investment. The Asian crisis proved many things. One of those things was that price advantage is no longer enough. Globalisation means that even countries which one perceives as being ultra-competitive because of a large labour force and low production costs, such as China, will come under increasing competition, in part from technological advances which make higher-wage countries more cost competitive, in part from other areas within the emerging markets such as India, and even potentially Africa.

China is at a crucial point in its history, certainly in its economic history and potentially even in its political history. In **China on the Brink**, I sought to examine not only what has happened to China's economy but what relevance that has for the world and where China is likely to go from here. No easy task! Certainly one which is full of available pitfalls. For many, China is the other shoe to drop, the Asian country which has yet to suffer its own crisis. I questioned this view then and I do now. While China could well face an economic crisis in the not too distant future given the complexity and size of its current problems, one should also take into account the excellent job the authorities have done just to get this far, to first create the fastest growing economy over the last two decades, once freed from the tyranny of Mao-ism, and then to navigate a path through the treacherous narrows of the Asian crisis. Given that most Asian currencies devalued by some 40% against the Chinese *yuan*, it is no surprise that the Chinese economy felt considerable economic pain resulting from this. What is remarkable is that the authorities have put in place a set of policies which have so far managed to support economic growth and avoid a devaluation of their currency. Whether they will be able to hold the line and produce a rebound in growth on a self-sustainable basis is another matter. It is to this subject that we now turn to the next chapter.

CHAPTER 6

THE RISK – CHINA ON THE BRINK

There can be little doubt that China's economy has come under severe strain as a direct result of the Asian crisis. With Asian currencies devaluing significantly against the dollar, and thus against the *yuan* since the *yuan* is to all intents and purposes not allowed to move against the dollar, China's exports lost a significant degree of competitiveness.

THE COMPETITIVE THREAT

This is important to the overall economy because trade has become such a large part of that economy. In 1978, China's exports were just over USD7 billion, not much more than the actual trade surplus for 1994. By 1998, that trade surplus had risen to USD43.6 billion. Trade has been one of the main engines of China's astonishing growth over the last two decades. Today, trade amounts to around 20% of China's economy, and that is the third largest economy in the world. China's bilateral trade surplus with the U.S. has overtaken that of Japan's. Consequently, the Asian currency devaluations against the *yuan* had a direct and significant impact on Chinese exports, and thus on the economy as a whole. Furthermore, as we saw earlier, countries which compete on price alone are eventually likely to get undercut - if you live by the sword, you are likely to die by it. Chinese exported goods are known for their volume and for their cheap prices, but they are not necessarily synonymous with quality and they are certainly not known for their technological content. In an increasingly open global trading environment, bringing value-added to the table of global commerce is the sine qua non of long-term business and economic survival. In 1989, according to data from the IMF's Direction of Trade Statistics, China represented 13% of all Asian (ex-Japan) exports going to the U.S. market. By 1996, that figure was 29%. Note that this does not include Hong Kong or Taiwan in the figure for China. If they were to be included, the figure would be 51%. In 1994, China took a further step to deregulate its currency, merging the official and swap rates and in the process allowing a 35% devaluation of the *yuan* against the dollar. While this was not the only factor in the subsequent Asian crisis from mid-1997, it was a significant one. Without question, it meant a loss of Asian export competitiveness to third world markets relative to that of China. In turn, the Asian currency devaluations of 1997-1998 have more than offset that initial *yuan* devaluation, thus reducing or eliminating the competitiveness gap between China and the rest of Asia once more.

China's authorities have tried to offset the effect of this by introducing export subsidies in specific industries such as shipping, iron and steel, coal, cement and textiles. In addition, they have increased the amount of export licenses for companies, both joint ventures and wholly-owned Chinese companies, and have encouraged areas of the economy which up until recently were not allowed to export to do so, most notably the Chinese domestic private sector. There is no doubting the amount of pain that the export sector has gone through however. In 1998, exports grew only 0.5% and for the first half of 1999 they actually contracted 4.6%. Since then, things have got better. In August, 1999, exports rose 17.8% year-on-year, followed by 20.2% in September and around 30% in October. A combination of factors is at work. First off, the Asian recovery which gradually took shape throughout 1999 resulted in rising demand for Chinese exports. Given that around 60% of China's exports go to Asia, the Asian recovery has helped China's export sector itself to recover. Within that 60%, just under 20% points worth go to Japan. Japan's recovery is also helping, clearly, and thus need to be sustained both for the benefit of Japan and also China. In addition to the Asian recovery, which is clearly the main factor for the revival of China's exports, U.S. demand has remained strong and the European Union appears to be reviving slowly. Finally, China's export subsidies have kept its export sector competitive in the face of the Asian currency devaluations.

On November 14, 1999, however, the game changed crucially, for both China and the rest of the world. On that day, China and the U.S. signed a bilateral trade deal, according to which the U.S. now supported China's proposal for entry to the World Trade Organisation, the WTO. As part of that bilateral trade deal, China granted U.S. companies greater access to its financial and manufacturing markets. In addition, a pre-condition to the WTO entry is that export subsidies have to be scrapped, and eliminated completely. Furthermore, import tariffs which were cut to 17% on average from 23% will also have to be eliminated, albeit gradually. China cannot enter the WTO without pledging not to reduce them but to eliminate them. While these measures will not be implemented immediately but instead will be phased in over the next 5 years, financial markets are already anticipating that this will mean reduced exports and increased imports. In other words, the bottom line of this deal in terms of the external sector is that it will cause China's trade surpluses to shrink. China has to give the same terms of its deal with the U.S. to other WTO members including Canada and the European Union before it can gain full accession to the WTO which is likely to happen some time in the first half of this year. Entry to the WTO, if indeed it is achieved will mean that the U.S. "normalises" trade relations with China, and that as a result China will no longer have to seek Most Favoured Nation (MFN) status on an annual basis with the U.S.. In addition, greater access to China's markets should eventually mean further expansion of global trade at the macroeconomic level. At the microeconomic level, it will mean even hotter competition for China's exporters. It will mean that many will go out of business due to that increased competition, while others will be forced to go higher up the value-added chain just in order to survive. Price will no longer be a sufficient advantage in many industries.

Somewhat offsetting this, however, if China does achieve WTO entry, this should cause a significant rebound in foreign direct investment into China. FDI, both on an actual and a contracted basis fell sharply during 1999 due to investor uncertainty as to whether or not the *yuan* would devalue and also how the economy would fair. In addition, given that some 80% of FDI into China before the Asian crisis came from Asia, it should have been no surprise that it fell sharply in the wake of the crisis as many Asian companies were more concerned with merely trying to survive, less on investing in new plants in China. From this year on, however, a China which is a member of the WTO should attract an FDI boom, enticing many companies which have not yet invested in China due to a lack of a legal and transparency framework, a framework which will be mandated by a WTO membership. Some of this investment will be for the purpose of producing factories which then re-export goods. The trend of the last few years, however, excluding the effects of the Asian crisis, has been that the FDI into China has been increasingly directed at the Chinese domestic consumer market itself.

BOOSTING CONSUMPTION

As one consultancy put it, China has experienced a "consumer revolution". It is estimated that as a result of the ongoing economic reform process in China, by the end of the decade some 450 million people will have annual household income of USD3,000 per year and 100 million will have annual household income of USD9,000 or more. Needless to say, China also has its rich, its "*dakuan*" or fat cats, and their "household income" is substantially more than USD9,000! Consumption now represents 50% of China's economy, relative to 20% for trade. At no time in China's history has consumer choice been so great - and that is part of the problem. China has historically relied on external policies to a significant extent to boost its growth, first using import substitution and then targeting strategic export sectors, in much the same way as the rest of Asia. Indeed, this seems the standard model for almost all developing countries which have prospered. Yet, this policy produces external over-reliance. China has become greatly dependent on external demand to support its economy. The slowdown in that external demand produced massive over-capacity in 1998. In addition, this happened at a time when the domestic economy also was continuing to slow down. In 1992, economic growth was some 14.2%. Rising inflation caused the authorities to stamp down hard on the brakes. The economy has slowed ever since. In 1998, growth was 7.8%, still a remarkable result given that it happened at the height of the Asian crisis but still a slowdown relative to the 8.8% growth rate achieved in 1997. The performance of inflation in China has mirrored this slowdown. After peaking at 24.3% in 1994, the CPI index fell gradually until it actually showed a contraction of 0.8% in 1998.

China has tried a number of measures to boost domestic demand. The PBOC has cut interest rates sharply, from around 11% in 1995 to around 3%, as measured by the 1-year deposit rate as of late 1999. On the fiscal side, the government has enacted a number of fiscal packages, specifically aimed at boosting infrastructure spending in the hope that rising consumption will follow. As a result, the fiscal deficit has expanded from -1.2% of the GDP in 1998 to around -1.8% for 1999. In 2000, it is expected to expand again to around -2.0%. Note that these deficit figures do not include government subsidies to the state-owned enterprises (SOEs) or to the State banks. If such subsidies were to be included, the budget deficit could be as much as -6% of the GDP, a worrying figure. Despite such measures, inflation data continues to show contractions, both in terms of the Retail Price Index (RPI) and the CPI. The RPI in China has been contracting since October of 1997. For the full year of 1998, it showed a contraction of -2.8%, which was followed by a contraction of just over -3% for the first half of 1999. In short, deflationary pressures remain rampant within China's economy. What is causing this deflation? The answer is a combination of factors. First off, we have massive over-capacity within China's economy. Theoretically, this can be reached in one of two ways. One is that demand chases supply, thus creating inflation until such a point where despite shortages people are no longer prepared to pay such high prices, in which case supply follows demand on a sharply downward track. The other is that demand can be artificially deflated, such as by tighter credit conditions through interest rate hikes by a central bank or through tighter fiscal conditions as a result of tax hikes or spending cuts or both. In China's case, the austerity measures put in place in 1994 have almost worked too well. Demand has received a body blow. Looking at the demand side in greater detail, there are two sorts of demand, fundamental and speculative. The first is concerned with buying essential goods and services needed for every day life, the second, usually financed by margin credit, is focused on buying luxuries. Speculative demand, needless to say, is usually the first victim of tighter fiscal or monetary conditions. It is when fundamental demand starts to be affected that the slowdown becomes a recession or even a depression.

In the case of China, however, another variable distorts the usually market-oriented and market-sensitive supply-demand equation: state-directed credit. As was the case in Korea, this artificially inflates the supply side. As long as this combination of state credit and speculative demand can offset this apparent over-capacity, the equation remains balanced for a time. Yet, both in theory and practice, this is unsustainable. This is particularly the case when the government decides to change the game. This is exactly what happened in China in 1994 and more recently at the 15th Party Congress in September of 1997 when President Jiang Zemin announced that the entire state-owned enterprise (SOE) sector would have to restructure within three years. Critically, the policy of state-directed credit was ended and companies would have to restructure themselves in such a way that they could support their own cost base without state aid. While the economy was already slowing beforehand, the result of this policy statement aimed at restructuring the SOEs was that millions were thrown out of work. Over the last three years, speculative demand has collapsed and even fundamental demand appears to be slowing. The result has been a widening gap between supply and demand, which we call over-capacity. You can look at the statistics and see that in 97% of manufactured goods in China there is over-capacity; that is excess supply relative to available demand. Far more effective however is if you actually see for yourself. In 1996 and 1997, the skyline of Shanghai was a sea of cranes as far as the eye could see, vivid testimony to over-capacity within the construction industry. In 10 years, Shanghai built as many buildings as it took Hong Kong four decades. The results should have been predictable, though this does not detract in any way from the pain they represent. Property prices have collapsed in the past three years. In some places, they have fallen by two thirds. Potentially good news for consumers although people are naturally reluctant to start buying until they are convinced that prices have bottomed. This is a chicken and egg scenario. Because people want to wait until prices bottom, prices keep falling. Meanwhile, the government which was to enact full deregulation of the housing market in July 1998 balked from doing that for fear of causing a social backlash. The population has already been stripped of the lifetime employment ethos and also of the "iron ricebowl" social security benefit package. To, in addition to those losses, strip it also of subsidised housing and force it to buy its house or apartment might be too much. As a result, housing deregulation in China has been partial at best. The government should know however that it cannot avoid indefinitely such tough choices. In such circumstances, it is a case of pain now or more pain later.

Deregulation of the housing market should in theory help to boost consumption since it also involves consumers buying things with which to fill their houses. However, with unemployment still rising and the iron rice bowl of benefits now gone, people are afraid to make such a monetary outlay just in case they too are made unemployed or "*xia gang*" - literally "stood down", meaning workers who have been sent home on partial pay. Job insecurity is not only adding to the problem of over-capacity, it is exacerbating it. In order to bring consumers back into the shops, particularly the "little emperors", those families who only have one child who they usually spoil rotten and thus consume avidly in order to do so, consumers have to feel that prices have bottomed and that they no longer face the threat of unemployment. How to achieve that? As the various efforts of the government testify, it is no easy task. Over-capacity and falling prices result in diminishing returns. The first part of the answer to the problem must surely lie in reducing the supply side. In terms of the property market, this must entail a temporary cessation of building houses, apartment blocks and commercial buildings. When I went to Shanghai in October of 1999, I was encouraged. The traffic jams may have been horrendous (a two mile journey to the Bund took forty-five minutes. We could have walked faster!), but of cranes there was no sign. In terms of Shanghai, this is quite a statement. In a way very much reminiscent of Bangkok, Shanghai's vista has long been splendid testimony to excess, over-indulgence and over-capacity. Now, Shanghai is a glorious site at night, all lit up, but the building has stopped, at least for now. So far so good. Next, the quickest way of getting rid of over-capacity is to have a sale. This may sound more appropriate for a village fete than an economy, but most assuredly the principle works at the macroeconomic level as well! The concept of the "fire-sale", that is a sale at rock bottom prices is a tried and tested method of reducing over-capacity. That is exactly what has been going on in the rest of Asia for the last two years. The only reason the process has seemed slow or inadequate is because the seller has not accepted the fire-sale price asked by the buyer. This process also has to happen in China. In 1997, roughly 40% of the office space in Beijing was unused and buildings were still being put up. Luckily, this seems to have stopped, but there is only one way to fill that office space and that is to drop one's prices dramatically. It will happen one way or another. The market will either force prices gradually lower over time, a painfully long and protracted process which is the hallmark of deflation, or the seller can drop his/her prices immediately. The latter is the better option to take.

Just in case the point has been lost, I make it clearly here: I am a true believer in free market principles, not necessarily because it is the best option, but because, as Sir Winston Churchill put it, it is the worst, apart from all the rest. History has proved better than any theoretician that communism, aside from its other numerous faults, does not work in producing an efficient economy. This realisation is no doubt why Deng Xiaoping decided to embark in 1978 on the road to economic reform, to develop what has been subsequently called the "socialist market economy". The Chinese government continues to maintain absolute power while at the same time seeking to introduce free market practices, albeit a gradual pace. While it better than anyone must surely understand the paradox of that situation, this combination has so far proved of a much more stable and sustainable sort than has the reform process in Russia. Yet, just as in Japan, the time and the place for gradual economic reform in China must surely be over. China is not currently experiencing a crisis and its leaders have coped admirably well with the economic challenges of the past two years, yet the rigidity of the Chinese economy remains a major fundamental problem, one which continues to hold it back. Opponents of radical reform in China either argue that the entire process is ideologically wrong - there are gradually less of such people around as the old Leftists gradually due off - or that it is actually going too fast and causing too much pain to the population, thus risking a social and political backlash. I would argue on the contrary: that it is not going fast enough! Restructuring the SOEs and the four state banks risks putting yet more millions of people in the lines of the unemployed. That does indeed risk a backlash. Yet, not doing so surely does risk a crisis, one whereby the entire economic system gradually grinds to a halt under the weight of over-capacity and ever diminishing returns. It is no secret. The State banking system is bankrupt several times over. That is not my estimate, but that of one of the credit rating agencies and they should surely know?! Non-performing loans at the state banks represent roughly 30% of the total loans, or around CNY2 trillion. The financial situation within China's state banks is every bit as bad as Korea or Thailand or even Indonesia. Over the last decade, their return on assets has fallen by some 80%. They make inadequate loan loss provisions and they have the highest cost structure of any banking system in the world as measured by assets per employee. What keeps the state banks afloat is the fact that the *yuan* is not yet freely convertible on the capital account, and thus the Chinese population has little alternative but to put its money on deposit at these state banks given the lack of other options. Yet China is seeking to develop its asset markets. In addition, it is likely to take further measures soon, perhaps as early as this year, to deregulate further the foreign exchange market in China and thus the currency as part of its long-term strategy to develop a fully convertible currency and as part of its commitment to join the WTO. The most likely option would seem to be the creation of currency trading which is bad for the dollar-*yuan* exchange rate, but allows greater financial and policy flexibility. Developing China's asset and foreign exchange markets would clearly offer alternatives for China's would-be depositors, hence the need for speed in the reform and restructuring process of China's banks. To this end, the government has instructed the heads of the four state banks to restructure their banks along more market oriented lines.

While there can be no doubting the efforts of these individuals, given that their jobs most likely rest on their success in the matter, this is surely not the most efficient way of achieving this aim. The creation of the Minsheng Bank, China's first truly private bank free from state control, has proved not only that domestic private finance can work in China, but that it does so to an extraordinary extent. In its first two years of operation, Minsheng Bank built up around USD2.4 billion in assets with a staff of only 800 people. China's financial authorities may be nervous that further private competition to the state banks in the form of other Minsheng Banks may put an intolerable strain on the deposit base of the state banking system. That may well be the case. On the other hand, nothing is more likely to force the state banks to restructure themselves and at a speedy rate than increased competition. Just as with the SOEs, there is no greater incentive to improve than survival itself. The financial authorities have sought to put a floor under the banking system through a CNY270 billion special bond issue with which it has sought to go some way to repair the balance sheet of the state banks, yet as the level of non-performing loans show, this is not nearly enough to do the job. However, just pumping more money into the banking system will not solve the problem. More likely, it will actually add to the problem since the policy of state-directed credit is why China's banking system is in such a mess in the first place. To this end, the government appears to be considering increasing private competition within the banking system, albeit cautiously, and at the same time has set up asset management corporations, much in the same mould as KAMCO in Korea or the Resolution Trust Corporation in the U.S. during the banking crisis there in the early 1990s, in order to reduce the total level of non-performing loans on the books of the state banks. In addition, the concept of debt-for-equity swaps has been introduced.

Under the veneer of government caution, radical reforms are being enacted. This is just as well for the clock is ticking. As a result of the WTO's bilateral deal with the U.S. and future full accession to the WTO, China will allow foreign banks to lend to the domestic corporate base in 2001 and to lend to individual Chinese in 2004. Then the Chinese state banks will be faced with real competition. In the intervening one and four years, they will have to restructure radically in order merely to be able to compete in such an environment, let alone come out on top. This is no doubt exactly what the government had in mind and this is indeed a more effective way of obliging banks to restructure rather than having government bureaucrats trying to enforce the process. The state banks face a dire threat in 2001 and then again in 2004. They have little choice but to savage their cost base, and that will include dramatically reducing their work force. The WTO's deal with the U.S. has thus become a major boost to the reform process.

THE BATTLE FOR REFORM

In truth, the reform process needed a boost. Given the amount of pain that it was causing, the process appeared to be slowing down. In April of 1999, it received a severe blow when Premier Zhu Rongji, the leader of the economic reform process, came home to Beijing empty-handed after offering the U.S. major concessions to try to achieve entry to the WTO. This offered a perfect opportunity to those within the cabinet, the Party and the parliament, the National People's Congress, who oppose the reform process to seek to slow it down further or even to reverse it. The reality of Premier Zhu being publicly criticised by Li Peng, former Premier and current Chairman of the NPC, for supposedly selling out the interests of the people of China to the U.S. through the concessions he offered and then returning with nothing must have been stunning to most ordinary Chinese. The subsequent bombing of the Chinese Embassy in Belgrade by the U.S. and the subsequent anti-U.S. riots in China were further opportunity for those who opposed the reform process to seek to damage it. The change in the political climate was discernible in the fact that Premier Zhu was seen far less at public meetings. In addition, President Jiang Zemin, ever the pragmatist like his predecessor Deng, made increasingly hawkish comments both on the political and the economic side. On the latter, he publicly took charge of the economic reform process, a move which caused some to take the view that Zhu Rongji's days as Premier were numbered. That said, Jiang staked his reputation, albeit indirectly, on the success of China's proposal for entry to the WTO, a risky move by Chinese political standards, but one which paid off in the end thanks to Zhu. For it was Zhu Rongji who saved the WTO talks with the U.S. at the eleventh hour, just when many on the U.S. side thought that all was lost, that a deal would not be signed. That may or may not have been merely a negotiating tactic on the part of the Chinese government, it actually does not matter. What happened was that a WTO deal was signed with the U.S. thanks to the personal intervention of Premier Zhu. As a result, the reform process has received a boost, as indeed has the Presidency of Jiang Zemin. People will look back on November 14, 1999 and realise its important as a crucial day in Chinese history, a day the reform process which had been flagging received a much needed boost, from which it accelerated to become eventually a true global economic power, the "workshop of the world" as someone will some day call it. This is of course based on the view that the forces which oppose reform will not revive, a view which is more hope than expectation. Yet, November 14, 1999 may become as important as the introduction of the economic reforms of 1978, or as the Party Congress in 1992 when the Leftists within the Party were finally and roundly defeated by Deng, securing the base for extension of the reforms.

Meanwhile, there remain problems to be addressed. In terms of the economy, there remains the issue of the exchange rate, which throughout the crisis has been overvalued on a Real Effective Exchange Rate (REER) basis, that is on the basis of the trade-weighted exchange rate adjusted for inflation. In addition, there remains the issue of inadequate fiscal revenue. As a result of the decentralisation process which the government has pushed through, tax revenue available to the national government has fallen to around 11% as of 1998 from 35% in 1978. Finally, there remains the mammoth task of restructuring the SOEs. There are around 305,000 SOEs which together still make up over 40% of the national industrial output and employ around 100 million people out of a total workforce of 685 million. On average, even during the economic reform years from 1978-1996, they took up to 85% of all loans from the state banks. The result has been massive over-capacity and falling profits, or rather mounting losses, at the SOEs and rising non-performing loans at the state banks. First, let us deal with the issue of the exchange rate.

AN OVERVALUED CURRENCY?

In terms of its Real Effective Exchange Rate, or REER, the Chinese *yuan* was significantly overvalued in the wake of the Asian currency devaluations. Given that many of these were key competitors of China's third world markets, the devaluation of their currencies against the dollar, and thus against the *yuan* since the *yuan* was to all intents and purposes not allowed to move against the dollar, made their exports much more competitive against those of China. In such circumstances, either the currency has to adjust or the export sector has to suffer, in order to compensate. China did not allow its currency to adjust, but instead tried a number of measures in order to help its export sector, as we have already seen. However, the *yuan*'s overvaluation meant in the short term that export growth first slowed and then exports started to contract. Meanwhile, RPI and CPI contraction, in other words deflation, is also symptomatic of an overvalued currency. What is an overvalued currency after all but excessive monetary tightening?! It is for this reason that the People's Bank of China has been cutting interest rates for the past four years. Will it be enough or will China eventually have to devalue? If fiscal and monetary easing do not work in boosting the economy, the government might run out of alternatives in terms of trying to boost demand. Yet some may seem curious that such a question could arise at all. For the full year of 1999, China had a trade surplus of around USD25 billion. Granted, this was down substantially from the USD43.6 billion trade surplus for 1998, but nevertheless it is still a significant trade surplus, indeed it is greater than the entire annual trade for many developing nations. In addition, at the end of 1999, China had foreign exchange reserves just under USD160 billion, almost four times the size of the reserves in the U.S.. Meanwhile, foreign direct investment totalled over USD25 billion. The reason there is the concern about the valuation of the exchange rate and why there has been concern in the past is that foreign exchange reserves only rose by some USD10 billion for the year of 1999. Taking the trade surplus and the FDI figure, they should have risen by some USD50 billion, excluding capital outflows.

It is the capital outflows that is exactly the problem. While some of it has been in the form of legitimate outflows of portfolio and FDI investment, much of it has been smuggled out, either across the border into the Hong Kong banking system or in suitcases on planes. The State Administration of Foreign Exchange (SAFE) has done much to try to close the available loopholes which have allowed such capital outflows, while simultaneously the People's Bank of China (PBOC) has cracked down on the black market in foreign exchange. For all their efforts, the black market exchange rate for the dollar against the *yuan* is still around 9, reflecting an anticipated devaluation of the *yuan* of around 10%. The authorities are faced with a policy dilemma. They can maintain their foreign exchange reserves at a high level, they can maintain the stability of the *yuan* or they can maintain the economy's growth rate, but they cannot do all three for any significant length of time. One of them has to go. Maintaining such high foreign exchange reserves is not necessarily appropriate. While it guards against future uncertainty or in the worst event against an economic or financial crisis, in the meantime it actually represents a wasted resource. The government needs to maintain the level of economic growth, and hopefully above the 8% level given that below this it is thought that China is not producing enough growth to support the job market and to absorb the unemployed resulting from the restructuring process. On the exchange rate, the authorities have pledged not to devalue the *yuan* for 2000, just as they did for 1998 and 1999. While a devaluation of the *yuan* could cause major financial instability in China, causing in the process a revaluation of

China's external debt, the current regime which approximates a fixed exchange rate is not necessarily the optimum arrangement to have over the long term. China's financial authorities are of course well aware of this. From September of last year, there appeared an intriguing debate within the Chinese press as to which exchange rate regime might be appropriate and what policy the authorities might eventually adopt. No less than the "People's Daily", the mouth-piece of the Chinese Communist Party, said that if China's trade surplus were to become a deficit, an "adjustment" to the exchange rate regime might be appropriate. In China, such public utterances in newspapers do not happen by accident, and if they are in the People's Daily it can be assumed that such considerations are coming from the top, or at the very least being launched by the most senior Party officials as trial balloons for debate within Chinese financial and economic circles.

The U.S.-China deal over the WTO has heightened the need for reconsidering China's exchange rate policy. By 2004, as a result of the deal, foreign banks will be able to lend to ordinary Chinese. Note that this is also the unofficial target of the Chinese authorities for full convertibility of the *yuan* on the capital account. China can go back on what was in any case an unofficial pledge, but the WTO deal makes it harder to do that for the simple reason that the deal is likely to make eventual convertibility a necessity rather than merely desirable. The bottom line is that China will indeed have to adjust its exchange rate regime. To the Chinese authorities, such a realisation will come as no surprise. Indeed, they argue that the history of China's exchange rate policy has in any case been one of gradual deregulation and liberalisation towards convertibility, first on the current account and then on the capital account. To this end, China last year widened the daily volatility band around which the dollar-*yuan* (USD-CNY in market terminology) exchange rate is allowed to trade to 1.0% from 0.3%. As a result of the WTO deal, is our strongly held conviction of our bank that China will widen that band still further, probably some time either in 2000 or 2001, perhaps say to 5% or 10%, thus creating a much freer exchange rate market to develop. Dai Xianglong, Governor of the People's Bank of China, gave a hint of this late last year when he said that the market determined the value of the *yuan* exchange rate rather than the authorities. For a Chinese high-ranking official to make such a comment was indeed truly revolutionary. It not only shows how far China has come, it also shows what they intend. The *yuan* exchange rate market will indeed be market-driven and it will eventually be a fully convertible market on the capital as well as the current account. The process will continue to be gradual by Western standards. One must remember however that relative to the length of Chinese history, the economic reform process from 1978 has moved at light speed. It is no doubt for this reason that Chinese officials sometimes get exasperated with Western commentators who say that China is moving too slowly to reform. Returning to the issue of the exchange rate, a wider trading band is likely to be created, perhaps along the lines of the ERM or the current trading band for the Polish zloty, which is allowed to trade 15% either side of a central parity against a basket of currencies. The authorities will then allow the *yuan* to trade freely within that band. It will be up to the market to decide where to take the *yuan*, whether to cause it to appreciate or to depreciate. The authorities will thus avoid being seen to devalue the *yuan* and this will give them considerably more monetary policy flexibility.

While there remain market concerns about the valuation of the *yuan*, not least in China's own black market, the movements of other Asian currencies against the dollar, including the *yen*, during the second half of 1999 have somewhat helped China in maintaining the stability of its currency. For instance, the decline in the dollar-*yen* exchange rate from a 1999 high of just under 125 to just above 100, dragging down with it many dollar exchange rates against Asian currencies, has resulted in a general revaluation of Asian currencies against the *yuan*, almost offsetting that initial devaluation of Asian currencies and thus causing China's REER valuation of its exchange rate also to decline from its greatly overvalued state. The *yuan* is thus now substantially less overvalued than it was in 1998, with the result that the authorities should have greater freedom to ease fiscal and monetary policy and to deregulate the foreign exchange market without fear of causing a major *yuan* devaluation.

TIGHTENING THE FISCAL SIDE

China has traditionally been known, at least in the past decade or so, for relative fiscal prudence, rarely having a budget deficit to the GDP which greatly exceeded 1.0%. The recent efforts to boost the economy through infrastructure projects and through deficit spending have caused the fiscal deficit to widen. This is not an immediate concern, but neither is the ability of China to spend its way out of the *rouble* unlimited, particularly when that fiscal deficit is coupled with a bankrupt state banking system. In short, China has to overcome the medium- to long-term deficit by spending less, putting more of the burden for supporting state industries and banks onto the private sector, and at the same time by collecting more tax. Tax collection has historically been a major problem of the emerging markets and China is no exception. Indeed, somewhat worryingly, if you look at the examples of many of the recent emerging market crises, inadequate tax collection and therefore rising fiscal deficits have played a major part in that crisis, notably in the case of Russia and Brazil.

As noted earlier, tax revenue available to the National government has fallen drastically in the last 22 years, from around 35% to 11%. The provinces continue to oppose fiercely any attempt by the central government to reclaim some of this revenue, somewhat predictably. Meanwhile, in terms of the contribution to the fiscal account of tax revenue, this remains quite low at just above 10% of the GDP. Over the long term, either China has to cut spending drastically or it has to hike taxes. On the spending side, it is trying get the state banks and the SOEs off its books, yet China will still have to upgrade the infrastructure of its middle and western areas, a task which will cost hundreds of billions of *yuan*. The bottom line therefore is that the government has to collect more tax. On the face of it the answer is simple: hike taxes. Yet, it is equally obvious that this is not the answer. If you create a nation of high taxes, you create a nation of tax cheats. It is that simple. The national tax system has to be restructured in order to recoup the maximum amount without providing any major incentive for tax evasion. In China, this is no easy task. What is necessary are modern national income and capital gains' tax codes. A consumption tax might be necessary at a national level at some future stage, but at present clearly it is inappropriate as demand continues to struggle.

Dealing with the tax system in China also means dealing with the issue of corruption. In China, the issue of corruption is not a small one. The authorities have periodically cracked down severely, imprisoning and even executing transgressors. As with most things in the economy, however, it is a matter of incentive. Corruption in any country does not happen out of a vacuum, but instead it emerges when market forces are not working or rather that they are not being allowed to work. If people are given sufficient incentive to pay taxes, they will. The Hong Kong tax code could be an excellent example for China to follow in theory. In practice, regulating and supervising such a tax code is a somewhat different enterprise in the HKSAR with some 6 million people, as it is in a country with some 1.2 billion. Still, it is an example of what can be done. Whatever form the restructuring of the national tax codes take in China, they have to be deemed fair, or else they will simply cause an increased level of corruption resulting from tax evasion.

RESTRUCTURING CHINA INC

Finally, we come back to the issue of the SOEs. At the 15th Party Congress in September 1997, Jiang Zemin said that all the SOEs must restructure over a three-year time period. Needless to say, this was then an enormous undertaking and so it remains. What we are talking about is nothing less than the largest corporate restructuring in the history of the world achieved in the shortest time period ever envisaged. The restructuring of the SOEs has been a process which has had its successes and failures and has gone through its peaks and troughs. The initial plan was that around 1,000 out of the 305,000 would be obliged to be listed on the A- and B- share markets, the first which is aimed solely at local Chinese investors, the second which allows the participation of foreign investors. Late last year, President Jiang made clear that the State would maintain control in key and strategic industries and that such corporate giants would not seek public listing, but instead would endeavour to restructure along market lines, albeit remaining within the grip of the state. This was in line with the phrase first used in 1997 of "grabbing the large and freeing the small" to describe the restructuring effort of the SOEs. While this is perhaps understandable given the socialist nature of the Chinese government, it does not necessarily bode well for the restructuring of these key industries. In all countries, the historical road of restructuring within the state is paved with good intentions. A much more effective and efficient way of achieving what is surely the same result as desired by the authorities is through free and open competition. Companies are never better at restructuring than when they have to. The government has however been quite clear. It is seeking to reduce the influence of the state within the economy, and to act more as an administrator of economic policy rather than in the past when it was an economic dictator of command policies. However, the Chinese government is most certainly not seeking to eliminate that influence, for that could spell anarchy, as well as eliminating the Party itself. Rather, it seeks to continue with its economic experiment, by freeing up the smaller SOEs, which amount to some 87,000, to see how they do and to allow the relatively young Chinese asset markets to get used to the privatisation process. It remains to be seen whether or not China has the luxury of such a lengthy approach. The large SOEs after all employ around 100 million out of the urban workforce of 175 million. They have debts which are casually estimated at USD120 billion. By the start of 1999, half of all the SOEs were estimated to be loss-making and the sector as a whole was increasingly being starved of credit in order to proceed with the restructuring process of the state banking system. Debt-to-equity ratios of the SOE sector have been put as high as 550%.

If any of this sounds at all familiar, readers have only to turn to chapter 4. This bears a marked resemblance to the situation in Korea in the immediate aftermath of the crisis there, and China has not even faced a devaluation. It is no coincidence then that Premier Zhu Rongji's model for the SOE restructuring was initially that of the *chaebol*. It is to be hoped that he has reconsidered, in the wake of the crisis in Korea. China's SOEs have all of the faults of the *chaebol* and more: high debt-to-equity ratios, low profitability, complete lack of balance sheet transparency or consolidated accounts. This is the task which stands before the Chinese regulatory authorities. To use the Korean analogy, China is still putting in the hardware. It will take years to put in the software. Ahead of such events, investors will have a difficult time in establishing real value. For the time being, the focus appears to be on creating *chaebol*-like conglomerates as the next stage of development. It is to be questioned whether China has the luxury in terms of time to do this rather than moving further ahead to the type of restructuring the *chaebol* themselves are undergoing. China's officials have long argued that China is still a developing country. Until such time as the government builds both the hardware and the software which can protect the interests of shareholders as well as depositors, their assessment will remain accurate.

CHINA, HONG KONG AND TAIWAN

In December of last year, the dependency of Macao, run by Portuguese administration, was handed over, just as Hong Kong had been handed over by the United Kingdom on July 1, 1997, returned to the sovereignty of China. There thus remains but one major territory which China claims ownership of and which it demands must be handed back to its control, Taiwan or the Chinese province of Taipei as some would have it. While some fret for the future of Hong Kong, whether for political reasons or because of a concern that China might change Hong Kong's legal framework, there can be little doubt that the focus in China itself is of seeking to persuade Taiwan that one country-two systems is a potentially viable future for Taiwan. In order to do that, China will have to make sure not only that this works in Hong Kong but that it is seen to be working. Ultimately, that is a key safety line for Hong Kong. The HKSAR does face threats however. No longer a British colony, its high cost structure means that it will not be able to compete as just another port in China, albeit an important one. Hong Kong thus has to remake itself in terms of both its roles, both as a centre of international finance and as a prosperous port in southern China which fulfils the trading needs of the mainland. Last year's deal with the Walt Disney Company to build a theme park on Lantau Island goes some way to helping Hong Kong diversify, yet it still faces increasing competition from the likes of Singapore and, more ominously, increasingly from Shanghai.

The government has long argued that Shanghai is not a threat to the future of Hong Kong. Those who automatically agree should remember an important piece of history: Philadelphia was once the capital of the United States and also its most important trading city. While it no doubt remains important, it has long since been bypassed by Washington DC in terms of politics and New York and even Chicago in terms of the economy. Whether the Chinese government likes it or not, Shanghai does represent a threat to the future of Hong Kong and that threat concerns price. For instance, real estate prices and shipping handling fee prices remain sharply lower in Shanghai compared to what they are in Hong Kong. In addition, Hong Kong has long been the gateway to China. However, as China continues to open up, the necessity of having such a gateway will increasingly come into question, particularly as China continues to expand its export sector and at the same time open up its domestic markets. Why be in

Hong Kong when your current and future clients are and will be in Shanghai. Hong Kong has a major advantage for now and that is that it already has in place much of the hardware and software which China is seeking to build. Hong Kong's historical adherence to the rule of law and to prudent and rigorous regulation and supervision has served it well. Those who seek to interfere with or to damage that do so at the risk of doing irreparable damage to the good name of Hong Kong and ultimately themselves. Not only that, the prize of regaining Taiwan might be threatened as well.

Hong Kong cannot compete with China on price so in order to remain both viable and vibrant it must move further up the value-added chain in terms of both technology and services. On the service side, the Disney deal should help. In terms of technology, the creation of the Cyberport should also help in providing renewed economic impetus and focus. Technology, value-added within services will be key in maintaining Hong's edge over the short term. The territory can become a mature, market economy, much as in the mould of Singapore albeit with the advantage of having mainland China on its doorstep, or it can sink back into oblivion, once more a barren rock, on the south China coast. The choice is partly Hong Kong's, but it is ultimately China which will decide the fate of this splendid place. Just in case the reader takes the view that authors stay in their studies all day and don't have a pulse, I say without any reservation or inhibition for that matter that I moved to Hong Kong at the start of 1996 and immediately fell in love with the place. Hong Kong is special. There is nowhere like it, anywhere else in the world. Thinking of this, I stand on my hotel balcony, in the Mandarin Oriental, and survey Hong Kong's Victoria Harbour, what is surely the most glorious harbour view anywhere. Personally, I take the view that a people who built such a city, the people of Hong Kong will have no problem in competing in this new and more difficult environment - if they are allowed to. Hong Kong will always be a special place. It will always be an important financial centre. What it may no longer be is the gateway to China. For that role, it seems there is little question that the future is in Shanghai.

Just as with Hong Kong, or with Shanghai over a longer time period, Asia still possesses major fundamental strengths which should help it to pull through this present crisis, as well as weaknesses which need to be restructured. It is to this subject that we turn to next.

CHAPTER 7

THE FUNDAMENTALS – ASIA'S LONG-TERM STRENGTHS

There is no question that the speed and extent of Asia's recovery has been truly phenomenal, much faster and much greater than most people expected, including me! While much of that has been due to the massive degree of fiscal and monetary easing undertaken by the national governments of Asian countries, this is not the whole story. One also has to give credit where credit is due to the much-maligned International Monetary Fund. Many blamed their painful policies for the degree of financial catastrophe, which occurred in 1997 and the first half of 1998. For a start, that was simply not true.

Granted, the IMF's initial policies did not take into account the degree to which economies would collapse. To a large extent, the emphasis they put on establishing social safety nets in 1998 was an admission of the lack of attention they had paid to microeconomic detail during 1997. This was pretty understandable given the panic which was occurring in the second half of 1997 and the consequent need to focus on stabilising the macroeconomic situation in Asia. Now however, it has to be said that those painful policies have worked. Yet, this is also not the whole answer. As we saw from the example of Korea, national pride and determination can also play a part. The ingredient we are missing with all these answers however is to an extent what made the Asian "Miracle" in the first place. To a great extent, Paul Krugman was right in his influential 1994 article in the sense that the policies which Asia had undertaken were not particularly "miraculous" and furthermore that the model was indeed flawed. Where this analysis comes up short however is that if the Asian boom years of the last two decades prior to the 1997-1998 crisis were merely a question of inputs, if the answer were that easy, why did it not happen elsewhere. In fact, why did we not witness the Asian boom everywhere in the emerging world? The fact that we didn't, or haven't yet, suggests that there might indeed have been something particularly Asian about this period of economic elevation. A "Miracle" it might not have been, but it was more than just a question of investment. In addition, where other emerging markets floundered or under-performed, the Asian boom or whatever one likes to call it reduced the number of people in Asia in absolute poverty - that is, making less than USD1 a day - to 350 million as of 1993 from 720 million at the start of the 1960s. If that isn't miraculous, I don't know what is! Yes, investment played a major part in this, but merely creating the foundation whereby investment could drive growth was major progress in itself, progress which others did not achieve.

Long-term fundamental strengths were behind the Asian boom of the last two decades and these same long-term fundamental strengths should help the region recover and prosper in going forward. In addition to these, Asia has learned many lessons as a result of the Asian crisis, not least that capital flows can be dangerous to an economy's health if not managed properly, as well as the fact that supervision and regulation of the national banking systems is important.

In **Asia Falling**, I wrote the following:
..."The doomsayers out there will say this region has past its prime. Don't believe them. A detailed look at the long-term fundamentals strongly suggests otherwise. That said, Asia must also face up to a number of serious fundamental problems and challenges."

I strongly believe in this. The Asian "Miracle", flawed as it was, happened for a number of reasons. Asian governments put together a platform of economic policies which provided a growth boom, the likes of which have not been seen anywhere else in the emerging markets. Those who scoff at this, who suggest that the peak of Asian economic performance has already been seen or that Asia is no different to other emerging markets should check out the economic mess that is Africa. Relative to its promise, Latin America has also under-performed significantly and as for Russia, it is in a class of its own political and economic ineptitude and corruption. Only in Asia have we seen a boom for *three decades*, followed by an almighty bust...followed by the most dramatic of recoveries. Just because Asia crashed in 1997, many have dismissed the previous thirty years of economic work. This is nonsense. Many lessons have to be learned, yes. But there is no question that Asia got the foundations of economic development absolutely right; so right in fact that it was part of the problem. Too much capital was attracted; too much growth created relative to the quality of that growth. To find out where we go from here, we have to go back to those foundations, to what exactly Asia did get right.

Asia did Get the Basics Right

The Asian success story - and in this, I include Japan - reflected a unique combination of market and government-led policies, a balance which did not exist in the mature Western nations to the same degree. Key behind this success story was prudent macroeconomic management - "getting the basics right" as the World Bank research report, "The East Asian Miracle" famously described it. What were those basics? Asian governments fostered an environment in which private domestic investment could grow rapidly. At the same time, these governments created strong primary and secondary education systems - or, in pure economic terms, "expanded the human capital base" - albeit to varying levels depending on the country. Extraordinarily high domestic savings' levels provided the bedrock for supporting that private investment, but this too did not happen by chance - governments created the environment in which savings could flourish.

Inflation was kept low and with tight fiscal policy, most Asian governments were running budget surpluses. In addition, while Asian authorities sought to expand strategic industries, they taxed their citizens less and maintained smaller-sized governments. Asians saved more and were taxed less than their counterparts anywhere else in the emerging markets or in the Western world. Equally, there was little or no social provision by the government for its citizenry. Consequently, Asian budgets did not suffer from the same degree of social spending burden as was - and is - seen in the West, and moreover Asians had to rely on the family rather than the government as the main institution for social safety and protection. The necessity of self-reliance resulted in fast, flexible and dynamic family-owned enterprises at the microeconomic level, providing a major spur for the macro-economy. Asian countries sought to increase productivity in both agricultural and industrial sectors, moving up the value-added chain from labour-intensive production to high technology. Moreover, the skills which Asian countries did not consider they had, they imported; Asian governments sought to provide attractive environments for foreign direct investment through tax and investment subsidies. The two measures of "success" which Asian governments held up as virtues were exports and GDP growth. The results they achieved were astounding. From 1960-1993, the more advanced Asian economies grew three times as fast as Latin America and five times faster than sub-Saharan Africa.

WHERE ASIA WENT WRONG

While Asia got the basics right, it also made what we can now see - a number of mistakes. At the very least, it did not move sufficiently quickly to eliminate the fundamental flaws in the Asian model of capitalism, to restructure and seek to continuously re-invent itself so as to be able to extend its economic success. During the period of Asian economic and financial boom, such fundamental flaws were either ignored or considered irrelevant. Only when the Asian crisis occurred were they seen as reflecting structural weaknesses. The Asian boom years were bound to end. As it lasted long in Asia, no boom time can go on forever. The way that it ended however suggests that Asia went wrong in a number of specific ways and that improvements to the Asian model can and should be made.

■ Quantity versus quality

By focusing on headline growth and export figures as the standards of national "success" at the expense of everything else, the foundations of a boom-bust cycle were created. Growth was seen as the "end" rather than the "means". Given the impoverished state of Asia after World War II, this emphasis on growth, whatever the cost, was clearly understandable. However, such a disproportionate focus on headline growth figures led to financial and political authorities ignoring the quality, and thus the sustainability of that growth. Symptomatic of this focus was the fact that many Asian corporations focused not on the bottom line, not on net profit, but on sales and on market share. A key reason why they could afford to take this dubious approach was the ever present endless cheap credit from local state and commercial banks or directly from the government. Such targeted credit policies, for instance, led to the creation of the Korean *chaebol.* However the competitiveness of such companies relied almost exclusively on the maintenance of favourable credit, exchange rate and external demand conditions. In other words, they weren't competitive at all, relying on artificially improved conditions that were in the end unsustainable. Cheap credit led to massive, uncompetitive companies, massive over-capacity and poor quality. Why? Because human beings if they do not have to make a profit, if they receive cheap and endless credit whether or not they need it, will in the end produce ever diminishing returns. That is by no means an Asian phenomenon, but one that can be liberally and generally applied to our species. Companies that are receiving such targeted credit are not competing. They are getting handouts. They might as well be receiving social security. The concepts of quality and profit come only with competition, where there is a necessity, and where there is sufficient incentive to avoid failure. Turn off the tap of cheap credit, just as you turn off the drug supply of a junky, and you will quickly get a different result. Either the company concerned will be forced to become efficient and profitable, to the eventual benefit of its employees and shareholders, or it will go under in which case it is no longer a burden to the state, that is to taxpayers like you and me.

■ A lack of productivity?

An issue of much interest prior to the Asian crisis and in the wake of it was concerned with whether the Asian success story was due solely to investment, indeed whether or not the Asian "Miracle" was in fact real as we noted earlier. Ever since the Krugman article, there has been widespread debate as to whether or not Asian growth was solely due to inputs, or rather that it did in fact include Total Factor

Productivity (TFP), or the total residuals when all inputs from GDP growth are taken out. TFP residuals are most commonly seen as coming from technology and innovation processes, that is those (grey) accelerating factors that cause growth to leap forward without any accompanying equal input.

Precisely because TFP is a residual, rather than a primary element of growth, it is notoriously hard to measure, which is probably why the debate on Asian TFP or the lack thereof continues to rage without much sign of progress. I have no intention in this section to go into the specific and detailed arguments of the economists who suggest strong TFP existence in Asia or those who deny that very existence, looking at such concepts as factor accumulation, capital to labour output ratios and the like. I strongly suspect that the reader who is not particularly used to the subtle complexities of such economic waffle would rather have conducted upon him or her root canal surgery than have to wade through it. I shall endeavour to save them from either task, taking a rather different approach. Whatever Krugman's contribution to the Asian TFP debate, that of his to the cause of readable, first-class economics has been immeasurable. His is unquestionably one of several key benchmarks by which we have to steer our attempt to make economics comprehensible and interesting. Most of what you read out there is pretty dire stuff indeed. Returning to the concept of TFP, this is actually a pretty important and interesting subject. No, really!

For my part, I take the following view: TFP readings from anyone are imprecise, however valid the scholarly work supporting them, and thus should be taken with a grain of salt. Whether an economy possesses TFP is another matter. TFP is clearly a vitally important concept for the continued economic development of a country. With the data itself so unreliable, anecdotal evidence and common sense, through necessity, can play a greater role, not least in the very understanding of the concept. Ever since that article, coincidentally or not, Singapore has been on a productivity drive. Rather than just through labour and investment, growth is now propelled by technological advancement. The creation of Singapore's infrastructure, surely the most developed in the Asian region, is also a TFP-type event in the sense that it creates growth which is not *directly* caused by the initial investment. Prior to the crisis, the likes of Singapore, Hong Kong, Taiwan and Korea experienced major improvement in terms of technological advancement, innovation and education that cannot simply be explained by input or funding. In a sense, education itself is an TFP-orientated process given that you can get a lot more out of it than the sum of what you put in.

Yet, there is some validity to the argument put by Krugman and others that Asian growth, notably elsewhere in the ASEAN apart from the countries that have already been mentioned was the result of "perspiration" rather than "inspiration". Growing labour forces due to demographic changes and rising capital investment were the chief drivers of growth in these countries, supported by high savings' rates rather than technology advances or productivity increases. In several reports, it would appear that the IMF has come to the same conclusion. Several economists, including from within Asia itself question that suggestion however. On balance, it would appear that the debate goes on without definitive resolution. In the end, whether Asia generated TFP in the past is not as important as the per capita income increases it *did* generate, whatever their source, which far outpaced any other region. Going forward, whatever the situation in the past, TFP will matter increasingly in the future if Asia is merely to keep up with the innovations of the present in the West.

■ Family problems

Asia's focus on not insulating its citizens from the hazards of economic reality has had many benefits. It has created a dynamic entrepreneurial class, particularly in the ethnic Chinese communities within Asia, outside of China. In addition, as a result, governments have been able to maintain strong and healthy fiscal surpluses, unburdened by the need to provide significant social security transfer payments. However, one detrimental aspect of this focusing on the family as the sole institution of security has been that there has until recently been little attention paid towards adopting prudential regulation which might otherwise provide a legal framework for the efficient running of society. Reliance on the family, but more generally on contacts, or *guanxi* as it is put in Chinese, has been a replacement for sound law and regulation - an impressive way of making do in the face of adverse conditions.

To a certain extent, this is a chicken and egg situation - because people have relied on the family as the sole institution of security and as the main institution for driving forward the economy at the microeconomic level, there has been little need or emphasis on regulation or law. Conversely, because there has been little emphasis on regulation, others have had no choice but to rely on the family rather than the government or the courts. It is no coincidence that many ASEAN countries, with the exception of Singapore had inadequate or non-existent bankruptcy laws in the run up to the crisis. Equally, while there have been not inconsiderable efforts to create or extend bankruptcy laws and courts, the practical application of such progress has been at best patchy. The natural instinct in many cases has been for the authorities to side with the family company or the debtor, in the context of an insolvency case whereby the creditors, in many cases foreigners, are seeking to take over the assets of the company. Taking a company away from the family that used to rule it is seen in the same light as severing a limb. In addition, in many cases the legal infrastructure that is supposed to enact this progress is either inadequately trained to execute the process or under paid and thus vulnerable to corruption. Here again, the institutional framework that Singapore has put in place serves it well.

How does one get around this problem? Clearly, Asia is not going to reject completely its previous model of developing family-owned companies, nor should it. That said, one of the many lessons of the Asian crisis is that a lack of appropriate regulation and law does have a cost, and in some cases that cost can be quite significant. In this context, it is up to Asian authorities to provide the lead in the matter, creating the appropriate regulatory framework as well as incentives to ensure that it works in practice.

■ External over-reliance

In a world of anything approximating free trade, it is of course impossible to be "free" of external factors. In Asia's case however, it has been over-dependent on the outside world in a number of key ways, which have both shaped its initial growth phase - reliance on exports for industrial expansion - and played a key role in the Asian crisis. First off, on the manufacturing side, Asia's dependence on the electronics industry, and more specifically on high volume but not necessarily highly value-added technology, was graphically demonstrated by the events of 1996-1997 when semiconductor prices collapsed, thus severely hitting Asian exports. In 1995 and 1996, electronics, including most notably semiconductor chips, made up an increasingly large proportion of Asian exports - an average of 34% taking Singapore, Malaysia, Korea, the Philippines, Thailand, Taiwan and Hong Kong as a group. As the Asian Development Bank noted, manufacturers in Singapore prior to the crisis made up 40% of the world's disk drives, while one third of PC microprocessors were packaged in Malaysia. Some 8 out of every 10 circuit boards in the world and half the world's keyboards were made in Taiwan. By the beginning of 1996, Asia accounted for over 50% of world memory chip sales.

In the end, there has been a major rebound in semiconductor prices and sales which has in turn contributed in a not so insignificant way to the rebound in Asian exports, but this is a cyclical rebound. It does not give an answer as to how Asia deals with the problem going forward. Over the long term, Asian manufacturers have clearly to go further up the value-added chain, producing more technologically advanced products. In addition, they need to be the manufacturers of those chips rather than just an export base of Japanese or U.S. companies. Short term - in order to build a base to achieve those worthy aims - the industry has to be rationalised. Asia still has far too much capacity relative to *domestic* demand, thus making it persistently vulnerable to downturns in external demand, for instance, a marked slowdown in the U.S. In addition, Asia as a whole has to build up its own technological capacity, much as Taiwan, Korea and Singapore have done in specific examples. Neither the U.S. nor Japan - especially not Japan - are going to hand this technology over to Asia on a platter. Note that I am talking about Asian industry developing it, with a (modest) helping hand from the government. I am most certainly not talking about government-directed national technology drives - which can be variously called "white elephants" or perhaps more accurately "black holes", sucking in finances and producing little if any return.

Asian external over-reliance took many forms. On the finance side, the most obvious example was exposure to foreign-currency denominated debt which occurred largely because domestic capital markets were not sufficiently developed and many central banks did not have much track record of inflation fighting with the result that domestic risk premiums were substantially higher than in dollar assets, thus causing dollar debt to be attractive, particularly in an environment of perceived lack of foreign exchange risk. The Asian institutional investor base remained lamentably small, thus causing Asia to remain dependent on foreign investors.

Building a New Growth Platform Based on Lessons and Long-Term Strengths

■ Lessons

The first lesson from the crisis is that Asia made tremendous progress in catching up with the Western economies, but that progress was not good enough and it will never be. When Asia started to pat itself on the back for its achievements, understandably, it was also the time when it stopped seeking to improve and stopped trying to catch up. For many in Asia, they had not only caught up but also surpassed the West, and certainly in terms of the GDP per capita that was true. Overall national advancement is more than just a question of GDP growth. That is a key lesson from the crisis.

The second is that many of Asia's supposedly competitive markets were not free markets at all. What asset markets were available were in many cases greatly distorted by targeted credit policies. The market pricing mechanism was not allowed to function and thus valuations and reality diverged strongly from each other. The crash in Asian markets was simply a righting, a re-balancing of this process, an extremely painful experience to be sure, but a necessary if not crucial one in the development of Asia. Within this, the main lesson is that Asia's lack of deep and developed bond markets was a critical weakness that cannot be allowed to continue. A bond market provides most importantly the requisite secondary market trading ability which ensures timely, inexpensive (in relative terms), long-term funding. It allows companies not only to grow, but also to invest for the future. The virtue of necessity will see that the events of 1997 and 1998 will in retrospect mark the birth of sustainable, liquid and deep domestic bond markets in Asia. In order to have one; a country needs to create a deep institutional investor base - the buyers of these bonds. Pension fund industries, which exist only in Singapore and Malaysia to any notable extent in the form of national provident funds, need to created and built up. Especially given that some Asian countries face demographic problems going forward - not as severe perhaps as those in Japan but significant nevertheless - pension funds need to be created in order to save for the future. Government budgets will not be sufficient to deal with the financial burden that the ageing of Asia will represent, nor should they be. For countries to have savings rates of 30-35% and not have a pension fund industry, national or private to better allocate the financial resources of that, both for the private individual and the economy, is almost criminal. Going forward, the creation of the Asian national domestic bond markets is one of the most important tasks, which faces national governments. To have a domestic bond market, the institutional infrastructure needs to be created. Hong Kong and Singapore have strong and well-respected central banks and regulators. In this regard, the development of the domestic bond markets in the likes of Thailand has been one of the truly positive aspects of the crisis and subsequently, helped in large part by the launch of benchmark government issues which has begun the process of developing a transparent domestic yield curve off which Thai corporates can price their own issues.

Asian corporate finance directors, who have largely used internal cash flow, bank loans and foreign currency-denominated bonds to meet their funding needs and focused on securing and maintaining revenue growth will have to change those mindsets. In the future, and in the wake of the massive corporate restructuring process which will take place over the next two years, they will have to take greater account of driving down costs, both in manufacturing and financial terms. From a funding perspective, this can best be achieved by issuing long-term debt. In addition, those that are already highly geared (which have high debt-to-equity ratios) will have to reduce that degree of leverage if they want to prosper, increasing their equity capital or reducing debt, or both. Either way, the degree of control that they exercised in the past will have to be reduced.

Along with the idea of the need for greater regulation and supervision, of the need for the strengthening of institutions in order to mitigate against the worst side effects of family/contact/crony capitalism, however one likes to define it, there must be the realisation that transparency is important. Prior to the crisis, Asia was the worst of the three main emerging market regions for corporate transparency. Family-run businesses that did not have to answer to anybody in the past will have to increasingly answer to shareholders and bond-buyers if they want their funding needs to be met. Business networks will not be able to meet their funding needs entirely, forcing them to tap the financial markets in one way or another. Institutional investors, whether domestic or international, are increasingly demanding a level playing field for issues such as corporate transparency. Any country in the world that says no to this will simply be bypassed and thus will not be able to achieve the requisite funding. This comes to the heart of the problem. "Crony capitalism" cannot go on. It has had its day. To allow it to go on is to risk a reversal of economic progress, to see such countries being bypassed by direct and portfolio investment, not necessarily (though justifiably) for any moral reason, but because crony capitalism inevitably produces a collapse in returns. It is what Marx and Lenin talked about when they predicted the demise of capitalism. Though they completely underestimated the ability of the market itself to develop and change to suit changing conditions, they saw that certain types of capitalism were inherently inefficient. Crony capitalism left unchecked will inevitably produce ever-decreasing rates of return. Why? Because it distorts the pricing mechanism. The market is not allowed to price goods and services correctly and this leads to incorrect pricing which has serious - and potentially fatal - consequences for business. Crony capitalism was indeed a major cause of the Asian crisis, not the only one, but an important one. It is for precisely this reason that Thailand, Indonesia and Korea suffered major structural damage to their economies - and equally why Hong Kong and Singapore did not.

Finally, there should be the recognition that the next stage of growth will be built not on exporting to the West, but on opening up Asian economies to free trade with each other. It will be based on self-reliance, on creating an Asian way rather than responding to the whims of Western consumer demand. The prospect of AFTA (Asian Free Trade Area) by 2003 remains in place. Asian governments can seek to direct the process, but the best way is to simply scrap all tariff and non-tariff barriers and allow market processes to flourish. The result would be an Asian economic and financial explosion the likes of which would make the achievements of the last two decades pail into insignificance. This would have the added benefit of restructuring their domestic economies in the process. Capital would be allocated more efficiently because it would seek the highest returns. Those with advanced markets and strong institutions would prosper, those without would have to run to catch up or risk falling behind. Intra-Asian trade already makes up some 40% of the total trade. Going forward, it is set to make up a majority of total Asian trade given the expectation that after a brief (in historical terms) lull of 1-2 years, the rise of the new Asian middle class will resume. Asian governments must seek to support domestic financial and manufacturing business through market-driven policies in order to ensure this rise will not simply renew Asian external dependency but lead to broad-based domestic prosperity. Given their successes to date, the events of the crisis notwithstanding, they are well capable of achieving these goals.

The next cycle will see the rise of the Asian shareholder - and none too soon! Up to now, stock markets have been vehicles for domestic speculation by retail investors. In relative terms, there has been little (or any) focus on corporate fundamentals. That will change. The challenge will be for governments to mould the needs of the global economy to the demands of Asian culture - neo-capitalism with Asian characteristics. That said, the market economy must be (once and for all) embraced. It is that simple. The age of the great Asian credit cycle is gone. The next cycle of growth, following the period of restructuring will be founded on (relative) returns, on the bottom line, on earnings per share.

■ Long-term strengths

While some see the previous Asian success story as merely the latest in a long line of national and regional improvement, I would offer a radically different argument. The Asian success story has not been a "Miracle" as the World Bank described, but it has not been any "mere" event either. The results of Asia's elevation from war and famine to near first-world status have indeed been miraculous, for want of a better word. They have been extraordinary, exceptional, out-performing any single event in the global emerging markets and many in the emerged world. As we saw earlier, the success story was built on a virtuous combination of high savings' and higher investment rates, a focus on exports, lean governments and a refusal to be compassionate to the domestic citizenry, thus forcing self-reliance and a ruthless, entrepreneurial spirit. Above all, it was built on sheer hard work. In addition, a key characteristic of all three stages of Asia's recent development - the success story, the crisis and the subsequent recovery - has been the remarkable flexibility of Asia and Asians to changing circumstances. Such flexibility is not universal, as the unemployed of the European Union, symptomatic of the fettered and rigid European labour markets could attest. The speed of the recovery is ample testimony of the flexibility with which Asian governments and their citizens reacted to the crisis.

Asia needs to be flexible if the recovery is to continue. As a result of the crisis, several Asian governments gained control of at least half the economy. In Indonesia, the figure is probably around 70%. In order to gain the necessary liquidity to re-capitalise itself, Asia needs the flexibility to allow for a reduction in influence and control through the privatisation of these assets. There will be a temptation as the recovery takes hold to demand prices that are not necessarily in line with the fundamental dynamics of supply and demand. That temptation must be resisted. As strange as it may sound for some, the nationality of the investor has no direct bearing to the health of the company in which the investment is made. In any case, companies that are protected will eventually go to the wall in the current environment due to diminishing returns. They will simply not be able to compete. A key ingredient of the success story in Asia was that Asians took Western technology and skills and used them for their own ends. This is not to negate the technology created in Asia itself. It is simply to recognise the contribution that Western technology made and the flexibility Asia employed to exploit it for Asia's gain. The same approach should be used this time to allow for the privatisation of assets and the increasing share of domestic capital foreign investors will own in Asian countries. Asia to a great extent built its success story on the back of high standards of education as the primary and secondary levels, yet it is at the university level where parts of Asia fall down in relative terms, resulting in an Asian brain drain where the sons and daughters of wealthy Asians go abroad to study - and many times do not come back! For Asia, this is a tragic waste of human capital. Education has been a traditional strength, but Asia needs to upgrade that educational capacity at the university level in order to stop this brain drain and in order to provide the knowledge base for the creation of its own regional technology base. In the meantime, it can learn from others, but that is not the answer over the long term.

If Asia continues to focus on maintaining lean governments, fostering a favourable environment for high savings' rates and creating budget surpluses or at the least minimising deficits, it will provide the same sort of solid platform which helped create the Asian success story in the first place. Once the remaining intra-Asian trade barriers are torn down, the rocket fuel for future expansion will be provided. In addition, this should help maintain regional security. If Asian countries are tied ever closer through means of free trade, they will have less incentive to go to war with each other. At the microeconomic level, there is a clear choice between maintaining the policies of the past or adopting a more flexible approach as to improve on the model.

We need to reflect on the political and economic after-effects of the Asian crisis and the subsequent recovery. In the 1980s, Latin America went through an earth-shattering crisis of its own, famously described as the "Lost Decade". In the wake of the Asian crisis, there were many that rushed to suggest that Asia would experience a similar fate. In truth, while the 1980s were a tough time for Latin American economies, the decade was not entirely "lost", because it was during that time that the economic reform finally took hold in the region. Granted, the Mexican crisis of 1994-1995 showed that the process of economic reform in Latin America was not yet complete by that stage, however it had achieved major successes. Mexico in 1995 remains a salutary lesson for those who think that Asia will never again experience financial or economic crisis, just as it should have been a lesson for Asia watchers from 1995-1997 (though sadly, it was ignored by many). So where does Asia go from here? For this, we turn to the shark-infested waters of prediction, in the next chapter.

CHAPTER 8

THE OUTLOOK – WHERE ASIA GOES FROM HERE

Make no mistake about it. I am a bull on Asia. In typical emerging market fashion, there is still a lot of corruption in some countries. The Asian crisis proved that there are a lot of badly run governments, businesses and banks in Asia. Markets were not free and capital was certainly not allocated efficiently. It will take time to make significant changes in this. However, as we looked at in the last chapter, Asia's flexibility, lessons it has learned from the Asian crisis and the region's long-term strengths should serve it well in dealing with this new decade.

Some of the reforms that has been undertaken already have been significant, not least in Korea and for the reason among many that it is leading the pack of Asian countries which are emerging from recession to economic recovery. Equally, some of the reforms have been little more than skin deep. Overall, however, the next few years should see a continuing process of restructuring and improvement in Asia, which should provide a more solid foundation for long-term growth than that which existed in the mid-1990s. The expectation of our bank is that Asian growth is likely to be even better in 2000 than it was in 1999, based on three factors. For a start, we have the prospect of improving the OECD growth, particularly in Japan and the

EU, coupled with a relatively mild slowdown in the U.S. In addition, inter-regional trade is back on track, after pulling the region down in 1997-1998. Presently, this contributes to around 40% of total Asian trade, but going forward it should soon represent a majority of Asian trade, and in any case should continue to aid fundamental economic recovery in the region. Finally, better than expected GDP growth in Asia and low nominal interest rates should actually boost the financial restructuring process in Asia in 2000 and 2001.

On the first point, U.S. growth is expected to slow only modestly from 4.2% in 1999 to 3.6% in 2000 and 3.1% in 2001. Japan, meanwhile, should grow 1.3% in 1999 and 1.9% in 2000 while the Euro area should see a growth of 2.0% in 1999 and 3.2% in 2000. The pickup in growth in Japan and the EU should be accompanied by persistently low price pressure. Continued deflation is expected in Japan with annual CPI for 2000 of -0.2%, and the CPI rising modestly in the euro area to 1.6% in 2000 from 1.1%. Together, this should provide a solid platform for Asian exports in 2000 and 2001. Granted, a slowdown in the U.S. will hurt those exporters which are exposed to the U.S. in particular - the Philippines - but there could well be a shift of company exports to the EU and Japan to meet rising demand there.

As regards Asian inter-regional trade, Asian exports should in particular be supported by Japan's recovery, however fragile that recovery remains at present. From 1985-1993, Asia's trade deficit with Japan rose from around USD9 billion to over USD54 billion. This was largely because Japanese manufacturers set up production capacity in the ASEAN in order to use this as an export platform for third markets such as the U.S. and Europe, avoiding the high cost base back home in Japan and the vigilance of the U.S. Trade Representative's office with regard to the bilateral U.S.-Japan trade deficit. These manufacturers subsequently imported parts from Japan which were then put together to form the finished product, which was exported elsewhere. Consequently, much of Asia's trade deficit with Japan was due to the Japanese manufacturing presence within Asia. The Asian crisis, which caused a collapse in Asian demand and political and economic stability in some parts, caused this trade deficit to be narrowed significantly, though not eliminated. Going forward, rising Japanese demand should narrow it further, though this will be offset by rising Japanese exports to Asia to meet the recovery. In any case, the volume of Asian exports to Japan and the rest of the region has been rising for some time, but this is now also the case in terms of value. Our view is that this strengthening trade picture is sustainable, though one concern is the electronics' cycle - which for now seems to be doing fine.

Nominal interest rates fell significantly in Asia in 1998-1999 and with significant spare capacity still in many economies they should be able to stay low through most of 2000 as demand pull pressures should remain absent for some time. Credit demand in the region has remained relatively muted given the burden to national banking systems of non-performing loans which has effectively meant that banks have sought first to repair their own balance sheets rather than lend to their corporate sectors. However, we expect credit demand to pick up. Certainly, we should now be able to say that we are no longer facing a credit crunch, which was certainly a major risk in the second half of 1998. Banks have been re-broadly capitalised, thus barring individual exceptions there should be growing liquidity going forward of local Asian banks to increase lending, albeit gradually and cautiously. Note that this is consistent with recoveries seen in other emerging markets where credit demand typically lagged by about 9 months.

Up until recently, this has been pretty much a "credit-less" recovery that we have seen in Asia with loan growth seen mainly in mortgages rather than in lending to industry. Despite this, economic growth has been on the strong side of general expectations and we see no reason why this should not continue, particularly as we anticipate modestly rising regional credit demand this year. Credit-less recovery reflects two key things - low investment demand, that is low capacity utilisation following over-investment in many Asian industries, and better cash flow due to currency depreciation, lower interest rates and lower tax bills. Credit-less recoveries have been the norm after banking crises in the emerging markets and the norm lag after which credit demand resumes has been between 9-12 months.

Better growth prospects and rising credit demand should mean a greater need for external finance, which in turn means dealing with existing creditors. These, mostly banks, are now better capitalised and hence better positioned than previously to restructure. Equally, better growth prospects mean fewer losses than earlier expected at the microeconomic level in terms of banks and corporations. Thus, we expect strategic non-performing loans to plummet in 2000, a further boost to recovery. Lastly, China no longer appears to be the potentially de-stabilising force for the Asian region it once seemed to be. Going into year-end, Chinese exports were still growing at a pace of over 20% year-on-year, helped in large part by the fall in the value of the dollar against the *yen* and the Asian regional recovery. China still recorded a trade surplus for the full year of 1999 of almost USD30 billion, more than the exports of many emerging markets. This and a significant reduction in the Chinese *yuan*'s over-valuation on a REER (Real Effective Exchange Rate) basis suggests a lessened likelihood of a *yuan* devaluation any time soon, which in turn should mean that the Asian recovery story should not be jeopardised, at least not from this source. In addition, the WTO should mean opportunities to invest in China and a faster domestic reform process. As noted earlier in this book, it should mean a move to greater exchange rate flexibility through the widening of the *yuan*'s trading band, though this should not cause too much concern.

	GDP				CPI		
	1998	1999	2000	2001	1999	2000	2001
China	7.8%	7.0	7.0	7.0	-1.4%	+0.2	+1.5
Hong Kong	-5.1	+1.3	2.7	4.0	-3.9	+1.3	2.5
Indonesia	-13.2	+0.2	2.4	3.7	22.0	5.0	13.0
Korea	-5.8	+10.5	8.9	6.2	1.0	4.0	3.5
Malaysia	-7.5	+4.8	5.2	6.0	2.8	3.0	3.5
Philippine	-0.5	+2.9	3.4	3.9	7.0	6.6	7.5
Singapore	0.3	5.2	6.0	5.6	0.6	1.8	2.0
Taiwan	4.7	5.3	6.2	5.8	0.4	1.8	1.8
Thailand	-9.4	+4.0	5.2	6.0	0.2	1.2	2.0

Source: Market data/forecasts

In terms of individual country outlooks, I present these below:

INDONESIA

The first signs of economic stabilisation were seen in the second half of last year and this year should see confirmed economic recovery, at least in terms of the headline growth figure. The country's shattered banking system remains a drag on growth given its relative inability to lend. On the positive side, this should cause domestic price pressures to remain muted for some time to come, a positive for the local fixed income market. The efforts of the Indonesian Bank Restructuring Agency should finally pay some dividends this year and the next in terms of re-capitalising the system as a whole. In addition, the fact that the domestic economy remains so fragile should keep the trade and current account balances in surplus, an important consideration both for the *rupiah* and the fiscal account. A number of issues have to be cleared up before Indonesia can truly emerge into fundamental recovery, both political and economic. On the political side, the election of President Wahid under the country's new and more democratic electoral system has clearly been a positive move, giving the Indonesian people a greater degree of influence than arguably they have ever had. However, the issues of east Timor and the Aceh province remain divisive within Indonesia and still have the potential to cause instability. On the economic side, the degree of corporate and banking debt restructuring remains inadequate, as does the framework for resolving bankruptcy issues. It will take some considerable time for this to be worked out. Fundamentally, the *rupiah* looks to have a cautiously positive outlook as the economy crawls its way out of the mire of recession.

KOREA

Korea is the leader of the pack and there is little prospect of that changing any time soon. After contracting almost 6% in 1998, the economy expanded over 10% in 1999, a truly remarkable performance. The issue of the collapse of Daewoo Group justifiably caused some concern among investors in the second half of last year, however this appears to have merely spurred on the authorities towards greater effort at restructuring the *chaebol* and the banking system. This is not to say that such efforts are anywhere near complete, however they appear further advanced than elsewhere in the region, and consequently Korea's status as leader of the recovery is no coincidence. Korean exports are booming as a result of three factors: the strong *yen* that makes them more competitive against their Japanese counterparts for third markets, persistently strong U.S. demand and the Asian regional recovery. The domestic recovery in Korea should reduce the absolute levels of trade and current account surpluses Korea will record to 3.2% of the GDP in 2000 as against 5.7% in 1999 and 12.4% in 1998. However, rising portfolio and foreign direct investment, anticipating a persistently strong growth trajectory should still offset this decline in the current account surplus. Overall, 2000 and 2001 should be relatively positive years for the Korean *won* and Korean assets, barring further external shocks, though the basing effect of being compared to 1999's exceptional performance could disappoint some.

PHILIPPINES

I said in **Asia Falling** and I still maintain that the Philippines was lucky that the Asian crisis happened when it did, in 1997, given that the Philippine property market was only just starting to take off and thus the exposure of the local banking system to asset price deflation was significantly less. That said, the Philippine *peso* and the local asset markets did not have a particularly good second half of 1999, weighed down by initial broad Asian currency weakness and then domestic concerns regarding the rising budget deficit. In addition, the Philippines rarely takes well to tighter Fed policy in the U.S. given its dependency on dollar-based commodities, notably oil. The fiscal position of the Philippines remains the one main concern. Revenues have been disappointing as the main tax paying sectors - industrial and manufacturing - are still down. In addition, bumper agricultural crops have not fed through to a strong consumption recovery as farmers have focused on paying off debts accumulated during the El Nino period. Aside from the fiscal account, the overall economic outlook is relatively positive, with growth recovering slowly, albeit off a modest base, and the current account balance showing unusually healthy surpluses. Structurally, the Philippines has suffered far less than the likes of Korea, Indonesia or Thailand during the crisis, yet it remains plagued by its dependency on imported oil which necessitates that currency depreciation and inadequate tax collection be fought vigorously.

SINGAPORE

In the depths of the Asian crisis, Singapore's economy still showed positive growth in 1998. At the risk of repetition, this was a remarkable performance. For 2000-2001, the city-state should continue to see strong low-inflation growth following the performance of just over 5% in 1999. Despite this some degree of vigilance is warranted given the strength of the recovery in domestic demand. Given this, we could well see the authorities guiding the Singapore dollar modestly higher against other currencies in order to ward off any threat of future inflation. If the Singapore economy maintains good growth momentum, then a rapidly closing output gap, tighter labour market conditions and the enhanced imported inflation threat from higher oil prices could potentially lead to a modest interest rate tightening in the second half of this year. In terms of the trade account, strength in semiconductor prices is clearly helping boost Singapore's Non-Oil Domestic Exports, given that electronics make up around 70% of this. The current account surplus should decline modestly in 2000 and 2001 due to recovery in the domestic economy, however it should still be 14.7% and 12.4% of the GDP respectively.

TAIWAN

Taiwan's low corporate debt levels have served it well in terms of managing through the crisis. Even in 1998, Taiwan's economy by some 4.7% and over 6% growth is expected for 2000. Inflation wasn't a problem prior to the crisis and it is even less so now given that domestic demand continues to lag behind the recovery in the export sector. Taiwan has the advantage of producing high value-added technology, which makes it less dependent - though not completely free - of the need to import Japanese parts. The current account surplus should continue to show modest surpluses of just over 1% of the GDP even when the domestic economy finally achieves sustainable recovery given the strength of Taiwan's export sector, somewhat offsetting the budget deficit which should amount to 2.9%

of the GDP compared to around 2.5% in 1999. Going forward, there is little on the immediate economic horizon to dampen investor keenness, though the political aspect clearly has the potential to unsettle investors. Until the issue of reunification with China is solved once and for all, Taiwan will continue to have a higher risk premium than its economic fundamentals otherwise deserve.

THAILAND

Local interest rates remain soft and in the immediate term, this is unlikely to change. Prior to the year-end, the Bank of Thailand said it intended to build up its oversold forward swap book to some USD4 billion from USD3.1 billion in order to provide excess *baht* liquidity where and when needed going into the Y2K. After the year-end, paradoxically, there was a modest spike up in the market interest rates as such excess liquidity was withdrawn. On a 12-month view however, we expect interest rates to remain broadly steady. Certainly, there is no immediate prospect or need for monetary tightening in Thailand given the degree of slack still in the economy and the extent of non-performing loans in the banking system which acts as a burden on demand, albeit indirectly. Thailand's fundamental outlook remains positive. Both the external and domestic sectors are seeing fundamental recovery. In addition, NPLs appear to have finally peaked, falling for six straight months after a high of 47.70% reached in May last year. Going forward, should NPLs continue to decline, this might well act as an accelerator to growth, a prospect that is not yet necessarily priced into the local asset markets or the *baht*. Potential negatives are the high oil price and politics. In terms of the former, a high oil price is a fundamental negative for the *baht* given that over 90% of Thailand's oil needs are imported, which could lead to imported inflation going forward. On the latter, the government of Chuan Leepkai appears secure ahead of upcoming elections given its parliamentary majority, however efforts by the opposition to stall the reform process show that there is still potential for occasional market upsets.

CHALLENGES AHEAD

As I said, I remain bullish on the region, with the consistent qualification that hard decisions have to continue to be taken, not least in the realms of corporate and bank restructuring. That said, Asia will, going forward face a number of important challenges, the most important could be the demographic challenge. While Asia benefited as a region in the last two decades from the so-called "demographic transition", that is the period when a previous increase in the birth rate and improving life conditions result in a rapid increase in the labour force. However, going forward, these same countries will potentially face an increasing financial burden that will be the result of the ageing of their populations. Prior to the Asian crisis, few countries provided much of a social safety net for the reasons that I have already gone into. However, helping the poor and providing such a social safety net was part of the programmes constructed by the IMF and World Bank for programme countries. Equally, the need to develop pension systems will require some degree of government intervention since the domestic corporate base of some countries cannot presently afford this burden. As Asian populations get older, these social expenses will become increasingly expensive, a hitherto unfamiliar burden to Asian governments. This is not yet a problem and will not be for some time, but it is well worth considering ahead of time. Furthermore, rising proportions of retirees will have a profound effect on savings rates and growth - hurting both. As countries achieve a certain degree of wealth, birth rates start to fall back - either because of government-oriented policies or through improving living conditions which serve to provide a lesser necessity and focus for procreation - as economies advance, women gain greater equality, freedom and choice. This causes changes in the overall demographic make up - from having lots of infants and a relatively small elderly population, there is a shift to a declining proportion of children, and a far higher proportion of adults who are then free (or not) to join the labour force. It is this that provides the demographic boost to the country's economy. This means that the country's government is able to gain greater tax revenues, a more available (and thus cheaper) workforce and less dependent elements - children and the elderly - within the economy, thus reducing any financial burden on the budget. This demographic change or transition not only benefits the budget and the economy but also serves as a boost to savings' rates - thus providing the necessary financial fuel for private and government investment. When this significant increase in the adult labour force moves further down the line, becoming elderly, the financial burden on the economy becomes greater as the dependants make up a greater proportion of the population.

As countries become older, savings' rates are bound to decline. The key is how investment performs while this is happening. If investment is maintained at high levels and savings' rates fall, then the country will be condemning itself to import capital rather than export it. Investment rates have to be cut when this happens in order to ensure that external over-reliance is avoided. This however in turn affects the growth rate, which as a consequence is bound to slow. All this sounds quite gloomy, adding to Asia's economic woes. There are two reasons why this is not the case however. Firstly, because the next wave of children will be hitting the labour market as the first (major) wave goes on to the elderly/dependent stage. While the second wave might be smaller in actual numbers, given those declining birth rates, it will still act as a catalyst for future growth. In addition, attempts to improve TFP and education should mean that the quality would more than make up for lack of quantity. The countries of the more developed East Asia will face this problem - and this opportunity - just as Japan does right now. The second reason to be optimistic is because there are countries that have yet to go through this demographic transition or at least have not yet fully experienced it. This is most notably the case in South Asia - in India, Pakistan, Bangladesh and Sri Lanka - and to a certain extent in South East Asia and China - though one could argue in China's case that it has excessive labour potential rather than a deficit given the massive corporate restructuring which is needed there. India and Pakistan in particular are only just starting to see the economic benefits of this demographic transition period, if they don't let politics or war interfere with economic progress. Finally, the lesson of the U.S. boom in the 1990s is that ageing populations within mature economies that do not expect to receive much of a state pension when they retire increasingly seek to finance their own retirement through asset market investment.

A further challenge for Asia will be to deal with its dependency on external energy sources. Given the relative paucity of available (and easily tapped) energy in Asia, Asia faces a number of energy shortages - and thus external over-reliance - including oil, coal and natural gas. Japan, China and all the South East Asian nations, apart from Malaysia and Indonesia which have their own resources in sufficient quantity, are thus forced to import their needs. This is costly and opens them up to foreign exchange and inflation risk - for instance, the Philippines imports 95% of its energy needs and thus the economy experiences major inflationary pressures when the dollar rises sharply against the Philippine *peso*, which then have to be offset by monetary and/or fiscal policy. Lack of immediately available energy resources causes countries to search elsewhere or at least in areas, which are not immediately obvious. This in turn can cause confrontation with other countries who dispute land/sea claims as their own - witness the dispute between China and Vietnam over sea territory in the South China sea, as well as the Diaoyu island dispute between China, Taiwan and Japan. Without tapping new sources of energy reserves, such as those in the South China sea elsewhere - and thus resolving conflicts in rapid order for mutual benefit - Asia's dependence will not only be maintained but will actually increase. At present, Asia consumes around a quarter of the global energy production. As a result of the ongoing period of economic consolidation, the Asian demand is likely to continue to increase.

A by-product of the Asian demand for energy and Asia's ascendancy over the past two decades has been a proportional ascendancy in the levels of pollution in Asia. Asian rivers are estimated to contain 3-4 times the world average of faecal pollutants. Over the last three decades, Asia has lost some 50% of its forests and 50% of its fish stocks. Urban pollution will continue to increase because an ever-increasing proportion of Asian population will migrate to the cities. Over the next two decades, if we look back, then extrapolate and also add on for anticipated acceleration of this process, around 50-55% of Asian populations could live in cities by the end of that period. This is potentially good news for growth and productivity, but awful news in terms of pollution. Asia is not far away from seeing its pollution levels acting as a dampener on growth. In addition, the longer Asian countries wait to do something about the pollution levels being created, the more it will cost them to clean the mess up and thus the greater the financial burden on the government budget and on savings. Japan was in a similar situation when it went through its own initial demographic transition phase in the 60s and early 70s.

Eventually, popular demand for change resulted in government action. The hope is that the same will happen in Asia.

A further challenge that Asia faces is to reduce poverty and make national income distribution more equitable. After all, what is economic development about if it is not about improving people's standards and conditions of living, and thus in turn reducing poverty? Growth in India and Pakistan in particular, despite the improvements made to date and the consequent emergence of a substantial (powerful and vocal) middle class in both countries, continues to be felt by an insufficient number of people. The trickle down effect does not trickle down - or rather it is in the form of minute drops rather than a torrent. How can this be alleviated? As someone who believes profoundly in the benefits of the market my answer has to be to open up the economy more fully to market-driven forces. Government can aid the worst off, in the process not only giving them financial and social aid, but providing training and education so that they do not remain dependent and thus provide a greater contribution, both to themselves and the economy.

Finally, Asian governments face the challenge of having to pay the bill for the fiscal expansion of 1998-2000, while seeking to avoid stamping on the fiscal brakes too hard and damaging the recovery. They will thus be faced with three choices: hike taxes, cut spending or accelerate the privatisation programme. While the recoveries remain fragile, increasing corporate taxes is the least dangerous option, avoiding the sort of popular backlash that a hike in personal income taxes might cause. Equally, spending cuts will be difficult while the worst effects of the Asian crisis remain significant. Thus, on a rather bullish note, the necessity of paying down debt, both interest and principle could cause an acceleration in the privatisation process, overcoming the reluctance of some governments to let go of control of these nationalised assets. That said, this alone would not be enough. At some point, there will have to be a trend change in Asian regional fiscal policy towards consolidation and rationalisation. Given the degree of fiscal expansion that we have seen to date, even if Asian governments begin cutting budget deficits earnestly from 2001 onwards, the burden of interest payments will mean that total government debt continues to rise for several years, barring a major fire-sale of nationalised assets. Either way, Asia is faced with Japan's choice of letting go a greater amount of control and thus paying down debt or taking on an increasing share of the economy within the state. Let us hope it makes the right choice.

Can growth resume at pre-crisis rates over the long term? The most likely answer is "no", but I would suggest that that is no bad thing. Such growth rates were to a large extent a reflection of Asia's stage of development. Going forward, the quality of growth will be more important than the quantity per se. High savings' rates and hard work will be important drivers of growth, but it will necessitate free and open trade and capital markets as the next major catalyst for regional economic expansion to be found. The medium-term need for fiscal consolidation, coupled with the ageing of Asia's population will also present further obstacles to maintaining high growth rates. In addition, at the microeconomic level, the complete restructuring of corporate and banking sectors will take years rather than months. Asia's over-reliance on external demand will mean that other sources of growth will be looked for. This should mean that domestic competition would be rapidly increased in those countries where it remains limited. While we continue to see the initial stages of the Asian recovery, the opportunity for participating in that recovery and in that restructuring process is abound. Investing in the new Asia is indeed the subject of the next chapter.

CHAPTER 9

THE OPPORTUNITY - WHERE TO INVEST (AND WHERE NOT TO)

The Asian recovery that we are now seeing will offer a tremendous opportunity for the investor, big and small. For a banker, this is an extremely exciting time to be focusing on Asia. Granted, to many it may not seem like that. Pause for a moment and think if you will: if you were given the opportunity, however humble and insignificant, to participate in trying to help the lives of two thirds of the world's people. I make no exaggeration and do not over-dramatise. When I come into work every day that is what I believe in. Banks like ours are providing the liquidity for the Asian recovery.

Focusing on money alone does not create wealth, prosperity and self-sufficiency. Having a vision creates them. The vision I have is that I can play a small part in guiding the investment to those areas of high value - and equally keeping it away from where value is insufficient. Bankers have responsibility. We have a responsibility to inform and guide, where possible and appropriate, the governments and financial authorities of emerging markets to the extent that they no longer need such guidance. We have a responsibility to our shareholders and to our customers. Asia is where Latin America was in the wake of the debt crisis of 1980-82, only more stable politically. The opportunity for us as a bank to work in partnership with governments, customers and shareholders to help rebuild Asia is monumental. It is not just an opportunity, but a responsibility. To shirk it would be unthinkable. Value, opportunity, and ultimately wealth will come out of this work - this hard work. Its root, its wellspring is the vision of helping to rebuild Asia, of having the commitment to remain in hard times. The manufacturers of Asia make the "widgets", banks like us the liquidity. The cynics, the greedy, the corrupt have gone the way of the Asian crisis. Those who give a damn now have the opportunity to stand up and be counted.

Market capitalism is not only about self-enrichment, or even mainly so. It is about freedom from the slavery of tyranny, of vested interests, and of politics. Ask the poor whether they would rather eat or vote. Until you have enough to eat, there is no point in voting. It is an irrelevance relative to the threat of extinction. Freeing up trade and making investment decisions based solely on market pricing enables, empowers and levels the playing field as command economics has never done and will never do. The protestors at the Seattle WTO conference late last year argued against globalisation, saying that it caused massive environmental pollution. They may have a point, to the extent that environmental waste and degradation are by-products of consumption. Yet, what is the alternative? They should visit areas of the former Soviet Union and see environmental catastrophe in its purest form, the result not of free trade but of a planned economy, protected, bound and gagged. Environmental improvement cannot come at the expense of the economy. That is not an alternative. Equally, environmental pollution cannot be allowed to continue the way it is going. Consequently, a way must be found to use economic growth to reduce environmental pollution and degradation. If people are given sufficient incentive to reduce pollution, they will do so. While some may do it for ideology, the biggest incentive - and thus the most likely to succeed on a sustained basis if given the chance - is money. What relevance does this have to a chapter on investment opportunities? Think back to Japan in the 1960s and early 1970s, when it also was a polluted country. Those who had invested in pollution reduction companies in Japan at that time would have made a fortune. Asia's pollution problem stands ready, waiting for someone to clean it up and make money doing so.

WHAT THIS CHAPTER IS NOT!

Now, anyone who is reading this section for specific stock recommendations would be advised to bypass it altogether. I am not a stock market analyst and therefore I am not the person to give specific stock market and company recommendations.

LIKELY TRENDS AND OPPORTUNITIES

What I can do however is to look at the current macroeconomic conditions and suggest likely general trends, in terms of investment classes, currencies and economies. Within this, the most obvious thing to say about Asian economies is that those which experience major, fundamental recoveries will see their currencies prosper. This is not necessarily always the case. However, with regard to Asia, the region is generally experiencing a virtuous combination of current account and capital account surpluses, resulting in rising balance of payments' surpluses. The Korean *won* is the perfect example of this. Korea experienced a dramatic economic recovery in 1999, with its economy growing around 10%. As a result, substantial capital flows were attracted into the Korean stock market. Korea's recovery in 1999 led to a reduction in its trade surplus from around USD40 billion to USD25 billion. However, the combination of current and capital account surpluses was a very powerful, positive force for the Korean *won*, so much so that the dollar-*won* exchange rate fell in the second half of the year from around 1,220 to 1,124. Indeed, the *won* strengthened so much that the Korean authorities fought such strengthening through direct and indirect foreign exchange intervention, albeit with mixed success, to try to keep Korean exports competitive. Similar currency strength could be seen this year in other Asian currencies, notably the Thai *baht* and the Indonesian *rupiah*. Equally, at some stage the Singaporean authorities are likely to engineer a slightly stronger currency in order to avert inflationary pressure in 2000 and 2001.

While domestic recovery should be a spearhead for Asian currency and asset market gains, external factors will also play a part. Much will depend on the *yen* and the *yuan*. On the former, our bullish expectation for Japanese economic performance necessitates that we anticipate further, albeit modest *yen* strengthening, despite Ministry of Finance warnings and the occasional bout of Bank of Japan intervention. Fundamental strength in the *yen* should simply be too strong for such efforts to meddle with the exchange rate. As for the *yuan*, as suggested earlier the November 14 WTO bilateral trade-deal between the U.S. and China makes the creation of a dollar-Chinese *yuan*-trading band more likely. Technically, the *yuan* already has a daily volatility trading band of 1%, but what we could see this year is the expansion of that band to perhaps 5-10%, allowing market forces a much greater role in the determination of the currency's value.

ASIAN INTERNET FEVER

Within the Asian recovery, we could see a number of important trend changes. For a start, Asia is just trying to get to grips with the internet and the high tech boom which is sweeping the U.S. Corporate IPOs of internet start-ups in China are a symptom of this. Just as has been the case for some time in the U.S. where such IPOs are a daily event and anecdotes surrounding them are increasingly wild, there would appear to be no shortage of interest or money to invest in such ventures. Asia is behind the curve in terms of the hi-tech boom which has been sweeping the Silicon Valley for the last few years, but it is seeking to catch up fast. Given that it has just started in Asia, there would appear to be greater growth potential. However, as ever, there remains a danger that some companies will be listed on the Asian markets merely to capture such investor demand, rather than to boost working capital in order to expand their businesses. Such interest is coming on the back of the hi-tech boom in the U.S. Given that fact, should the U.S. "dot com" fever decline, this could quickly cause the recent increase internet in technology in Asia to fizzle out, albeit temporarily, hitting Asian companies early on in their investment and growth cycles. That said, if this does not occur, Asian investor and corporate interest in Internet technology is likely to continue to grow exponentially.

Within this, internet-friendly digital devices and gadgets could well be a new fad. The common thread will be value-added rather than price alone. Market research companies forecast that the global market for Internet appliances will be just under USD19 billion worth by 2003, compared to USD4.5 billion in 1999. Most of the digital Internet gadgets and appliances are actually made in Asia. Thus, whether or not Asian companies make them, Asian economies should benefit. In terms of Asian competition in the high-tech markets, Japan, followed by Korea and Taiwan should benefit the most given that they themselves produce substantial value-added technology, they are the inventors. Only countries and corporations which can be innovative and creative will be able to maintain and develop pricing power. This comes back to the issue of freeing up the market to create and price rather than relying on past policies which have focused on the government directing growth. Countries, which continue to rely on the state to provide economic development and direction, will fall by the wayside, the difference between them and free and open market economies getting ever wider by the day. The nature of globalisation, involving exponentially increasing competition, means that those who do not add value but merely imitate or rely on price will quickly see their margins eliminated. Even those who do add value will have to go ever higher up the value-added chain in order merely to remain profitable. Time stands still for no man, country or technology.

THE RETURN OF THE ASIAN CONSUMER

Before the crash, consumption was King in Hong Kong. Not only was the priority to buy the brightest and most glaring of consumer goods, it was also most assuredly to buy the most expensive. There was a definite stigma in buying bargains. While for the wealthiest, who were relatively unaffected by the crisis, this might still be the case, it is probably not for the majority. Indeed, many can no longer afford the luxury of only buying the most expensive items, while the shock of the financial and economic crash that was the Asian crisis has caused many to be more cautious about consuming given the threat of unemployment. The jobless rate in Hong Kong is currently above 6%, or treble what it was before the crisis and this picture is mirrored elsewhere in Asia, notably in Korea, Indonesia and Thailand. During the Asian Miracle years, Western consumer goods' companies set up and developed in Asia to meet exploding demand and offset weak demand back at home. Needless to say, the Asian crisis changed this scenario somewhat. Long-term fundamentals suggest that this will only be a blip in the development of an Asian consumer market though the confluence of several factors have to take place for this to happen. The Asian Miracle probably lifted some 500 million people out of poverty, not including Japan. The Asian crisis will not reverse that. While trend growth is likely to be slower in 2000-10 than it was in the 1990s, this is no bad thing if it is more sustainable and built on more fundamentally solid foundations. The Asian consumer will play an important part in this because this is naturally the next stage of economic development, following on from import substitution and the export platform for growth. In order for that to happen, trade barriers between Asian countries have to be torn down. The idea of an Asian Free Trade Area has to become a reality. It will. Asia has no choice given the creation of the European Union and the North-American Free Trade Area (NAFTA). Asian governments will soon realise, if they do not do so already, that this in the interests of their citizens and their countries.

The streets of Seoul were packed with shoppers, so were those of Shanghai, when I went there last October; so much for the crisis. Rumours of the death of Asian consumption are greatly exaggerated, as Mark Twain might have put it. Demographic forces are likely to propel it forward once more in any case. While the population of Japan is rapidly ageing, those of the ASEAN are generally younger. The one child policy in China has effectively increased the average age of the country, but the "little emperors", the progeny and latest generation of this policy still number around 100 million or 45% of the U.S. population. Those countries in Asia which are at a more advanced stage of economic development, the so-called new industrialised economies (NIEs) such as Hong Kong, Singapore, Taiwan and Korea generally have older populations relative to the likes of Thailand, Indonesia, the Philippines and India. After a sustainable base of growth has once again been created in these NIEs, the consumer focus is likely to be less on basic consumer goods, and rather on improving the quality of life. Naturally, to poor Asians, such an idea is an unaffordable luxury. The focus for them will remain firstly on survival and then on improving their living conditions if they can. For Asia's middle classes, such as they remain after the crisis, reducing pollution, increasing leisure time and boosting savings are likely to take on greater importance going forward.

Prior to the crisis, it was already starting to happen. After all, what industries focus on leisure? -- Airlines, the hotel industry and sports and recreation, along with fashion and high-end autos. At the height of the Asian boom, it is probably fair to say that Asian consumers were not getting a fair deal in terms of price. Indeed, in some cases they were getting completely ripped off, one of many reasons why the "bust" happened. The mushrooming of domestic airlines and hotels all over Asia did not only represent external tourist and business interest in the region, but also the rise of domestic Asian interest in travel and leisure activities. Clearly, the Asian crisis has put a severe dent in this process, however it is unlikely to derail it over the long term. Asia has so far avoided the threat of depression, which it faced in 1998. Consequently, the very nature of economic development and advancement should mean that such industries and trends prosper over the long term. This is not to say that Asian consumers will necessarily have the same priorities or focus as their Western counterparts. Indeed, within this, if there is a trend it is likely to be that Asian consumers focus increasingly on Asian brands. The rationalisation that is taking place in leisure-based industries in the wake of the crisis will only serve to make them more competitive. In turn, as an increasing proportion of Asians grow older, health care spending will increase markedly.

PROFITING IN THE RESTRUCTURING OF ASIA

The restructuring process is not only being conducted by the IMF and the Asian governments, but also in the private sector by management consultants, banks and educational companies which are increasing their presence in Asia in order to cope with the demand for knowledge on how to restructure. In the wake of the Asian crisis, there has been a substantial increase in demand for insolvency and corporate turnaround services. The demand by the IMF and acceptance by many Asian governments for the need for higher standards of corporate governance potentially offers a substantial opportunity for those with the appropriate set skills to provide this. Indeed, the World Bank and belatedly the IMF view the leading consultants and to a certain extent the banks as partners in the restructuring process of Asia.

Talk of the Asia or Pacific Century was clearly premature, as the Asian crisis has proved somewhat painful. However, this does not change the fact that Asia represents a substantial opportunity for the careful investor. The maxi devaluations of Asian currencies and economic collapses destroyed much of the Asian regional economy, but its foundations remain in place and it will simply return to be much more competitive than before. Many analysts make such statements and don't do anything about. For my part in mid-1998, I immediately put a quarter of my pension into Asian stocks. At the end of the day, you either believe or you don't and if you do, you put your money where your mouth is. This is not a trading position. That is a wholly different sort of investment. This is my pension: a put it away and don't look at it for the next 10 years kind of investment. The rationale behind this is that firstly I believe in the Asian story and secondly I remember the panic in the wake of the 1987 Crash. The golden rule of investment, "Buy from the desperate and sell to the greedy" is tried and tested. Baron de Rothschild adopted a similar strategy somewhat earlier when he was responsible for the advice, "the time to buy is when there is blood running in the streets".

Clearly, there is a risk to this bullish scenario and that risk is that Asia may take the wrong road and follow the one that Japan took in 1991. Personally, I don't think this will happen, not least for the reason that Asia has Japan's fine example to show it what not to do. In addition, Asian economies have followed a model of capitalism, which at the microeconomic level relies more on the small, and the flexible rather than developing *keiretsu* and bank networks. While this also has negative consequences in that there is a reluctance to allow small, family-owned businesses to be taken over by creditors for the purposes of face or tradition, small companies are the foundation for an entrepreneurial spirit and that is clearly needed to foster a true, fundamental and economic rebound. The Asian model of capitalism, which to a large extent in ASEAN is one dominated by the overseas Chinese communities, appears more flexible and much quicker to react to fundamental change. Hong Kong itself is a perfect example. Many considered that it had too many small companies, too many banks with China continuing to show an over-reliance on mainland growth. Despite the relative handicap of a currency board - it can't devalue its way to prosperity - Hong Kong's economy should still grow by 3.5% in 2000 after a 1.0% growth in 2000. Unlike Japan, non-performing loans remain relatively low. The banking system continues to be supervised by the vigilant HKMA. While one could argue that Hong Kong relies excessively on the property sector, with the result that the banking sector might have an excessive exposure to this, there is little question that Hong Kong's banking system is substantially more healthy than Japan's and was at this stage in its own crisis. Granted, the same cannot be said for the likes of Thailand and Indonesia, but there would appear to be no question that the authorities there fully realise the importance of speed in dealing with non-performing loans. Remember that historically, the banks are usually the last sector to emerge from a recession.

SORTING THE WHEAT FROM THE CHAFF

Television and the Internet mean that the economic cycles of the past, particularly with regard to economic booms and busts will occur more quickly. This is not to say that they will happen more frequently, but the pace by which an economy goes from boom to bust and back to boom will accelerate. Just as the Czech and the East German citizens switching on their TV sets in 1989 realised they had been lied to for the last 50 years changed the very nature of eastern Europe, so the delivery of all information, everywhere, instantly means those in recession are allowed much less time to recover. They have to recover quickly just to stay in the game. Unlike with corporations, national economics is not a zero sum game. International trade can potentially benefit all concerned and a substantial part of the rise of living standards globally over the past three decades is due to it. Yet globalisation demands that national economies "keep up" with the standards and performance of others, otherwise capital simply flows elsewhere, which in turn has real macroeconomic effects on the economy of the country concerned. The danger to this scenario in turn is that eventually countries reject the ideas of free trade. This risk should not be underestimated. The failure at the Seattle WTO conference last year was an important setback for the ideals of free trade, the gains from which should never be taken for granted. A rejection of free trade would be catastrophic for the global economy and for global asset markets. This is NOT my expectation, but the risk should never be underestimated. That way, one best avoids facing the situation.

At a national level, those which are likely to prosper within the Asian region are those which bring value-added quality to the table, those which develop their own skill and technology bases, and those which increase Total Factor Productivity (TFP) within an economy. If one has to pick countries within Asia that are likely to outperform over the next decade, one first has to base the idea of economic out-performance on that idea of the maintenance of political stability. While there remain threats to free trade, there also remain threats to the maintenance of political stability in the Asian region. The testing of nuclear devices last year by India and Pakistan and the ongoing conflict between the two nations over Kashmir is a case in point, but by no means the only one. There is substantial conflict over territorial claims in the South China Sea, an area through which Japan receives the vast majority of its oil from the Arabian Gulf. Indonesia, in the wake of the removal of the Soeharto regime, continues to see ethnic and religious conflict in several of its provinces and outlying islands. The threat there of escalation is real. China continues to threaten military conflict against Taiwan should the latter seek any form of independence from the mainland, at times conducting military exercises just off the Taiwan coast to make its point. Finally, there remains the thorny issue of North Korea, a country which most probably has nuclear, chemical and biological weapons and which continues to have an open hostility to its southern neighbour, requiring a heavy U.S. military presence in South Korea as a result.

As incomplete as such an analysis is, anticipating economic performance in a region cannot be inclusive of such possible military or political conflicts given their very unpredictable nature. As a result, I will put them to one side and give my expectation for the region based on the view that the current, relative political stability which has existed for the two decades in Asia - relative that is to the 1950s and 60s - will be maintained. Given that presumption, let's look at my predictions for those countries in Asia that are likely to out-perform:

TAIWAN

While the likes of computer company Acer are a major presence in the global markets, the secret of Taiwan's success would have been well familiar to Joseph Schumpeter: small is beautiful. In the past 40 years, Taiwan has transformed itself from an agricultural backwater to a major economic presence in the global economy, one of the four New Industrialised Economies that Asia has so far managed to produce. With a population of around 22 million, it has a per capita GDP income of around USD12,000. While Korea emphasised the building up of large conglomerates, the *chaebol*, Taiwan's path to growth emphasised a more traditionally Chinese model, one more focused on smaller and more flexible companies, built around families and with relatively low debt levels, both domestic and external. The main platform for Taiwan's growth for the past two decades has clearly been exports, however Taiwan has also placed a special emphasis on developing its own technology base with the creation of the computer and electronic development parks and research centres. While one could argue that Taiwan remains critically dependent on Japan for key components for its exports, it has achieved a substantially greater degree of technological self-sufficiency than many of its Asian competitors. Taiwan is not without faults, like any country. The state still takes up too much of the economy. Equally, corruption, as epitomised by triad gangs, is a problem. However, the ferocious nature of competition within Taiwan's private sector is a major reason why inflation has remained extremely low, even in the wake of the Asian crisis.

Unlike many of its competitors, Taiwan did not suffer from major external imbalances prior to the Asian crisis. Indeed, in the period 1995-1997, its current account *surplus* averaged 2.9% of the GDP. Its currency and asset markets were hit by contagion resulting from the crisis, however the Taiwanese authorities took an appropriately flexible approach, allowing the Taiwan dollar to depreciate modestly in order to restore export competitiveness, but on the other hand cracking down on speculative activities in the non-deliverable forward market. The government enacted fiscal and stabilisation measures to support the economy and the stock market. In addition to not having a current account deficit prior to the crisis, Taiwan also did not have a public external debt problem. As of 1999, public external debt was a mere USD100 million, peanuts in relative terms within the Asian region, while private external debt is only around 8% of foreign exchange reserves, easily manageable. Equally, public domestic debt is only around 25% of the GDP. The capital account has been gradually liberalised with a target date of some time in 2000 set for complete liberalisation. The banking system appears relatively well capitalised, with foreign currency liabilities matched by foreign currency assets.

The real story of Taiwan remains however in the sector of small and medium-sized enterprises (SME), which had an average debt-to-equity ratio of 0.8 as of 1998. Crucially, well-functioning bankruptcy procedures allow for the relatively easy exit of insolvent firms. In short, Taiwan is a very good story indeed, a model for high value-added and efficient economic growth. If China followed the model of Taiwan rather than seeking the bigger-is-better approach, its economy would already be twice the size of that of the U.S., food for thought indeed. Below, I present an overview of Taiwan's economic performance and our bank's forecasts going forward.

Taiwan - Macroeconomic performance and outlook

Indicator	1995	1996	1997	1998	1999F	2000F
GDP growth	6.0%	5.7	6.8	4.7	5.3	6.2
Domestic demand	4.5%	4.7	8.9	6.2	4.6	6.5
Industrial growth	4.7%	2.1	7.4	2.6	7.0	8.0
Export growth	20.0%	3.8	5.3	-9.4	5.2	8.0
Import growth	21.3%	-1.1	11.8	-8.5	3.6	10.0
Current Account	2.1% of GDP	4.0	2.5	1.3	1.9	1.6
CPI	3.7%	3.1	0.9	1.7	0.5	1.0
90-day CP yield (average)	6.7%	5.8	6.8	6.8	5.1	5.4
USD-TWD (average)	26.5	27.5	28.7	33.5	32.4	31.8

Source: Market data/forecasts

The last 40 years have been a remarkable success story for Taiwan, albeit at the expense of substantial pollution. It is notable that since 1970, the annual growth rate of Taiwan has gradually slowed, the usual and inevitable result of a decline in investment inputs (such levels are not sustainable). In addition, just as it is more difficult for a corporation to grow at a rapid pace once it becomes large, so it is for a country's economy. Once a certain level of wealth is reached, there is no longer the absolute necessity to grow. Other priorities become more important, such as enjoying life more and leisure pursuits. Looking at a graph of Taiwanese growth since 1970, one might think that one is witnessing a secular economic decline. Not so. What is taking place is a change in focus. The one concern that an economist might have is that Taiwan traditionally ran substantial budget deficits in the 1990s, however this was largely the result of the massive infrastructure programme it began in 1991. That and the government's effort to reverse the usual brain-drain effect that has been happening in Asia - students study in the West and stay there rather than returning home - should provide a major platform for renewed growth in this decade to come.

In addition, China's entry into the WTO has major implications for Taiwan. Beijing has never been opposed to Taiwan's entry to the WTO as long as it is on a provincial, trading basis rather than that of a separate country. Indeed, if anything, China's WTO entry is likely to hasten that of Taiwan. Once that occurs, China will most likely turn around to Taiwan and demand free trade between the two countries. This will present the Taiwanese government with a political as well as an economic dilemma, but in the end my bet is that Taiwan will choose free trade with China, accepting the eventual political implications of that. Consequently, direct trade between China and Taiwan is set to explode. In China, Taiwan will be able to access a huge, cheaper labour force for new production facilities, as well as the Chinese consuming public, which now make up half the Chinese economy. In Taiwan, China will be able to access state-of-the art technology. At least in economic terms, the merger makes perfect sense and has great synergies. If it doesn't happen, it will be because of political obstacles. For the economies of both countries, that would be a tragedy. But if it does, Taiwan's growth up to now will be as nothing.

At this stage, it is well worth mentioning the other two main components of Greater China, China itself and Hong Kong. There is no question that China is likely to be a great economic power, not just a powerful economic country and if the efforts of the government are successful it could well challenge the U.S. over the long-term for global economic dominance. In the short term, however, as the country undergoes the largest corporate restructuring process in the history of economics, and as it tries to reform its banking system, it is too early to give a definitive forecast. China still has substantial economic and financial problems to work out. It possesses many of the problems that are now seen as the leading causes of the Asian crisis. This is not to give a bearish view on the country, rather to be realistic as to near-term prospects. The good news however is that China's entry into the WTO will act as a major catalyst to domestic economic reform, while attracting substantial foreign direct investment.

As for Hong Kong, the former colony and current Hong Kong Special Administrative Region - as Macau has also achieved that status after having been handed back in December by Portugal - the key issue remains as to how it can re-model itself. Being just another port in southern China, albeit an important one, is not an option as down that road lies the extinction of the territory as a major economic presence of any sort. Hong Kong cannot compete on price. Rather, it has to develop new industries and services to meet the changing needs of the global economy, while simultaneously servicing China's ongoing restructuring process. It is a truly daunting task. While the currency board provides for financial stability, it is a straight jacket in terms of the economy. The long-term consideration must be for currency unification with the *yuan*, in order to provide the territory with greater price competitiveness. New efforts to set up hi-tech and leisure industries are part of the ongoing restructuring of Hong Kong. It is too early to say how successful this will be, though if China is wise it will maintain the HSAR as its advance guard of economic development. Having had the good fortune to live there during both the boom and bust years, I have a soft spot for the territory. I have full faith in the Hong Kong people's ability and determination to restructure and reform in order to reposition the territory. What needs to be maintained however is Hong Kong's emphasis on the rule of law. Any substantial signs that it is being whittled away as a result of its incorporation into China - for whatever excuse - would do irreparable harm to Hong Kong's ability to attract investment and compete in the global economy. This point cannot be sufficiently emphasised. In China, corruption is a national consequence of its state of economic development and evolution. In Hong Kong, it cannot be tolerated. To do so would be to sign the death warrant of Hong Kong, simply because in a global economy no-one *has* to be in one place, in particular if there are other alternatives.

SINGAPORE

The city-state has the best infrastructure in Asia, including Japan. Infrastructure matters because it un-blocks potential economic bottlenecks, making the economy more efficient and allowing for a more sound platform for high level growth. Economic management also matters and in Singapore, you have some of the best economic managers in Asia. The Singapore model of high investment in human and manufacturing capital, rejection of the welfare state, welcoming of foreign technology and investment and stern efforts to achieve the complete elimination of corruption, has proved a brilliantly successful one. Estimates vary as to Singapore's TFP, but most suggest that it is among the highest in the region. Singapore's emphasis on education and high-end technology, some of it created locally, some imported, suggests anecdotally that this is indeed the case.

Where Singapore's challenge will be going forward is developing the kind of entrepreneurial flair found elsewhere in Asia, notably in Greater China. The government's emphasis on growth from above has not necessarily left the population well equipped to develop growth for themselves. This is a problem with which the authorities are well aware. The challenge will be in opening up the economy in this way, indeed in freeing up the population while maintaining government control not only on the economy, but also on social order. Globalisation demands ever-increasing flexibility and rapid response to change. This can be best and most efficiently achieved not by governments but by the people with sufficient incentive. Hong Kong may be grateful that it would appear to have an entrepreneurial lead over Singapore - though Singapore has a clear technology lead over Hong Kong - but that lead will not necessarily last for long. A people and a set of authorities that built Asia's most modern city out of nothing are well capable of overhauling that lead. There are those who say that Singapore's fellow ASEAN members could well be dangerous competitors to the city state in terms of price. Some time in the future, that may be so, but only once they have developed the same kind of infrastructure and technology capacity. In the meantime, it would appear that the gap is widening rather than narrowing in Singapore's favour.

INDIA

Just as when I suggested this in **Asia Falling**, the idea of India as an opportunity for investment produces shock. The Indian political scene remains potentially volatile. The streets of New Delhi and Mumbai are clogged to overflowing, as anyone who has taken a business trip there knows to their cost, pollution is appalling and poverty levels surpass those seen in sub-Saharan Africa. Yet India has a number of comparative advantages that make it look like a good long-term bet. First is education. At the university level, the Indian education system, both that was created by the country since independence in 1948 and that was left over from its colonial past, remains superior to that say of China. Education is a cornerstone of growth and prosperity and such an advantage is a major positive regarding economic prospects. That said, on balance, the story of Indian education is a mixed one. Below university level, it is no exaggeration to say that Indian education is appalling. Unlike the ASEAN countries that first sought first to build up primary and secondary education, India placed its education emphasis at the university level. The result has led to sharp education and economic disparity - over half the country's adults are illiterate. Successive Indian governments have promised to raise spending on education, yet it remains mired at a paltry 4% of the GDP, less than half of many of its Asian neighbours. In the likes of Thailand and Indonesia, large, cheap and moderately skilled workforces have been developed, but with the economy lacking the requisite number of higher-skilled workers and managers. In India, it is the other way around. This has one advantage in that the managers can theoretically solve the problem. Of course, putting theory into practice is no easy task in India, plagued as it is by a tortuous political system. That said, by Indian standards, the last two years have shown some signs of developing stability, despite the regrettable decision to test a nuclear weapon by India which then resulted in a similar test by Pakistan. The current administration remains committed to the cause of economic reform.

A further positive is that India should benefit from demographic change. South Asia as a whole is just starting to go through its demographic transition, just starting to feel the benefits of a generation hitting the labour market. While East Asian populations age, India will outperform in demographic terms - as will Pakistan, Sri Lanka and Bangladesh. The contribution to the economy from this will - peace and political stability allowing - drive the Indian economy for a decade. Given the political chaos that is the norm in India, it is indeed incredible how far India has come and not least how fast the economy is growing. In the last three years, India has been averaging at a 5.8% growth, even while the Asian crisis was taking place, a substantial achievement. Just think what it could achieve if the politicians ever got their act together!

Yet India still has massive problems, not least the appalling poverty that one witnesses on the streets, the levels of illiteracy, and the lack of infrastructure. What should it do? The government should set a course of gradually withdrawing from the economy, freeing up assets to perform efficiently through privatisation. Despite cuts in the last 10 years, import tariffs remain too high. In effect, they are a tax on the domestic population in that they are inflationary. Barriers to free trade need to be cut down with a scythe. In the last 30 years up until the Asian crisis, Indonesia raised half its population out of a state of abject poverty, a remarkable achievement. At the starting point, Indonesia and India were at roughly the same stage in their economic development, but Indonesia left India far behind in the dust. That is an indictment on the political administrations of India during that period. The crisis caused a partial reversal of the gains made in Indonesia. At the least, India should use this as an opportunity to try and catch up. Despite the fact that its population could overtake that of China's some time this century due to China's one-child policy, there is no talk of India becoming an economic superpower. Why not? Because up until 1991, India suffered from inadequate and inept economic policies, relying mainly on a socialist model. In many ways, the economic and financial crisis of 1991 was a blessing in disguise. It forced the Indian authorities to realise the bankruptcy of those policies - though there remain some that cling to the past, just as there remain people who believe the earth is flat.

Perhaps the most pressing need is to develop infrastructure. India's roads and ports were not built for the amount of traffic that is flowing through them. The result is delays - frustrating for individuals but extremely costly for business - and thus for the country because such delays act as a deterrent in terms of foreign investors going to India in the first place. Returning to the issue of import tariffs, they are no doubt intended to protect domestic export industries. However, in practice they actually damage the Indian export sector, since they act as an incentive for companies to simply sell goods at home rather than take the effort to export. India's overall trade balance would benefit greatly from its import tariffs being slashed. Exports make up only around 10% of the GDP and for this reason India continues to have a structural current account deficit. Indeed, the combination of a substantial fiscal deficit and a current account deficit could at some stage be a fundamental deficit. That current account deficit is currently only around 1% of the GDP, but it could widen if India's capital account surplus increases. Setting up special economic zones where trade barriers are eliminated would be a good way of reducing and reversing this fundamental weakness. Traditionally, the politicians have held India back from its rightful destiny, not the business community and certainly not the heads of the Finance Ministry and Reserve Bank of India, both of whom have been at the forefront of the reform movement. It is the politicians who need to change. Though India is rightly and fiercely proud of its status as the world's largest democracy, that does not mean to say it cannot learn from others. Thailand also faced political chaos. It took a crisis for the Thai politicians to realise that change was necessary and thus for a new constitution to be enacted. India could undoubtedly benefit from a similar approach to altering the political makeup. With the present administration, there would appear to be cause for hope that some of those lessons might be learned.

Concerning the economy, the ninth five-year plan that takes account of the period 1997-2001 aims at surpassing what has become known as the "Hindu growth at an average of 7-8%, with strong contributions from both industry and agriculture. In order to achieve this, it will have to be financed. That can be achieved in two ways: through liberalising and deregulating further and by seeking ways to raise the savings rate and to reduce the state's presence, thus putting more of the burden of investment on the private sector rather than the public sector. Restrictions on rupee foreign exchange trading and the fact that India did not see anything like the amount of capital flows before the crisis to a large extent protected the country from the worst effects of the crisis. In addition, from July 1997 to August 1998, the rupee depreciated by some 17% against the dollar, thus providing some support for Indian export competitiveness. The authorities are fully aware that in order to achieve desired growth and advancement levels, they have to push through a second wave of policy reforms, covering a broad spectrum including the revitalisation of the agricultural sector, on fiscal policy, the financial sector, trade, foreign investment, infrastructure, downsizing of the government and privatisation of the public enterprises. While India is an increasing recipient of foreign direct investment as a result of deregulation of investment laws and the gradual opening up of the Indian economy, it has to become a favourite among the emerging markets among the global investor community as have Korea, Brazil, Mexico and Poland at various times.

I have just given a few examples of the countries I like. Korea and Indonesia should also do well though they continue to have major structural problems that must be dealt with. Investors should pick carefully. So far, we have looked at the various issues of the Asian crisis and the subsequent recovery solely in an Asian context. Both the crisis and the recovery have major importance and implication for the global economy as a whole however. It is to this that we turn to next.

CHAPTER 10

THE IMPLICATION – GLOBAL SIGNIFICANCE OF THE ASIAN EXPERIENCE

Cast your mind back if you will to a single day, October 23, 1997. To many of you, this day will not be familiar. To the people of Hong Kong and particularly to those who participated in the stock market - it is well remembered. It was the day, a Thursday, that the Hang Seng experienced up until that point its largest one day fall in history, a day of horror, of panic, of despair and of financial catastrophe.

In the first three days of the week, in the wake of the free-floating of the Taiwan dollar, speculators had turned their guns on Hong Kong and the Hong Kong dollar peg, "certain" that its currency would be forced ultimately to devalue, just as had so many of Asia's currencies, the latest being that of Taiwan. In those first three days, the Hong Kong dollar came under tremendous pressure. The HKMA, the Hong Kong Monetary Authority, held the line at 7.7500 Hong Kong dollars to the U.S. dollar, selling at that level against wave after wave of speculative attack. It stepped out of the interest rate market, allowing interest rates to skyrocket. In those first three days, the Hang Seng, Hong Kong's benchmark stock index lost almost 2,000 points. More was to come. Trading opened on that Thursday and within the first few hours the Hang Seng had plummeted by a further 1,699.3 points, losing some 14.6% of its value. That Thursday, in

Hong Kong, people from all walks of life stared up in horror at the stock monitors of bank branches, or looked in dazed shock at their price trackers as billions were simply wiped off the value of the shares they owned. By the end of the session, the Hang Seng had managed to crawl its way back from the lows, but still ended the day down some 1,211.47 points, the largest one-day fall in unit terms in the Hong Kong Stock Exchange's history. Why do I mention this? What relevance does it have, other than a painful reminder of a dire day in the markets?

Because, on the Thursday and Friday, October 23 and 24, 1997, the Dow Jones Industrial Average, the benchmark of the U.S. stock market on Wall Street, fell almost 320 points, largely on the back of the fall in the Hang Seng. Up until that point, it would have been inconceivable for events in the likes of Hong Kong to have even troubled the U.S. stock market, the benchmark of global capitalism. Worse was to come. On the Monday, the Dow experienced its largest one-day fall in unit terms and on a closing basis in history, surpassing the 508-point fall on the day of the Crash, October 19, 1987. On that Monday, October 27, 1997, the Dow plunged 554.26 points, losing 7.18% at the close. There was no question at the time. The fall in the Hang Seng had been a butterfly flapping its wings, a ripple that had become the tidal-wave which had crashed upon Wall Street that Monday. People were in shock that events thousands of miles away could trigger such devastation in the U.S. If there were any doubters, such doubts were dispelled for good the following year, when on August 31, 1998 the Hang Seng lost 554.70 points on closing basis or 7.08%, at the height of the battle by the speculators against the HKMA for supremacy in the Hong Kong markets, and the Dow promptly lost 512.61 points, or 6.37%, also surpassing the total unit losses on the day of the Crash. We live in a global village, a global world, a global market. Right there is the proof. I could wax lyrical about the global significance of the Asian crisis and recovery to the global markets and the global economy, but I would humbly suggest that those few statistics demonstrate the point rather powerfully, certainly more powerfully than any such waffle could.

THE ASIAN CRISIS CONFIRMED THE GLOBALISATION OF FINANCIAL MARKETS...

The Asian crisis of 1997-98 must not only be seen for what it was, the bursting of a financial bubble which showed up the economic flaws of the Asian "Miracle". It must also be put in context - in the context of other crises in emerging and emerged markets, down the ages, and also in the context of its significance to and implication for global markets. The crisis in Asia had of course particularly Asian characteristics, but it was also part of a wider process of financial and economic deregulation without the necessary infrastructure to cope with that deregulation. Such inadequacy of infrastructure (institutional and "real") was also seen in the Mexican crisis of 1994/95, in the Czech crisis of 1996-97, in Russia and finally in much of Latin America in both the 1980s and 1990s. Indeed, the bursting of the Japanese bubble in 1990 also has similarities with the Asian crisis. Asia differs however from these crises in some important ways. The initial reaction in the West to the Asian crisis was frankly, largely indifference, followed by the view, expressed by none other than the Federal Reserve Board Chairman Alan Greenspan, that it might actually help to keep Western inflationary pressures muted; a thought that had perhaps escaped those in Asia who were at the time suffering the worst effects of the crisis. By the Autumn of 1998, as the Asian crisis had been followed by the Russian default in August of that year, and pressures were building up elsewhere, not least in Brazil, Western commentators could no longer afford the luxury of saying that the Asian crisis did not matter. Certainly, it was no longer seen as beneficial! The Asian crisis was seen as a financial crisis, which had spread throughout the global financial system, infecting where it went, endangering the very existence of that global system. The idea of "Contagion" was no mere hysterical talk. When the first signs of the credit crunch appeared within the U.S. economy in late August of 1998, such talk had clearly become a reality, a very dangerous reality indeed. Without exaggeration, the Federal Reserve responded magnificently, cutting interest rates three times. Such extraordinary easing of the monetary settings was followed by similar action by the bank of Japan and the European Central Bank. The result was that the threat of global financial meltdown was averted. There was no longer a question however of the significance of the Asian crisis to the global economy and to global markets.

Globalisation means that the financial crisis can potentially be transferred across the globe at light speed. Losses in Hong Kong can mean losses on the floor of the New York Stock Exchange the same day or on the computer screens of the NASDAQ system. Default in Russia can mean a run on the currency of Brazil. An attack on the currency board of Argentina can mean an attack on all currency board systems globally. The world in which we live is one whereby at least in theory all information is available everywhere, instantly. Needless to say, in practice it doesn't quite work out like that. For a start, we don't ever get *all* the available information. There are usually parts missing, potentially important parts. In addition, information is value-added so it has to be paid for. Finally, technological inadequacy means that some parts of the globe are fighting an uphill battle from the start. The Internet however is helping to change that. For instance. Anyone with a computer in the UK now knows for certain that they have been ripped off (for years) when they buy any average consumer good compared to the prices available across the Atlantic. Markets operate on the basis of information. Thus, with the Internet, the free market of ideas and prices will in this case be able to operate across a significant portion of the British population for the first time. The result, despite the efforts of some to fight the process, is likely to be that UK-U.S. price differentials shrink rapidly. In the context of Asia, the significance of the Asian crisis and recovery is now easily available and accessible to a much greater proportion of the global population than ever before. Individual day traders in the U.S. can quickly appreciate the impact on the NASDAQ, for example, of a slide in the Nikkei 225 and take the appropriate action or not, as the case may be.

The globalisation of financial markets, which has been taking place due to the deregulation and liberalisation of the capital markets, has been happening at an astounding pace. For the emerging markets, this has had a profound effect. From 1990 to 1997, just before the Asian crisis, it is estimated by international authorities including the IMF and the World Bank that the volume of private capital flows to emerging markets rose more than five-fold, to USD255 billion from USD42 billion in 1990. In that time, world trade grew by around 5% a year, but private capital flows increased 30% a year! Within those private capital flows, those headed for emerging markets took up an increasingly large portion, albeit off a relatively low base.

...AND ECONOMIES

The Asian crisis triggered financial disruptions elsewhere in the world, or at the very least caused investors, once burned in Asia, to take a hard look at the fundamentals of other countries in the emerged and emerging markets. Anticipation of a major slowdown in global growth at the end of 1998 and into early 1999 caused oil and other commodities - the price of which is after all linked directly and cyclically to global growth expectations - to fall dramatically. On NYMEX, the New York Mercantile Exchange, the front month futures' contract fell to a low of just above 10 dollars a barrel on December 10, 1998 as global markets priced in a U.S. and Japanese slowdown, with U.S. and Japanese exports to Asia likely to be hurt significantly by the collapse in Asian regional demand. As of Friday, December 17, 1999, it closed at 26.74 dollars a barrel. What had happened? Clearly, there had been a major change in financial market sentiment. However, what took place occurred not only in financial markets, but also in real economies. The extraordinary monetary easing by the Fed in late 1998 allowed the necessary increased liquidity for global financial markets, but it also gave potential house-buyers cheaper mortgages, cut the funding costs' of corporations and encouraged people to consume rather than save. Oil, like other key commodities, is a reflection of economic growth expectations. When economies are doing well, there is more demand for such key commodities. Equally, when global growth is slowing this reflects on the oil price. Oil and growth are thus both cause and effect.

When the Asian crisis occurred, this was one of the factors that led to a slump in global growth expectations and thus the price in such commodities as oil. Equally, when the Asian recovery began in the first quarter of 1999, a recovery in global growth expectations and commodity prices ensued. Many may point to the OPEC product agreement in early 1999 as being the main factor behind the rally in oil. Undoubtedly, it was a crucial one, but it was not the only factor. The recovery of Asian economies had major global significance, not least for the oil market given that most Asian countries, including of course Japan, are significant oil importers rather than producers. Rising demand for oil from Asia as the region recovered was undoubtedly a factor in the oil price more than doubling in 1999.

THE TITANIC AND THE ICEBERG

In the conclusion of **Asia Falling**, I made the suggestion that the U.S. economy was equivalent to the "Titanic" - the largest, fastest and supposedly the most efficient ship of its time - and the Asian crisis was an iceberg which had at least the potential to damage if not actually sink the U.S. economic boom. Thankfully, the "ship" was not sunk. Some damage was suffered, but the ship has sailed by, rewriting history at least in economic terms. How did this happen and do risks remain? On the first, the Fed's monetary easing was clearly the major reason why we did not see the kind of financial meltdown, which could well have occurred. As the Federal Reserve Board Chairman himself noted in 1997, the Asian crisis played a significant part in dampening global price pressures. Indeed, while the threat of deflation was averted by timely Fed action, the crisis induced dis-inflation. Even the Fed was surprised by how muted PPI and CPI data were in the first half of 1999. After all, this was the eighth consecutive year of strong economic growth. Price pressures should have been developing. Asia could have exported deflation to global markets and economies and to a certain extent the Asian crisis did just that. However, the fact that trade remains only around 14% of the U.S. economy and in any case price competition was already intensely ferocious within the U.S. before the Asian crisis saved U.S. manufacturers from the threat of seeing their margins hit by cheap Asian imports.

The Asian crisis did however mean that the U.S. current account deficit grew further, from some 2.7% of the GDP in 1998 to 3.6% in 1999, or around USD330 billion, as U.S. exports to Asia fell while imports from Asia rose substantially given persistently strong U.S. demand. Incidentally, we as a bank expect the U.S. current account deficit to be USD393 billion in 2000, or 4.1% of the GDP. Thus, while the "iceberg" that was the Asian crisis did not cause the U.S. economy to go into recession, it did greatly exacerbate the already existing large U.S. external imbalance. That imbalance is seen in the U.S. trade deficit, but it can also be expressed by the savings' deficit relative to investment. The U.S. savings' rate is presently barely above zero and at one time late last year it dipped into negative territory, implying that U.S. citizens were in effect eating into their savings on an overall basis rather than adding to them. Over-consumption relative to savings is a key reason why the U.S. has a current account deficit and conversely why Japan has a current account surplus given its high savings' rate relative to that of consumption. Such levels of economic imbalance, as Thailand proved in 1997 and others have proved both earlier and later, are unsustainable on a long-term view. Either the dollar has to reflect the needed adjustment to close that imbalance or the U.S. economy does. While the U.S. economy appears to have escaped the worst effects of the Asian crisis and indeed the Asian recovery should help to boost U.S. exports to Asia, it is by no means out of the woods yet.

THE NEED FOR MULTIPLE CHANNELS OF FINANCE: A KEY LESSON OF THE ASIAN CRISIS

Yet, why did a credit crunch happen in Asia and not in the U.S.? After all, Asia suffered from current account deficits and high consumption rates prior to the crisis, as does the U.S. The easy answer is that Asian financial systems were weak, while that of the U.S. is vigilantly patrolled by the Federal Reserve. While that may be true, it does not tell the whole story. In a speech before the World Bank and IMF on September 27, 1999, Fed Chairman Alan Greenspan gave his view on what occurred. I quote his speech at length here below because of the unique insight of the man.

"With the benefit of hindsight, we have been endeavouring for nearly two years to distil the critical lessons from the global crises of 1997 and 1998. From what seemed at the time to be isolated and contained disruptions in Thailand and Indonesia, economic turmoil deepened and spread, ultimately engulfing the emerging-market economies of East Asia and other parts of the globe and then the financial markets of industrial countries...

...Following the Russian default of August 1998, public capital markets in the United States virtually seized up. For a time not even investment-grade bond issuers could find reasonable takers. While Federal Reserve easing shortly thereafter doubtless was a factor, it is not credible that this move was the whole explanation of the dramatic restoration of most, though not all markets in a matter of weeks. The seizure appeared too deep seated to be readily unwound solely by a cumulative 75 basis point ease in overnight rates....

...Arguably, at least as relevant was the existence of backup financial institutions, especially commercial banks that replaced the inter-mediation function of the public capital markets. As public debt issuance fell, commercial bank lending accelerated, effectively filling in some of the funding gap. Even though bankers also moved significantly to risk aversion, previously committed lines of credit, in junction with Federal Reserve ease, were an adequate backstop to business financing. With the process of credit creation able to continue, the impact on the real economy of the capital market turmoil was blunted. Firms were able to sustain production, business and consumer confidence were not threatened, and a vicious circle--an initial disruption in financial markets leading to losses and bankruptcies among their borrowers and thus further erosion in the financial sector--never got established....

...What we perceived in the United States in 1998 may be an important general principle: Multiple alternatives to transform an economy's savings into capital investment offer a set of backup facilities should the primary form of inter-mediation fail. In 1998 in the United States, banking replaced the capital markets. Far more often it has been the other way around, as it was most recently in the United States a decade ago."[1]

As the Chairman noted, when the U.S. banks faltered in 1990-1991 in the wake of the collapse of property markets, the financial capital markets which were largely unaffected by this were able to substitute for the loss of bank inter-mediation in the financial market place, thus averting the threat of a fully-fledged credit crunch. Similarly, in 1998, when the global markets looked like seizing up, including those in the U.S., U.S. commercial banks stepped in to provide the needed finance, effectively saving the day. In the case of Asia, while the massive IMF bailouts and significant monetary and fiscal easing have been the key reasons for the Asian regional economic recovery, the growth of the Asian bond markets should not be overlooked. Prior to the crisis, most Asian countries outside of Japan had budget surpluses and hence there was little incentive for Asia to develop little more than token bond markets. After the crisis, with most of Asia running substantial budget deficits, there is needless to say a far greater incentive. Asian authorities have responded vigorously by making benchmark issues, thus seeking to develop yield curves off which corporate issues can be priced. It is not too much to say that one of the as yet unsung benefits of the Asian crisis has been the development and improvement of the Asian capital markets. The success of the U.S. and Europe in avoiding a credit crunch was due to the fact that both had mature and developed capital markets as well as bank and financial intermediary loan finance available. The existence of multiple channels of finance was not only a crucial aspect behind the subsequent recovery in markets and economies in 1999; it was most likely *the* crucial aspect.

The speed with which Asia has been able to overcome the crisis offers a stark contrast with the long-lasting problems of Japan. A major reason for this is that Japan's financial system has traditionally been the archetype of virtually bank-only financial inter-mediation. The *keiretsu* corporate system focused on each *keiretsu* having a main bank around which this group of corporations was built, leaving these Japanese corporations almost solely dependent on bank credit. Given the Japanese banking crisis of the 1990s, which appeared to climax in the Winter of 1997, rising non-performing loans at Japanese banks meant the banks in turn were not willing or able to make new credits. Hence, Japanese corporations were starved of their *only* source of available domestic funding. It is for this reason that there has been a protected credit crunch in Japan. Creating multiple channels of available finance in Japan would undoubtedly accelerate the recovery, which is ongoing in Japan, as well as forcing the banks to deal with their remaining NPLs. The process has seen some progress with domestic corporate bonds outstanding in Japan more than doubling over the last decade while total bank loans have been almost flat, however banks remain such a dominant source of funding in Japan that this non-bank lending increase has not been sufficient to avert a credit crunch.

Had Asia developed capital markets prior to the crisis, rather than relying almost solely on bank lending and external private capital flows, the economic crisis which followed the Asian currency crisis might have been largely averted, a lesson upon which I would humbly suggest that Asian governments should ponder on. A further lesson is that quicker alternative channels of finance should be developed, the quicker the existing debt problems are dealt with and restructured, the less the eventual financial and economic cost. At the time, many predicted that Australia, which had become increasingly connected with Asian trade, would face a sharp slowdown if not outright recession in the wake of the Asian crisis of 1997-1998. Australia's economic performance in 1998 and 1999, growing 4.1% and 4.3% respectively, has needless to say completely disproved as nonsense such gloomy predictions. How did that happen? How did Australia escape when over half its trade went to Asia? For a start, because the authorities allowed a devaluation of the Australian dollar so as to regain export competitiveness. In addition, the existence of the well-developed multiple channels of finance in Australia protected the overall financial system against this type of exogenous shock.

The developments of the past three years, set off by the Asian crisis, have provided ample evidence that where a domestic financial system is not sufficiently robust and more specifically does not provide a variety of competing channels of finance, the consequences of a country participating in the new global economy can be hazardous. Needless to say, improving the deficiencies of the domestic banking systems within emerging markets should help to limit the toll of the next financial crisis on their real economies. In this regard, the development of free and open capital markets to compete against and compliment bank finance is of special importance and urgency. This must be a clear and unequivocal message to those countries within the emerging markets that have not yet experienced a full financial crisis. Perhaps this is a further reason why the authorities in China are seeking to develop and build up the Chinese stock and bond markets. If it isn't, then it should be. The consequences of having bank lending as the only available channel of finance are easily visible in the indebted state of many an SOE and state banks.

THE RELATIVE IMPORTANCE OF ASIA

By the mid-1990s, roughly 40% of global manufacturing output was being made in Asia. A majority of the world's largest container ports were in Asia and some 60% of all short-term capital flows bound for emerging markets in the 1990s went to Asia. In contrast to the apparent ascendancy of Asia during the early 1990s, in the initial aftermath of the Asian crisis, there were those who have questioned whether Asia was in fact globally significant. The global economy avoided recession let alone depression. The U.S. economy continues to grow strongly. The European Union is starting to grow again and even Japan is emerging from economic darkness. So presumably Asia does not actually matter to the global economy? To a great extent, such talk is a reaction to the previous over-hype of the Asian region, whereby Asia superiority and its by-product Western inferiority would inevitably lead to Asian rather than Western dominance in the global economy. The opposite of this is that Asia does not matter at all. Both views are nonsense.

The rise of Asia had profound significance for the global economy. For a start, it was symptomatic of the ending of the Cold War and of a refocusing on the economic rather than the military. If the 1980s marked the decade of *realpolitik*, the Cold War and developed world political and economic dominance, then the 1990s have seen the rise of a new focus, emerging markets. Countries which were previously mere pawns on the global chess game played out between the U.S. and the Soviet Union - with the occasional intrusion by China - are now players in the game. Indeed, the very nature of the game itself has changed. The rise of Asia was also reflective of a righting of the imbalance between Western colonial domination and Asian subordination. It is not without reason that China's government seeks a more appropriate role and responsibility for its country in a global context.

The subsequent financial crash in Asia, temporary economic decline and ensuing recovery are also significant, not least because Asia serves as an excellent example of what needs to be done in order to avert further major financial market disturbance such as we witnessed in 1997-1998. In addition, it is also a fine example of how it is possible to cope under the most extreme of conditions. The relative importance of Asia is an issue with which both Asia and the rest of the global economy have to deal. In a global setting, Asia is not nearly as important as many in Asia - both Western and Asian - thought prior to the crisis. Yet, equally, it is not as unimportant as many in the West thought. For those, the collapse of the Asian stock markets and the subsequent sickening declines in those in the West, not least the Dow, have been an important wake up call, a reality check. Equally, for those who anticipated Asian dominance in the global economy, either because of some sense of guilt at past Western colonisation and consequently a need for re-balancing, a Western sense of insecurity or simply an analysis which seemed to suggest the rise of Asia and the decline of the West - as many thought at the time - the actual events of 1997-1998 have been a sober reminder of the difficulty inherent in predicting financial markets and economies.

Asia has a key place and role in the global economy, a role that is neither trivial nor unimportant, nor a dominant one. The authorities of China are the first to acknowledge that theirs remains a developing country, or an emerging market however one likes to express it, despite the truly extraordinary progress they have made since the commencement of economic reform in 1978. This is no false modesty, nor an attempt merely to seek better trade terms, but an acceptance of how far they still have to go to achieve "developed" world status. Asia's role should no longer be seen as a reversal of past colonisation. For an Asian to think that merely enslaves and condemns the thinker to a static and negative relationship with the rest of the world. Asia has gone far beyond reversing past humiliations. Future generations of Asians will in any case most likely not focus on such considerations, nor should they. They will focus on surviving and competing in the global economy, in the global marketplace, in whatever task or work they undertake. Asia does not have any sort of rightful place in the global economy, good or bad, elevated or lowly. It has the place it deserves, that it has earned and that alone. There is no such thing as a free lunch, even at the global economic level. In this regard, Asia is better placed than many to survive and prosper for the simple reason that the concept of handouts, of a welfare state is foreign to the Asian model of capitalism. Granted, there is a possibility that that may change over time.

Asia and the Welfare State

Some greater emphasis may be put on state provisions rather than individuals providing for themselves. Asia's anti-welfare state mentality was largely the result of necessity, along with a honed ruthlessness. On the necessity, many Asian countries, faced with war and famine in the period of 1950-70 simply could not afford to bail out their populations. On the ruthlessness, it is without doubt that Asian governments during and after that period have adopted a deliberate policy of rejecting the concept of the welfare state. Compassion for the needy and the downtrodden is minimised, has been the policy. Sink or swim. In such a ruthless, Darwinian environment, government is no longer the institution upon which people can rely in times of crisis. Rather, the family is the sole institution that affords some degree of protection. It is no coincidence that families are much more tightly bound in Asia than in the U.S. or Europe. The generation who remember much of Asia being used as a theatre of war relied on themselves, on their families, primarily for survival, but also as a network to rely on in order to prosper. Persecuted in Indonesia, Vietnam, Cambodia and at times Malaysia, it is for this reason that the "overseas Chinese" communities have thrived - because necessity forced them to rely on their own family structures and to thrive merely to survive. If the question is asked, "sink or swim" most will swim precisely because they have no choice.

While the Asian crisis has been traumatic, one has to put it into the context of the kinds of tragic conflict which were seen in Asia from the end of the Second World War - the Chinese Civil War, the invasion and occupation of Tibet, border clashes between China and the Soviet Union, the Korean War, the first Vietnam war with the French, the second Vietnam War with the U.S., Indian independence and the subsequent massacres of Hindu and Muslim people as the border was created, the bloody creation of Bangladesh, civil conflicts in Burma, Islamic and Communist insurgencies in the Philippines, the Borneo insurgency and the brief war between China and Vietnam to name but a few. Of the Asian crisis, there were many casualties, all of which are tragic, but such casualties should be seen against the context of the horror that has been Asia's reality for much of the time since what we in the West know of as the end of the Second World War. Asia's bloody past, together with Asian governments' focus on refusing to be compassionate, led to small governments, lack of benefits, tight family structures and a focusing on the absolute necessity of succeeding financially, a characteristic often seen in immigrant communities living in the West but which, in the form of the Asian Miracle, was seen across the region and at national level.

By comparison - and here I tread lightly, fully recognising the risks of generalising - today's generation of Asians are relatively well off. Most of them are not faced with imminent destruction or starvation. India may be an exception in that it still has sub-Saharan levels of absolute poverty, but much of Asia has become moderately well off, certainly in terms of the emerging markets. Some, notably Singapore and Hong Kong, have a GNP per capita that is substantially above much of the West. The Asian crisis derailed the process of Asia's elevation, but it will certainly not reverse it. Asia's very insistence on survival of the fittest rather than handouts will *necessitate* that Asia prospers once more from here. Today's Asians however, having it somewhat easier in general than their parents or grandparents, do not necessarily have the same feelings of necessity, particularly if they are supported by their families. There would appear to be the first signs within Asia, the effects of the Asian crisis notwithstanding, that wealth is leading to the start of a social breakdown. Again, this should be put in context. I am not talking about the collapse of the family as the leading social institution such as has been seen in the West. However, we do appear to be seeing a shifting of emphasis and focus, the natural evolutionary result of the creation of a certain degree of wealth with a society.

In addition, Asian governments are now faced with the hitherto unfamiliar reality of having budget deficits. The natural inclination is to eliminate these as quickly as possible, yet as discussed before they also now have the imperative to develop deep and transparent capital markets, which means that such deficits cannot and *should not* be eliminated entirely. Looking ahead, populations are starting to age within some of Asia's most advanced countries. Going forward, there will consequently be a greater emphasis put on developing efficient pension fund systems, such as that which exists in Singapore, in order to cope with the future need of pension payments being paid to an increasing amount of middle-aged and elderly within the population. The temptation might be that governments will seek to build up state pensions. This would be a mistake, and in any case one that Asia is not likely to make. One of the many reasons for the boom of the last 8 years in the U.S. stock market has been the realisation that the U.S. state pension will be effectively worthless when people retire and come to collect it. By that time, it will be so small and insignificant relative to an individual's cost base that it is not worth considering. Consequently, more and more people in the U.S. have been putting their money into stocks rather than into state pension plans, in the hope that they can provide for their own future rather than rely on the government to do so. Will there be an Asian welfare state? The most likely answer is that there will, as Asian economies transform into wealthy societies and as the focus changes from necessity to entitlement, but it will be nothing like the size of that in the West. Asia has watched the U.S., the UK and Europe make the mistake of providing massive social welfare packages, packages which are becoming increasingly more difficult for the national budgets to pay for. It is unlikely to be a mistake that Asia repeats.

Asia and Free Trade

In the immediate aftermath of the Asian crisis, there were those who feared that the very severity of the crisis would tempt some within Asia to reject the idea of free trade, causing them to put up new protectionist barriers in order to seek to protect their economies from the full ravages of competitive devaluations. The reality, thankfully, has been rather different. In no case has an Asian country, which went through the crisis, increased trade protectionism. Indeed, it has rightly acted as a spur to the ASEAN to develop the concept of AFTA, the Asian Free Trade Area about which it previously talked much but did little. At least from an Asian perspective, globalisation is here to stay. If anything, the process of globalisation, that is the approach to economic management based on global integration of trade and capital markets has been strengthened rather than weakened as a result of this crisis, as a result of this ordeal. This conclusion is not one of theory, but rather a reflection of the practical decisions taken by Asian policymakers as they confronted the crisis. In the specific case of Malaysia, the authorities imposed capital and exchange controls so as to eliminate the offshore market for the Malaysian *ringgit*, but they remained committed to free and open trade, and have reaped the benefits as a consequence. The fact that Asian governments decided to remain engaged in the global trading system should not have been that surprising. Looking at Asia ex-Japan as a whole, trade accounts for over 100% of the GDP. Just taking Hong Kong as an example, trade is 250% of that territory's GDP. By contrast, the figure is around 15% for both the U.S. and Japan. Asia simply did not have the luxury of rejecting free trade, even if it had wanted to. Indeed, it was not Asian governments which dragged their feet at the Seattle WTO conference. It has not been Asian governments that have been holding back the progress of global free trade. Rather, it is the protectionism of the U.S. and more particularly of Europe, which talk a good talk but in the end seek to protect their own bloated, vested interests rather than practise what they preach. The West called on Asia to maintain a commitment to free trade. What utter hypocrisy! Asia is committed to the idea of free trade. It is the West that is not sufficiently committed. The European Union should in theory be a free trade zone with no trade barriers within it, direct or indirect. It is of course nothing of the kind. National governments seek to protect their own for supposed national reasons or simply because they went to the same university as the chief executive of the company they are protecting. Eventually, however, there will be a day of reckoning. It is to be doubted as to whether or not the European governments who have committed to the euro realise what huge and seismic forces they have unleashed. Eventually, the market will overcome one way or the other. Either a truly free-trade zone will be created, or the euro zone will blow up. Asia made a commitment to the cause of free trade during the crisis. As a result, and with the future creation of AFTA, it will become a formidable competitive force.

If one is to take an optimistic road, one might well consider that Asia could be a progressive force for the continuation and extension of free trade in those parts of the globe where it does not yet exist sufficiently, emerging and emerged. There remains a threat however that the creation of regional trading blocks such as NAFTA, Mercosur, the EU and AFTA could bring forward a day of increased regional protectionism. It is a consideration upon which all the delegates of the Seattle WTO conference - who let us not beat around the bush, let us all down - should be made to ponder. Such regional protectionism could bring forward the depression that the emerging market crisis managed to avoid; a depression in equal if not greater severity to that of the 1930s.

The West's Responsibility: To Strengthen the Global Financial Architecture

The fact that Asian governments did remain committed to the cause of free trade despite the severity of the Asian crisis puts a greater responsibility upon the authorities of the industrialised world, national governments and multilateral organisations, to strengthen the international financial architecture so as to prevent or at the least limit the worst effects of future crises. That is surely the least that Asian countries can ask for while they seek to rebuild their national financial systems. Given the depth and breadth of the global emerging market crisis of 1997 to early 1999, of which the Asian crisis was just a part, it quickly became clear that while it was crucial to implement appropriate national economic responses, these by themselves were not enough. There was thus a need to develop an international economic and financial response to this situation. Mohamed el-Erian, current Global Emerging Market Portfolio manager at Pacific Investment Management Corporation, one of the biggest mutual funds in the U.S., defined these measures in terms of their crisis prevention and crisis management characteristics[2]:

- Improved information flows to the market - from national authorities, the international financial institutions and members of the private financial community such as hedge funds
- Better regulation and supervision of financial systems, including improved harmonised treatment of banking systems in emerging economies
- Ways to enhance the sustainability of private capital flows, including the minimising of large inflows of "hot money"
- Enhancing the ability of the IMF to react quickly to crises around the world
- Improving contingency funding lines which can be quickly drawn down to stem market panics and manias
- Lowering moral hazard and ensuring that the private sector participate in orderly financial workouts rather than aggravate the crises pressures and disruptions
- Look into ways of controlling huge capital outflows

With regard to some of these, the question of consideration and implementation of the ideas are of course two different things. It is one thing to say that capital flows must be controlled. It is another to try and control them, only to see them flee somewhere else, the benefit of these flows having been lost by the home country concerned, gained by the one to which they have fled. Nevertheless, it has to be said that the Asian crisis and subsequent crises elsewhere, have proved the necessity of strengthening the international financial system. Financial crises cannot and in many cases should not be avoided by the automatic stabilisers within a market pricing mechanism righting themselves after some degree of considerable imbalance. However, efforts can and should be made to militate against the worst effects of such crises. If this means that the issue of moral hazard be tackled specifically whereby investors have to realise that they will not of necessity be bailed out in the event of a national financial crisis and if that in turn reduces the extent as well as the volatility of capital flows into global emerging markets it is surely a price worth paying for in order to avoid a reoccurrence of the events of the last few years.

CONCLUSION

I can finally afford some degree of relaxation, at least in terms of this book. In these few pages, I have tried to explain my views on Asia, the relevance of the Asian crisis for both Asia and the global economy as a whole, the characteristics that caused the Asian "Miracle" and its subsequent crash and finally the emerging - and powerful - Asian recovery that is upon us. In terms of the region, dawn appears to be breaking, to mark the end of the darkness.

If the Asian crisis represented a time when the region plunged into financial and economic darkness, then what we are currently witnessing could surely be the dawn breaking once more, a fiery sun rising in the (eastern) sky to mark the end of that darkness. Is this a fitting analogy for where we are seeing today in Asia? I sincerely believe so, though how long this period of "light" will last depends heavily on the Asian authorities themselves, and also to some degree on the external environment, not least the U.S. economy.

There is no question that the years of 1997-1998 marked a catastrophic nightmare for Asia, but the darkness has gone, the light filling where darkness was. Only time will tell whether or not the appropriate lessons have been learned from the ordeal that was the Asian crisis. Many Asian governments, financial authorities, banks and businesses have been humbled in the process of the last couple of years and quite frankly this is no bad thing. No country or region has a right to be arrogant, not even the United States, even in its phase of the "new economy." No country is perfect and the day that a country or region thinks of itself as such is surely the day when it has peaked. Not that Asia thought of itself as such, but there was no little amount of gloating in the Asian Miracle. The story of Asia since de-colonisation is one of unparalleled success. The crisis of 1997-98 can be seen either as a turning point, or as merely a bump in the road. While external factors - such as the sustainability of U.S. economic growth and Japan's recovery - will have a part to play, it will be entirely Asia's choice as to which road it takes from here on.

A fitting analogy for where we are today in Asia? I sincerely believe so. There is no question that the years of 1997-1998 marked a catastrophic nightmare for Asia, but the darkness has gone, the light filling where darkness was. Only time will tell whether or not the appropriate lessons have been learned from the ordeal that was the Asian crisis. Many Asian governments, financial authorities, banks and businesses have been humbled in the process of the last couple of years and quite frankly this is no bad thing. No country or region has a right to be arrogant, not even the United States, even in its phase of the "new economy". No country is perfect and the day that a country or region thinks of itself as such is surely the day when it has peaked. Not that Asia thought of itself as such, but there was no little amount of gloating in the Asian Miracle. The story of Asia since de-colonisation is one of unparalleled success. The crisis of 1997-98 can be seen either as a turning point, or merely as a bump in the road. While external factors – such as the sustainability of U.S. economic growth and Japan's recovery – will have a part to play, it will be entirely Asia's choice as to which road it takes from here on.

Taking the Right Road – And Avoiding Japan's Mistake

The lesson of Japan is that there is indeed a wrong road to take. That is the bad news. The good news is that such a road can easily be avoided, but it comes back to taking tough decisions. The viable must be supported and re-capitalised. The non-viable should be left to fail. This means that the model of Asian capitalism, which helped cause the Asian boom, must itself change. It does not necessarily have to be replaced by a Western model, nor should it. No Westerner should be arrogant enough to believe that the West cannot learn from the East. As a result, developing a newer and better model of Asian capitalism is fully justifiable. Its phase of emphasising growth, in many cases at any price, is now surely over. Higher investment without higher productivity is no longer the answer in the age of the Internet and rapid technological change. Quality must be emphasised over mere quantity. Price alone can no longer be the defining characteristic, for it is an advantage which is all too rapidly eroded, and ultimately eliminated. The chief lesson of the Japanese example is that cutting debt significantly and early on is necessary to provide the foundation for growth. Without reduction in overall debt and more specifically non-performing loans, credit growth will remain muted at best and could even continue to contract, effectively asphyxiating the economy. New credit is the oxygen of any recovery, without which that recovery cannot be maintained.

This is a key test for Asia in 2000 and 2001. To date, there has been little sign of major reduction in non-performing loans. Indeed, the recoveries in Thailand and Indonesia have happened in the absence of such a reduction, despite other improvements in the economy. The danger of this is that it could suggest to some that debt reduction is not important. Without debt reduction however, the total debt and non-performing loan levels will rise, spreading like a virus throughout the financial system of the country concerned, poisoning, and even killing it. This is what happened to Japan and why Japan has found it so tough to recover without reducing debt. Indeed, the ultimate result of a lack of debt reduction is the "liquidity trap", an economic state whereby monetary and fiscal policy changes are no longer effective. Japan has been in this state since early 1998 and is only now struggling to break free, with the economy showing signs, albeit patchy, of fundamental economic recovery. While I believe in the recovery that is currently underway in Asia, the threat of deflation and liquidity trap is a real one for those who do not do enough to cut debt and NPL levels. One year of strong data - 1999 - is not enough to confirm the sustainability of this recovery. We need to see this extended into 2000 and 2001 before we can truly say that this recovery is self-sustaining. In turn, the only way for this to happen is for Asian countries to continue and extend the reform process.

The debt reduction process can only happen if the appropriate regulatory and supervisory framework is put in place. While Thailand, Indonesia and Korea, the three IMF programme-countries, have created and installed bankruptcy laws and courts, the practical effectiveness of these laws and courts remains in question. It will take some time for these to make a major impact on the economy's development, but these countries do not necessarily have the time to spare. This is not to be alarmist in any way. It is simply to point out that speed remains necessary in order to limit the damage done to the Asian regional economy resulting from the crisis.

The example of Japan holds many lessons for Asia. Japan's miserable economic performance during the 1990s, relative both to its potential and past growth rates, was rooted in the asset market bubble of the 1980s and the subsequent bursting of that bubble. The collapse of land and equity prices resulted in massive non-performing loans at Japanese financial institutions. Instead of dealing with that problem immediately, the authorities sought to preserve face and quietly shoved the problem under the carpet, where the rot proceeded to spread, thus gradually disabling the banking system and rendering monetary and fiscal policy levers increasingly ineffective. Of late, the authorities have acted with more vigour, with the Bank of Japan cutting interest rates to only fractionally above zero and the government enacting a series of substantial fiscal stimulus programmes, resulting in a budget deficit of around 7% of GDP. Only through such extraordinary measures has the economy shown any sign whatsoever of recovering. While we believe that recovery will in fact become self-sustaining, there is little question that business and individual sentiment remains fragile. The authorities, rather than the private sector are still contributing the lion's share of the rise in investment. From its peak through the end of the decade, business investment fell by around 20%, with residential investment down 30%. Even when the economic recovery does become self-sustaining, Japan will have to deal with its debt problem. Debt to GDP is now well over 100% at around 120% and is still rising. Unless the authorities deal with this now through fiscal rationalisation, Japan's citizens will ultimately be faced with the bill. Debt overhang is an especially important problem in Japan given the country's ageing population. Meanwhile, manufacturing companies continue to have excess capacity. What is interesting to see is that despite the political rhetoric suggesting that Japan should seek a third way rather than cut such excess capacity through job layoffs and plant reduction, Japanese corporations are finally taking up the corporate axe to the dead wood, the wasted human and production capital which remains within their businesses. The market is finally being allowed to work in Japan. It is about time.

Just as Japanese construction firms and banks continue to labour under the burden of bad debts resulting from the bursting of the asset bubble in 1991, so do Thai, Korean and Indonesian firms and banks from the fallout of the 1997-1998 Asian crisis. Equally, the fate of many a Japanese corporate golf club membership - which let us not forget were exchange-traded prior to Japan's crisis - is mirrored in the sea of loss-making golf courses throughout Asia. Extraordinary measures were needed to support the Asian regional recovery and it appears they have indeed been taken. Going forward, the tasks of reducing excess capacity, reducing debt and fiscal deficits and strengthening the regulatory framework lie ahead. For this to happen, it requires the political commitment from Asian governments, yet the temptation will be for the authorities to sit back on their laurels, to enjoy the recovery rather than to use it as a platform for further reform. The lesson of Japan is that the road of such laziness leads to gradual fundamental deterioration. Japan's financial crisis in late 1997 should be taken as a stark warning to the authorities of Asia that there is no time for complacency.

WITHDRAWING FROM THE ECONOMY

The best way that Asian governments can help secure the sustainability of this recovery is to help provide the regulatory and financial platform for growth, and then gradually withdraw from the scene. One of the many lessons of the Asian crisis is that Asia did not have free markets. They were for the most part casinos. The exceptions such as Singapore have prospered. While Asian governments have traditionally played a lesser role in terms of taxing their citizens than have their Western counterparts, they have been much more significant in terms of developing industry. To a large extent, this has been a characteristic of the stage they are currently at in their economic development. That stage is now past. One of the many painful lessons learned in the course of Western economic development is that governments are not good at running economies over the long term. The road to economic hell is paved with good intentions. Eventually their efforts fall victim to vested interest, to diminishing returns, to laziness. Because they do not have to succeed, they eventually don't. It is all about incentive.

It is a simple lesson, but one which many ignore or fail at. If companies or banks don't have to make money, they most certainly won't! The Asian Miracle was characterised by many of the same elements, the same stages of economic development as have been seen in other areas of the emerging markets -- such as import substitution, followed by strategic export development - only they developed these in a much more vigorous and focused way than elsewhere. We are now at the "dawn" of a new stage, of a new Asia. That is the potential. It will be up to Asian governments to see that it becomes a reality.

In this stage of development, a new contract will have to be written between Asian governments and populations. The old contract whereby universal suffrage was sacrificed on the altar of mammon was clearly torn up in the wake of the crisis, burning embers in the wake of the Jakarta riots. The new contract must involve greater trust placed upon the populations and less direction from on high. With that greater trust however comes greater responsibility. Setting aside for a moment the issue of the Asian crisis and the subsequent recovery and instead looking at the long term, for Asia to even get near Silicon Valley will require a seismic shift in mind-set, a shift which will require the population to be allowed to take up an increasing share of the burden of driving the economy. The U.S. authorities created the environment under which the Silicon Valley phenomenon could be established and thrive, but it is human ingenuity - talent - which has been the driving force for its subsequent explosion. Labour, the work force, in Asia is generally regarded as a component of production, necessary but ultimately replaceable. In the high tech industries of the U.S., labour is a source of human and intellectual capital. Innovation and individual brilliance cannot be imposed from above. The conditions for it to flourish have to be created by the government. The government must plant the seeds and then leave the scene, allowing it to grow by itself.

To achieve this shift in mind-set, the Asian work force must develop new, higher and more modern skill sets. Granted, it is a generalisation, but the very fact that wealthy Asians usually send their progeny to Europe or the U.S. for their higher and university education shows the relative lack of such resources in Asia itself. Governments created the Asian "Miracle". Individuals, if it is to occur, will create the next Asian boom. The Asian Miracle was a rags-to-riches story. To a certain extent, it was characterised by the desire of the poor to become wealthy and to "better oneself" at all costs. Wealth was not the means but the end in itself. The next Asian boom will, if it is allowed to do so, focus on wealth as a means for betterment and empowerment. The Asian middle class is a relatively recent historical phenomenon. Once institutionalised and entrenched, it will have new priorities, focuses and demands. This has major economic and even political implications. Western investors, corporate and individual, should think of the potential that the middle class would represent. It will be extraordinary. For this to happen, clearly the current era of peace in Asia - also a relatively recent phenomenon historically - will have to be maintained. Not only that. For Asian economies to be able to utilise effectively the opportunities available and to re-deploy wasted capital and capacity, less emphasis must be put on defence spending. It is thus an economic priority, in addition to a political and social one, that the perception of security must be enhanced so that it does not have to be created artificially through a new Asian arms' race. Here, bilateral relations between the U.S., the country that has maintained Asia's security since the end of World War II, and China will be paramount.

China, rightly, sees itself as a great power and wishes to play a greater part in influencing relations within Asia, effectively at the expense of the U.S. role as the global policeman and as the world's dominant superpower. China places great emphasis on developing "comprehensive national power" or "*zonghe guoli*". There are several definitions of this concept, but basically it reflects a desire to develop the ability of political, economic and military security and to raise China's international status to a more appropriate level relative to its history and its potential. Within Asia, this would appear to conflict theoretically with the U.S. national interest, which is deemed by the U.S. government as maintaining a dominant role in the region. Consequently, the very nature of the U.S.-China relationship will have to change if this dichotomy is to be managed satisfactorily for both sides. Naturally, the issue of Taiwan will be central to this change.

Assuming this is achieved satisfactorily, a platform for long-term economic development in Asia would be created. That development would in turn have to be based on quality rather than quantity, on value-addition rather than just investment. Such a future would offer unparalleled opportunity, not least for Asians themselves. In that case, the Asian "Miracle" of the last two decades could be repeated, only on substantially more secure foundations. The alternative scenario is one in which the technology, skill-base and ultimately prosperity differential between Asia and the West widens once more. This is the dilemma - and the opportunity - which Asian governments face. In the end, there is little choice. Yet the need for Asian governments to take a more backseat role and allow their populations to drive the economic growth from here on will have political implications. Sooner or later, those populations will ask for a similar role in the political sphere.

The Asian crisis and the subsequent recovery have lessons for the international community. Data transparency does matter. That was a lesson of Mexico 1995 and again a lesson from Asia 1997. Improving standards for dissemination of financial and economic data helps markets to price risk more appropriately, reducing the risk of bubbles being created. Stronger international surveillance is also needed. In theory, this might help alert policy makers to upcoming financial problems. In practice, the IMF warned the Thai authorities several times with regard to the *baht* and Thailand's external imbalances. Such warnings were ignored. The presentation and marketing of country reports by the IMF should be altered in such a way that it issues "alerts" when it is particularly concerned about a country's fundamentals. Hoping that national governments might solve the problems themselves is not enough.

In the wake of the Asian crisis, much talk was focused on the issue of private capital flows, with opinions varying from seeking to manage flows, to trying to imprison them. Capital flight is the symptom rather than the disease. Financial markets are not perfectly efficient - contrary to academic speculation. In addition, as Churchill might have said, they are the worst arbiters of risk, apart from all the rest. The law of market pricing is that capital always seeks the highest rate of return. This might be perfectly true all the time if we were dealing with computers rather than humans. Alas, we are not. Humans - fund managers, corporate leaders and yes, believe it or not - bankers - are fallible. The rule holds true over the long term however. Thus, we can say that over the long term, investment will be withheld from Asia unless it develops higher rates of return. Asia's ability to develop growth based solely on being an export platform is limited.

AN IMPROVED OUTLOOK FOR EMERGING MARKETS

Now may be a strange time to suggest that the outlook for emerging markets looks bright given the crises in Asia, Russia, Brazil, the Czech Republic and Mexico over the last few years, but this is my personal view. The various crises which have been seen in Latin America, Asia and Central and Eastern Europe should be seen as one stage in the process of national economic evolution and development, rather than as the end of an era. In a sense, emerging markets have been victims of their own popularity. International capital flows will play a major part in determining which countries achieve the highest rates of return. Governments, which fret about losing control over the market, should not be concerned - they've already lost anyway. To go back, through the imposition of capital controls or taxes can be an appropriate temporary measure, but is not an answer over the long term. Looking ahead, the stage seems set for relatively broad-based and balanced growth in the emerging world. In addition, as Y2K concerns fade, risk appetite within the global investor base should pick up again. Moreover, if Asia and other emerging markets build a platform for more sustainable growth, we might well see the end of emerging markets, only to see the birth of high yielding industrialised countries. Indeed, it will not be long before we are faced with the dilemma of an "emerging market" having a fully developed economy.

This will have major investment implications. A majority of the global investor base is as yet unwilling or unable to invest in emerging markets because of the associated risk premium, real or imagined. As "emerging markets" become "Higher Yielding Industrialised Countries", they will thus have access to this new and dramatically increased investor base. By that time, they would better have developed sufficient institutional infrastructure to cope with capital flows. The resulting boom could otherwise become a spectacular bust in short order. Reassessment of risk premium as a result of this process could be as important as the initial change from the so-called "Lesser developed Countries" to the slightly more catchy "Emerging Markets".

The emerging world of countries should see stronger growth going forward. Growth in this asset class is expected to be 4.5% in 2000 as against 2.5% in 1999, largely reflecting economic rebounds in Latin America and emerging Europe, following recessions in 1999. Strong growth is also likely to continue in Asia, helped by recovery in Japan. While growth should pick up, inflation should fall again in 2000 to around 8%. This good performance should reflect an improvement in underlying economic policies. Finally, the emerging world of countries used to have significant fundamental imbalances, most notably trade and current account deficits. For the most part, this is no longer the case. Either they have been eliminated as a result of financial and economic crises or the respective authorities have sought to reduce them through appropriate policy mix. Some exceptions remain and these are consequently likely to be given higher risk premiums than those where such imbalances no longer exist. As a result, the number of emerging market countries with sharply overvalued exchange rates has declined significantly. In addition, foreign direct investment appears to be taking up an increasing share of capital inflows to these countries, thus reducing the volatility of such flows.

On a long-term view, the reduced differential between emerging markets and the industrialised countries should lead to lower risk premiums for emerging markets, or higher yielding industrialised countries as they could become. This will also change the reason for investment. High interest rates will not be the sole or even the main reason for investing in emerging markets. Rates of return will not be able to rely on price alone, just as manufacturing goods. They will have to be boosted by productivity efficiencies, by what the respective countries bring to the investment table in terms of value-addition. The sustained pickup in industrial country growth which we expect in 2000 - the U.S. economic slowdown being more than offset by the recoveries in Japan and the EU - should also boost emerging market exports to the industrialised world, a further reason why emerging markets as an asset class should outperform.

What we have seen in the last three years is an adjustment, a restructuring along the way to industrialised country status for many emerging markets. Given that the Asian crisis has been a major part of this restructuring process, Asia is likely to play a leading role in the ongoing evolution of emerging markets to emerge market status.

This bullish scenario which I personally foresee is not without risks. China could devalue its currency - though in the end I don't expect it will have to - Japan's recovery could falter or Argentina's currency board could come under further stress. Clearly, the most dangerous risk to the bullish scenario for emerging markets on a medium to long-term basis however is the U.S. If U.S. inflationary pressures pick up to a greater-than expected extent, resulting in major monetary tightening by the Federal Reserve or the stock market experience a significant fall, that would have serious global implications, not least for the emerging markets. Given that the U.S. has effectively been the importer of last resort over the last three years, resulting in its present, massive trade and current account deficits, a sharp downturn in U.S. growth or even a U.S. recession would cause U.S. import demand to collapse, thus hurting those countries whose exports are significantly exposed to U.S. demand, many of whom are emerging markets. In addition, major disruption in the U.S. asset markets could cause severe declines in global asset markets.

While this is not my expectation - I expect a benign scenario where the U.S. economy experiences a soft landing guided by prudent Fed policy - the risk should not be underestimated. The U.S. is likely to have a current account deficit in 2000 of over 4% of GDP. That coupled with a zero or negative savings' rate reflects a substantial fundamental imbalance that will have to be corrected one way or another. Either the dollar corrects or the U.S. economy (i.e. the stock market) will. The good news is that the dollar has already corrected substantially lower against the *yen*, from a 1998 high of around 147.60 to just above 100. In 2000, it will have to correct lower also against the euro in order for the U.S. economy to avoid a substantial slowdown.

Overall, however, the outlook for global emerging markets looks bright, which should in turn benefit the citizens of those countries over the long term. The restructuring currently taking place in Asia will serve as a model for others in the emerging world, one way or another, hopefully for the positive. Some in the emerged world could also learn a thing or two from the speed and extent of the Asian recovery. If there were those who thought that the Asian crisis marked the demise of increased global competition for capital, they are in for a rude awakening.

NOTES

Introduction

1. Named after the U.S. Treasury Secretary at the time, Nicholas Brady, who devised the "Brady Plan" to restructure national debt payment streams in the wake of the 1982-83 Latin American debt crisis.
2. Callum Henderson, "Asia Falling" Making sense of the Asian Currency Crisis and its Aftermath", McGraw-Hill, 1998, page 275.

Chapter 2

1. "The IMF's Response to the Asian Crisis" (January 17, 1999), International Monetary Fund.
2. As reported by financial newswires.
3. Ibid
4. Ibid
5. World Bank report "East Asia: The Road to Recovery", World Bank, September 1998.

Chapter 3

1. Article by Paul Krugman, "Recovery: Don't Bet on it", Time Magazine, June 21, 1999.
2. MAS official comments as cited by international newswires.
3. World Bank report, "East Asia: The Road to Recovery" op cit., page 113.

4. Speech by IMF Managing Director Michel Camdessus, May 20, 1999, at the South East Asian Central Bank Governors' conference in Seoul, Korea.
5. Interview with World Bank Chief Economist Joseph Stiglitz with " Far Eastern Economic Review", November 4, 1999.

Chapter 4

1. Article by IMF Director of Asia Pacific Department Hubert Neiss in an article entitled "Public Sacrifice Serves as Driving Force for Recovery" reproduced by the "Korea Times", November 30, 1998, IMF Website.
2. Bank of Korea official comments.

Chapter 10

1. Speech by Federal Reserve Board Chairman Alan Greenspan, "Lessons from the global crises", before the World bank Group and the International Monetary Fund, Programme of Seminars, Washington DC, September, 1999.
2. Presentation by Mohamed el-Erian, December 1998.

BIOGRAPHY

Callum Henderson is an Emerging Market Currency Strategist at a global investment bank in London. He previously worked for independent research house Standard & Poor's MMS in both Hong Kong and New York. He is widely quoted in business publications including The Asian Wall Street Journal, New York Times, Business Week and the Financial Times and has appeared on CNN, CNBC-ABN, Reuters Financial Television and Bloomberg. His first book, *Asia Falling*, was critically lauded as the benchmark work on the Asian currency crisis, while his second book, *China on the Brink* was recently awarded "Best Business Book of 1999" by the Library Journal of the U.S.

The views expressed are the author's own and are not necessarily shared by his employer.